WILDLIFE CRIME

WILDLIFE
CRIME

THE MAKING OF AN
INVESTIGATIONS OFFICER

Dave Dick

Whittles Publishing

Published by
Whittles Publishing Ltd.,
Dunbeath,
Caithness, KW6 6EG,
Scotland, UK

www.whittlespublishing.com

ISBN 978-184995-036-7

Printed by Bell & Bain Ltd., Glasgow

CONTENTS

Foreword vii

Introduction ix

Acknowledgements xi

1 The making of a raptor fieldworker 1

2 The contract trail 12

3 A new start 35

4 First captures 48

5 Falcon theft 82

6 Poison 105

7 On becoming an expert 136

8 International investigations 152

9 Working with the media 176

10 Into the new millennium 184

Quotations 191

References and further reading 195

FOREWORD

by Sir John Lister-Kaye OBE

This is an important book. It is written by an expert who probably knows more about wildlife crime in the UK, and especially in Scotland, than anyone else. It is important because so little is known and understood about a widespread and deeply disturbing illegal practice, a disgrace which is both a blight on our society and a proliferating cancer upon some of our most precious and iconic wildlife.

I recommend that the reader turns to the excellent colour photographs before embarking upon Dave Dick's harrowing accounts of poisoning incidents in Scotland. If, as I have on many occasions, you have once seen a magnificent golden eagle lying in a ragged heap beneath its eyrie, its chick also dead in the nest, and if you have held in your hand the rigid corpse of that most exquisite of all our falcons – the peregrine – then you will understand how truly callous the perpetrators of these crimes are. If you have seen the mangled bodies of goshawks, hen harriers, red kites, buzzards, even kestrels and owls, thrown onto a gamekeeper's midden along with the rotting carcases of foxes, ravens, stoats, weasels, hedgehogs, and perhaps even a cat or two, you begin to understand how indiscriminate and devastating the use of poison is. Dave Dick's photographs and the carefully detailed accounts of his casework over the twenty-five years of his career are a wake-up call to all of us, whether we work with wildlife or not.

At the heart of this book is the over-riding question: why? Why do a very small minority of people who consider themselves to be sportsmen and women and countryside lovers, who even claim to be wildlife enthusiasts – namely sporting estate owners, their agents and their game-keeping employees – permit and in many instances continue to condone the blatant flaunting of the law against the clear enactments of Scottish, Westminster and European parliaments and in flagrant rejection of the settled will of the vast majority of the general population? The answer is because they can get away with it. Our culture of private landowning, which is over a thousand years old in Britain, has for most of those centuries been predicated upon the premise of 'I can do what I like on my own land'. This is overlaid by the ancient prejudicial dumping of all predators – all hooked beaks, talons and carnivorous teeth along with scavengers like crows, gulls and ravens – into the hate bin of ignorance labelled 'vermin'. Then it is endorsed by the fact that for the most part these crimes go undiscovered because they are so very difficult to witness and bring to court, even when the evidence appears to be irrefutable.

Prosecutions fail over and over again or are lightly dismissed, delivering no deterrent at all. The police are often indifferent or too busy with 'real' crimes, and the judiciary have often proved to be apathetic or even sympathetic to the interests of landowners. And yet if it were possible to take a census of the countryside-using general public in Scotland, the overwhelming majority – I suggest 99.9% – would tell you that the poisoning of wildlife is abhorrent and unacceptable.

I had the honour of serving the RSPB in Scotland and at a UK national level for a total of sixteen years. During that time I came to know Dave Dick well and to develop a deep respect for his dedication to duty in the face of the illegal destruction of wildlife, which is getting worse, not better. Today, despite new and supposedly more effective legislation, the problem of poisoning and trapping, to say nothing of illegal shooting of protected wildlife, is more widespread than I have known it for the fifty odd years I have been actively involved in nature conservation. It is a war: a constant struggle between those who seek to uphold the law in the interests of wildlife and the general public and those who choose to flaunt it in the interests of raising game birds, particularly pheasants and grouse.

It is often argued that conservationists are anti-shooting and would seek to have field sports banned, destroying jobs and crippling the rural economy. That is rubbish. I and all my family have actively supported and participated in field sports of all kinds, as have many of my conservation friends. I was a very keen shot myself and still occasionally turn out for a day's 'rough' with my sons. I do not accept that there is a necessary conflict at all. In fact I believe the reverse. I believe that the best indicator of a healthy grouse moor is the presence of natural predators taking out the halt, the lame and the unfit to breed – a natural selection process vital to the evolution of all wild animals. Where this goes wrong is when the artificial rearing and release of quarry species such as pheasants and partridges and the over protection of wild grouse creates 'honey pot' concentrations of prey, which understandably the predators are unable to resist. And there is only one answer to this: the shooting fraternity have to be less greedy and accept smaller and more varied bags, and even more importantly, farming and countryside management has to shift further towards an holistic regime of integrated land management so that there is better maintenance of habitats for wildlife – field margins, wetlands, marshes and native woods – and consequently less need for predatory species to target the honey pots. But that is a very big ask and I am not naïve enough to imagine that is going to happen overnight. Meanwhile, it is vital that the RSPB and the other agencies for nature conservation keep pressing for the law to be upheld and those flagrantly breaking it to be brought properly to justice.

My most earnest hope is that this book will re-ignite the public debate and that the media coverage it generates will lead to a wider appreciation of the problem, and concentrate the minds of politicians and the police to bring an end to these disgraceful practices. I want to see golden eagles and peregrine falcons flying free and unthreatened over our countryside, just as I want to see the sporting tradition of which we should be proud clean up its act for once and for all.

John Lister-Kaye
House of Aigas.

Sir John Lister-Kaye OBE is the founder-director of the internationally-acclaimed, award-winning Aigas Field Centre and is one of Scotland's best loved nature writers and conservationists.

INTRODUCTION

Throughout my career in conservation, I always enjoyed talking to my colleagues about my work. It provided a good outlet for the continuing frustrations of witnessing and recording wildlife crime on a daily basis. 'You should write that stuff down!' they'd say, but while I was working as an Investigations Officer, the job was far too demanding to allow me to stop and sit down at a desk to write a book.

Now retired from the fray after 25 years, I can at last try to put some perspective on what went on. Reviewing the incidents and court cases which follow has reinforced some of my ideas but has also, if anything, left me even angrier at what is still going on in the Scottish countryside. I make no apology for showing that anger: passion and confrontation are what got us through many of the situations I describe in this book. Without passion and anger, we would still have a country devoid of its top predatory birds. Conservation is about an emotional response to the world around us once our eyes have been opened to the beauty of nature. Some people never learn or feel that and I feel profoundly sorry for them – not that they will care a jot, safe in their world of 'virtual conservation'.

My first idea was simply to describe the different categories of wildlife crime using the mass of incidents and cases with which I was involved. I have been persuaded by my publisher to write an autobiographical account. While this allows me to expound my personal opinions on a subject which has been a lifelong passion, I sincerely hope that my own presence will not get in the way. My hope is that this book will be an education to those unfamiliar with what is really happening with wildlife crime in Scotland, particular where our open countryside is concerned. I also hope it will strengthen the resolve of those involved in the fight, with much of it showing what can be achieved when people genuinely work together.

Finally, while I hope that you will come away from this book sharing some of my anger against the wildlife criminals and those who protect or encourage them, I hope also that it will serve as an entertaining read rather than as a textbook.

ACKNOWLEDGEMENTS

I t is my strong hope that I have acknowledged those who helped form and inform me on my way to becoming an Investigations Officer, as described in the pages that follow. This was, however, a rollercoaster ride and I will inevitably have forgotten to mention many deserving people – I know I have only included a small fraction of the casework in which we were all involved.

On a more personal note, I know the all-absorbing nature of the work made life difficult for my nearest and dearest. I am acutely aware that I had the stability of a home to return to after the physical and mental traumas of witnessing and trying to deal with some pretty horrific situations. I would therefore like, very publicly, to thank Jayshree and Mel and Joanna. Those who have had the enormous pleasure and comfort of living with dogs will see no irony in my also acknowledging the companionship of Hayley and Tess, my faithful hill companions.

I sincerely hope that my dear Sarah, who has done so much to heal me in the last few years, will understand, by reading this book, why I still feel such rage at the destruction of our wildlife and the perversion of the system which should be protecting it.

Lastly, I dedicate this book to my mother, 90 years young and still 'a bonny fechter'.

1

THE MAKING OF A RAPTOR
FIELDWORKER

An 11-year-old boy, carrying a brown canvas rod case, walks out of his garden on a glorious early summer's morning and heads down a leafy tree-arched lane. He's wearing a blue nylon polo-neck jumper, its sleeves rolled up, while below his grey shorts a pair of bony knees are almost covered by the top of his black Wellington boots. He makes his way along the bottom of Leggat's Field, a meadow of long ungrazed grass and flowers, past the end of a line of tall beech, down the steep grass slope and over the Low Road – no traffic at this hour. Climbing a low stone wall, he walks over the wooden sleepers and shiny steel rails of the main line and stands gazing across the marsh.

This is paradise. He can see the water of Loch Libo in the distance, reflecting, flat calm, the woods and steep slopes of Caldwell Law. Between the boy and the loch lies a sea of green reeds, with here and there a clump of majestic bulrushes. This is no silent tableau – the songs of a hundred chattering sedge warblers fill the warm air and as he steps down into the faint water-filled path, through reeds taller than himself, he occasionally sees, clinging onto a nearby stem, a small brown bird with a thick creamy eye stripe, open-beaked and bursting with its efforts.

After a few minutes of careful, booted splashing through the jaggy-edged path, he reaches a small sluggish burn with a heavy wooden plank – almost certainly an old railway sleeper – laid across it. Who knows how deep the mud is below the slippery moving bridge? It's not a place to linger but the scariest part of his journey is about to come. He enters a bouncing, floating bog, where the reeds give way to strong-smelling bog myrtle and minty marsh plants and from where he can now see the 'islands', tantalisingly close.

The path which has spread out across the open bog narrows to a series of grass-covered clumps of earth, with open water around them. He is very near the lochside, hopscotching from one wobbly clump to the next as in a playground game of peevers. Away to one side, though, is an even more worrying danger. A loud hiss from a clump of reeds just feet away lets the boy know that the sitting mute swan has spotted him and is not amused. The easier route would have taken him past the huge nest but he had already learnt to be cautious: he'd heard tales of a swan's ability to break an arm or leg with a strike from its powerful wings and had seen how they dealt with straying moorhens and ducks.

And now the islands! Two tiny strips of grass-covered earth fringed with stunted bushes. On the landward side, an impassably deep bog often covered by water, and on the other, a wide inlet of open loch with a sea of lily pads, just within casting distance. The boy hurriedly pulls out his three-part whole-cane rod and pushes together the brass ends to make a 12-foot-long pole. He pulls off his green canvas satchel with its military webbing and pulls out a shiny round fishing reel, full of dark green nylon line. Fixing the reel onto the rod and walking down the length of the pole, he carefully threads the line through the rod's eyelets. Next comes the bubble float, a small plastic sphere through which he twists the line, leaving about two feet clear at the end; he pulls the little rubber plug out of its top and stoops down to hold the float under the green- tinged water of the lochside, waiting until it is nearly a quarter full before stopping it up again. Fishing once more into the bag, he removes a small piece of lead shot and, using a rusty pair of pliers, crimps it onto the line. He takes a sharp pointed hook and ties it onto the end of the line, with a blood knot and a reef knot for luck at the end. The knot he has learned from his big brother, who has also bought him the hooks and line in packets marked 'Alex Martin's Fishing Tackle, Royal Exchange Square, Glasgow'.

Next comes a jam jar with a bronzed pierced lid, carefully screwed on, full of earth and worms forked out of the sticky clay soil of his father's potato patch, not much good for potatoes but occasionally revealing a nice plump, wriggling, purple earthworm. Dispassionately, he spears the worm with the hook halfway up its length. Checking the line is flowing freely from the reel and through the eyelets, he swings the long cane pole level with his waist and lets the weight of the float pull the line out. The bubble turns in the sunlight before landing with a gentle splash a few yards out. The worm, hook and weighted line sink below the surface.

The young fisherman, early 1960s

As the ripples die away from the isolated bubble, the young boy starts to take note of his surroundings. The peace of the countryside, on this warm summer morning, is actually a continuous symphony of natural sounds. He can already distinguish the songs of the warblers and buntings, the soft quacks and clucks of ducks across the water, the sharper metallic calls of the coots, spaced out down the length of the loch, like black chequers in a vast gleaming board game. Nearer to hand are the purring notes of moorhens, foraging on the edges of the reeds and bog. Most intriguing of all is the occasional plopping sound of some unknown creature, dropping into the water close by. Eventually, putting his rod carefully down on the grass, he creeps up to watch the whiskered head and back of a water vole as it attempts to circumnavigate the islands. He has learned to distinguish between these benign rodents and the large brown rats occasionally glimpsed as they swim in the loch.

Most exotic of all, though, are the two pairs of great crested grebes, which always keep to the open waters of the loch. He has read about them in his *Observer's Book of Birds* but the reality of watching their spectacular and tender displays – head-shaking dances, breast to breast, with offers of weeds and always close together, creating a double reflection of chestnut, black and white feathers – is a rare treat.

Occasionally, a swan will drift past on its way to or from the supposedly concealed nest, carving its regal way through the squabbling and violence of ever-restless coots. But all the while, the boy is watching the bubble.

And then a moment's distraction, perhaps the faint sound of an early cuckoo calling from the woods up the hill, and when he turns back, a telltale circle is spreading out from the bubble: a quick bob, then under. Yanking the rod upwards, he can feel the thrilling vibration of a fish struggling, passing from the tight line through the cane rod and its cork handle to quicken his own young pulse. A rushed and excited scrabbling at his reel until he is lifting his catch onto the grass, a glowing russet, black-striped fish with its sail-like fin erect and sharp-tipped.

The roughness of the perch's scales, the sharp stab of a bony gill cover and the magical folding of its dorsal fin will live with him all his life. So, too, will the calls of singing birds in the ragged hawthorn across the marsh, the echo of the coots and cuckoos and the beat of the sun on the calm surface of the loch, filled with unknown fishy wonders waiting to be discovered.

Those early days of discovering nature first-hand, in 1950s rural Renfrewshire, were most definitely what lay behind my decision to work in full-time conservation. And it wasn't just that magical fishing loch, to which I returned right up until my mid-teens – so often, in fact, that my parents began to worry about my love of solitude – but the whole, idyllic countryside childhood and adolescence.

Looking back through windows in time, I see myself peering into hedgerows of hawthorn and privet and looking in wonder at the nests of blackbirds, thrushes, robins, dunnocks and yellowhammers; catching newts and water beetles from the fringes of drowned quarries, taking them home and keeping them in a weedy tank in my bedroom; playing in haylofts and byres with the farmers' kids and, later on, loading hay bales and mucking out those same byres; driving grey Fergie tractors with huge haystacks on a slipe – a flat-bed two-wheeled trailer- at the back; sitting in a favourite climbing tree, watching looper caterpillars disguised as twigs and listening to the wistful sound of a hundred willow warblers all around me; I see myself in that same tree in high summer, watching the shadows made by shoals of small perch, far below, as they swim across the sands of the north end of the loch; digging a hole with my brother in two-foot-thick loch ice in the Big Freeze of 1963 and catching a large pike on a treble hook baited with roast beef; hearing the distant yelps of geese in the autumn and looking up to see them, in long ragged 'V's, heading south; the wild trumpeting of whooper swans from the loch in the early dark of a winter's bedtime. That is what those years mean to me.

And all of that without belonging to any club or society. When the time came to join the local Cub Scouts, most of us were already expert in guerrilla tactics and were told little about nature that we hadn't already found out for ourselves. I could weep for what the restricted, spoon-fed and health-and-safety cosseted children of today have lost. We feed them virtual reality, including virtual conservation, and this book will explore what we are losing on the way.

So my Uplawmoor village childhood had sown in me a lifelong interest in natural history and love of the countryside, but there was still a long way to go before that young boy fishing at the side of a loch became the adult RSPB Investigations Officer.

Both my parents had grown up in urban environments, one on the north and one on the south side of Glasgow. As a result, they treated as a major event any slightly unusual nature sighting – a pheasant landing in the garden or a weasel eating one of the dog's bones on the front lawn – and God help anyone who even thought about harming any living creature, if my mother found out. My own obsession with birds and bugs, while regarded as eccentric, was at least tolerated.

Uplawmoor had no game-shooting tradition and no closed estate. Caldwell House, which in previous centuries had been the local seat of landed gentry, was by then a hospital and there was only one shooter that I knew of, who only shot rabbits. Most importantly of all, there were no restrictions on access to woods, fields, hills and lochside. As children, we roamed for miles. We, of course, knew to shut gates, to leave livestock in peace and to give bulls a wide berth. Our friends and companions were farmers' sons and we would no more have walked through the middle of a crop than through the middle of a flowerbed. With 50 years of hindsight, I see now that this lack of threatening gamekeepers and of a fear-based estate culture was a boon. And, what's more, nature flourished! No-one shot the crows or foxes, no-one trapped the stoats and weasels, and yet there were fields full of lapwings and hedgerows full of songbirds. This is always in my mind when I find myself faced with the modern, dressed-as-conservation, politically correct shooting propaganda that tells us that man must always destroy predators. Those childhood days always came back to me when I received calls in my office from frightened tenants who wanted to report a shooting or the poisoning of wildlife, a working dog or a pet, but who were desperately scared of being identified. I was very lucky but, of course, I thought back then that my experience was normal.

It is also worth noting at this point that I was unusual amongst my childhood companions. Not every young boy or girl knew the names of all the birds, or trees, or fish or bugs that we came across daily. They all undoubtedly knew some, but I most definitely do not go along with the dewy-eyed nonsense I regularly hear from defensive modern country dwellers, who write others off as 'ignorant townies'. Even back in the 1950s, surrounded by hedgerows, woods and fields crammed with wild birds, you would have been hard pressed to find more than half a dozen people who could put a name to all of them, who could recognise male and female, who could identify their songs, who could tell a robin's egg from a thrush's. That included farmers and other outdoor people, because why should they? These were busy, hard-working people, who may have enjoyed the song of a blackbird but who didn't need to know what it was. To me it is blindingly obvious that someone who pursues birdwatching as a hobby – or even, often, as an obsession, going out and looking for them at every opportunity – will gain a much deeper knowledge of wild birds than the man who works on the land. His main interest is the crop he is growing, whether it be wheat, cattle, sheep, pheasants or grouse.

So far, so good. I had learned to identify, appreciate and occasionally use the wild things around me. These skills were only reinforced after the age of 11, when I had to travel into Glasgow every day, at the tail end of the steam train era, to my secondary school. I can still remember the wide-eyed wonder with which the occasional city-based school friend, invited out for a weekend, viewed 'my' woods and fields. All that country knowledge was of little use, though, in a 1960s school which, as was the norm, offered neither a biology department nor any natural history teaching.

This was the era of the growth of nature programmes on television and David Attenborough and Peter Scott were early heroes. Perhaps the biggest influence in my early teens was the magazine *Animals*, a colour photo-filled, eagerly-awaited Saturday treat. Well ahead of its time, it introduced me to a world – the world, quite literally – of nature and conservation issues. This was no pretty postcard view of nature, although the photography was often superb: it carried in-depth articles about serious issues.

The two which I remember most clearly had a profound effect on my view of the world. The first dealt with the Kariba Dam project, carried out in what was then called Southern Rhodesia, now Zimbabwe. It was more correctly called Operation Noah, a huge animal rescue effort which took place in 1960 and 1961 as the dammed Zambesi River began to drown a huge area of African bush. It was obvious that a young boy already interested in nature would be drawn in by the stories and photos of animals, from rhinos to poisonous snakes, being rescued on small boats from dwindling islands. And there's no doubt that a seed was sown by the twin stories of man destroying the natural environment and then trying to do something about the mess he's made.

The second big story covered by *Animals* was its 1963 partial serialisation of Rachel Carson's recently-published book *Silent Spring*, the first serious attack on the newly-perceived danger to the environment of the application of untested chemical pesticides. The title was her description of a worst-case scenario, a spring without birdsong caused by the large-scale death of birds after the applications of substances such as DDT. It is difficult to think of any modern book which has equalled the impact of *Silent Spring*. It has been described as the starting point for the entire modern environmental movement, the starting point for the creation of the very science of ecology. It created uproar in the USA where she lived, provoking a huge over-reaction from the agrochemical industry and its government supporters. She was personally vilified by these people and their apologists, described as 'a hysterical woman' until the reality of what she had been describing began to get through to those in power. Knowing now how these things work, I am sure that it was the environmental awakening of a mass of voters which made the difference, rather than an acceptance by those at the top of the possible dangers to nature or even to human health. It still took until 1972 to get a ban on DDT in the USA.

Scientists and ornithologists in the UK had a large part to play in showing the effects of persistent chemical pesticides such as DDT , Dieldrin and Aldrin on a whole range of bird species. Peregrine falcons and golden eagles were particularly useful as indicator species. I feel honoured to have known and worked with, and for, some of that generation, including Ian Prestt, a scientist who became Director General of the RSPB, as well as 'amateur' raptor workers such as George Carse and Dick Roxburgh. Without the huge, unsung efforts of those fieldworkers, the pesticide story would have reached an even more damaging conclusion.

Of course, my life as a schoolboy in rural Renfrewshire was as far removed as it could have been from all of this, but the effect of Rachel Carson's words has never left me. I had been shown that nature was of indescribable beauty and complexity but also that it could be destroyed by greed and callous indifference. That was heady stuff for an adolescent. With hindsight, I can see why I later fought so hard against the poisoning gamekeepers who used similar toxic substances to produce their own, estate-based silent springs: woods where no buzzard or sparrowhawk calls, moorland missing the yelp of a golden eagle or the kekking of a triumphant peregrine on its kill.

I should emphasise, though, that the real driving force behind what became a lifetime battle was my growing appreciation of the sheer magic and stunning beauty of nature. Nature conservation at its best is a positive, civilising action. Leave aside, for the moment, the arguments about methods and priorities that cloud our adult lives: it is about allowing the survival of that connection with nature which we feel as children, or which an adult latecomer might experience as a childlike wonder. It is about allowing that connection to be carried on indefinitely, for future generations, elevating a wild flower, animal or bird beyond the level of a pretty object to be studied or photographed to its rightful place as an essential part of the world in which we live, leading us not just to look at the landscape but to become a part of it. As a young boy, those were instinctive, unexpressed thoughts, yet as an adult I increasingly found myself reverting to them during some interminable court case, as a defence lawyer described yet another wildlife killer as 'a true countryman, with a genuine love of nature'. I don't think so.

I was not 'a dull, bookish boy'. Although I learned to love books early on and had an ability to keep my own company, I had plenty of close friends and enjoyed a good laugh more than most. I enjoyed life. The one book which may have had more influence on me than any other is one which is full of sunshine and laughter: Gerald Durrell's *My Family and Other Animals*. Not surprisingly, I was captivated by the true story of a young boy obsessed with nature and living a carefree life on a sunny island. I still think of Durrell and his greatest book every time I manage to get a trip to the Mediterranean: with my rucksack, binoculars and camera, I become that boy again, and I know there must be thousands of others just like me.

There was a gap of more than a decade between my nature-obsessed childhood and early teens and my later arrival at the lower rungs of the conservationist ladder. These are the years when most young men, unless they take the 'marry in haste, repent at leisure' route, will give at least a passing nod to 'wine, women and song'. And I gave the 'song' part a good deal more than a passing nod. After hearing the first slide guitar riff of the Rolling Stones' *Little Red*

Rooster, I was lost forever. This was the era of the late 1960s and early 1970s. It's a truism that the Swinging Sixties didn't arrive in Scotland until the 1970s but, believe me, they arrived!

In between imitating my guitar heroes of the blues, folk and rock world, I somehow managed to gain two degrees: a BA in Geography and Geology from the University of Strathclyde and an MIBiol in Ecology and Animal Behaviour from Paisley College of Technology, now a university. I also travelled overland in a six-month epic drive to eastern Turkey, via Germany, Italy, the former Yugoslavia and Greece, and through the wilder parts of some of them, well before mass tourism had reached that far. I was a professional musician for a year, permanently short of money, despite having the young Eddi Reader as the singer in our band. Oh, and I managed to get married and then divorced. I can remember thinking on my 30th birthday, at the end of the 1970s: 'I'm lucky to have survived all that!' but little did I know what was just around the corner.

As an unemployed university graduate, I had signed on in 1979 to the Professional Executive Register, giving my occupation as 'ecologist'. I can't have been taking it very seriously, as it was a rare person indeed who knew what

First job as an ornithologist, Dean Castle Country Park, 1980

ecology was in the 1970s. I had actually studied the subject, mainly for my own interest, while working as a laboratory technician in the biology department of Paisley College of Technology, but with very little chance of ever using it professionally. Imagine my surprise, then, to receive a phone call. 'We don't have any jobs for ecologists but there is one here for an ornithologist ...' In 1979, I had never even heard of anyone being employed as an ornithologist in Scotland but, never one to miss an opportunity, I followed it up and began two very pleasant years surveying the bird population of what was to become Dean Castle Country Park, on the outskirts of Kilmarnock.

After a gap of a decade I had been given the ideal situation in which to refresh my abilities in bird identification and natural history generally, in countryside very similar to, and only 20 miles from, my home village. I was also working alongside other biology graduates – a zoologist, a botanist and an entomologist – all enthusiastic about using their knowledge. An added pleasure from my perspective was that I was by then living in a flat in Glasgow's West End. I had all the advantages of a city life in the evening and was able to watch the seasons change, in a rural setting, during the day. That contrast of lifestyles was to become the norm for me, in Glasgow and in Edinburgh, for the next 28 years. But, by the winter of 1980, this rather pleasant 9-to-5 lifestyle was coming to a temporary close as we prepared the reports which were to be used in creating the Park in an environmentally-aware manner.

I can't now recall where I saw the ad – probably in a copy of *Birds* magazine in some waiting room. 'Wanted: biologist to monitor breeding golden plover on Yorkshire Moors. Send CV to RSPB HQ.' I had never had any desire to work down south and I had recently re-married but by now I had caught the birdwatching bug. I had had a taste of working in bird conservation and liked it, so sent off my CV. To show willing, I also volunteered to help out for two weeks on the RSPB's Insh Marshes Reserve, near Aviemore – in December! My first work with the organisation was planting trees in sub-zero temperatures at the side of the River Spey. My fellow volunteer and I had literally to break the ice to get washed in our caravan each morning and I doubt if I've ever been so cold, before or since. (Note for RSPB volunteers: they built a nice snug heated cabin for volunteers at Insh a few years later.)

At the end of March 1981, when I had forgotten all about golden plovers and was at a loss as to what to try next, I got a phone call from Pete Ellis at the RSPB in Edinburgh. 'I've been sent your CV. We're sorry to tell you that the golden plover job has gone, but how would you feel about monitoring peregrines in Argyll?' I could not believe my luck.

Within a few days I was being interviewed in Pete's office at 17 Regent Terrace, Edinburgh, an address I came to know extremely well. At this time the RSPB had only five or six executive staff at their Scottish headquarters (today they have over 50) with Pete the Species Protection Officer for Scotland. In addition to his work helping to investigate wild bird crime, he also had to organise bird survey work. It can't have helped that he was also the first person in the post, created in 1979. His hard work early on, particularly in making contacts and in record keeping, was of immense use to me when I ended up sitting at the same desk a few years later.

Things began to move very rapidly – an end-of-March phenomenon which I grew to know only too well and whose effect I still feel in my retirement. The peregrine contract was due to start in a week's time.

FIRST RAPTOR WORK: PEREGRINE SURVEY, 1981

My crash course on peregrine falcons took place in the Borders Hills south of Edinburgh. Having obtained my NCC licence (the Nature Conservancy Council, the UK government's nature conservation advisers at the time), I was taken by Pete to my first peregrine nest. It was far from typical of what I was to face in Argyll but was ideal as a safe introduction, both for me and the birds.

My first nest was what I learned to refer to casually as a 'walk-in' site, a nest ledge that could be accessed without climbing equipment – 'you could take your granny into it!' Such macho jargon – for these were often pretty terrifying places – is common in the rarefied world of raptor monitoring. As I was already well acquainted with, and enjoyed, Glaswegian black humour, I found that I fitted into this world and its codes with ease. I was, however, totally un-prepared in terms of equipment, or even in knowing what was required. Pete gave me an RSPB telescope, an item which would now qualify as an antique: a draw-pull scope with a tendency to condensation at the first hint of dampness – so hardly ideal for Argyll. The whole area of optical equipment and hill clothing was to undergo radical changes over the next few years.

Clinging to a cliff face with a wonderful view: a pair of peregrines, almost deafening me as they performed high-speed manoeuvres just a few feet away, and a clutch of brick-red eggs: this was to become my obsession for every waking moment of the next four months.

I learned to identify peregrines in the sky at a distance, I learned their different calls, I learned to identify traditional nest crags, I learned to free climb (without ropes) into nests and to get back safely. I learned their habits and their preferences in feeding, nesting and roosting. I learned to age chicks

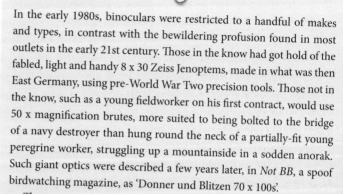

HISTORICAL NOTE
BINOCULARS

In the early 1980s, binoculars were restricted to a handful of makes and types, in contrast with the bewildering profusion found in most outlets in the early 21st century. Those in the know had got hold of the fabled, light and handy 8 x 30 Zeiss Jenoptems, made in what was then East Germany, using pre-World War Two precision tools. Those not in the know, such as a young fieldworker on his first contract, would use 50 x magnification brutes, more suited to being bolted to the bridge of a navy destroyer than hung round the neck of a partially-fit young peregrine worker, struggling up a mountainside in a sodden anorak. Such giant optics were described a few years later, in *Not BB*, a spoof birdwatching magazine, as 'Donner und Blitzen 70 x 100s'.

The common mistake made then, as now, was to associate large magnification with visual acuity. Binoculars are one area of life where there really is no substitute for quality.

MOUNTAIN DRESS CODE

When I began my career in bird of prey monitoring in Scotland at the start of the 1980s, there was no dress code amongst fieldworkers. Most walkers wore anoraks over woolly jumpers, shirts and woollen thermals. Over-trousers were uncommon and were bought from agricultural merchants, and most of us wore jeans or cords, over long johns in cold weather. When it rained you got wet and cold. By 1982 a new fashion had appeared – Barbour jackets, previously the domain of the huntin', shootin' and fishin' class, were discovered to have rugged qualities and good deep pockets for hiding your binoculars from the aforementioned huntin', shootin' and fishin' class. After a couple of seasons of hard wear and neglect, however, they began to fray round the bottom and cuffs. Splits across the back became the badge of honour for your hard-working eagle or peregrine man. They were also very heavy, after a couple of hours' struggling around nest crags. The Barbour had begun to appear as a yuppie accessory on the streets of Edinburgh in the same way that the 4 x 4 has recently become the 'Chelsea Tractor' and just as the modern era of cagoules, layered clothing and entire shops devoted to the needs of a growing army of Munro baggers and weekend hillwalkers had started.

and grown birds by their feathers. I also learned a great deal about the Argyll environment in which they were living.

There were other lessons I was learning, though, through experience, observation and received wisdom, which would prove invaluable in the unimagined future. I learned that not everyone loved these beautiful creatures, which I had so recently discovered. Gamekeepers shot, poisoned and trapped them; pigeon fanciers hated them; egg thieves wanted every eggshell from a nest and criminal falconers wanted to take live chicks. And all that in addition to the terrible losses they had so recently suffered as a result of pesticide pollution. The peregrine was a perfect species on which to start a career in conservation.

My patch for the 1981 national peregrine survey stretched from Ballachulish to the south of Kintyre, including all of mid-Argyll, Appin, Etive and Glencoe, bounded in the east by Crianlarich and Arrochar. Hilly, to say the least, and my early experience of walking those steep hills, many of which go straight from sea level up to over 2,500 feet, made hill work in other parts of Scotland in later years seem that little bit easier. The wet climate and the dreaded midgies didn't help, but if the picture I am painting is a gloomy one, my state of mind was anything but – I loved every minute of my time there.

The freedom of being given such a beautiful area to work in, to be given a vehicle, maps, telescope, a list of known nest sites and friendly contacts and to be more or less left to get on with it, has spoiled me for the rest of my life. I worked every hour possible in what was a labour of love. I turned myself from a wheezing wreck on my first long walks, into a fit and experienced 'mountain man'. I had at last found something, apart from my beloved acoustic guitar playing, which I could 'do right'. Perhaps the biggest lesson was a reminder that I could work alone and live alone for long periods, a pay-off from those long days' fishing on Loch Libo. I know now, from many years of employing others, that not everyone can handle long periods away from any human company.

Argyll is, for the most part, a harsh environment for anyone trying to make a living off the land. Just look out of the window during a sleet shower and imagine having to break open bales of feed, on an open hillside, in that kind of weather, for the rest of your life… I learned to respect the shepherds and farmers I met and who often gave me very welcome hospitality. Apart from a few weeks spent living in an old friend's spare room in the village of Strachur on Loch Fyne, I lived out of my car and tent, so the regular farmhouse cups of tea were very welcome. I learned that many shepherds were very protective of wildlife and it sometimes took several visits before I was trusted with information. (When working on golden eagles in later years, I was occasionally told about local nests only after I had known someone for at least three seasons. This has always pleased me: it reveals a caring attitude.) For the next 25 years I was always aware that, no matter what kind of stress I was under, no matter how bad a day I had had, no matter what plaudits I was getting from the public or from my peers, these are the really important people in the countryside.

Not everyone was welcoming, though. Back then, I approached everyone with the same youthful enthusiasm and optimism but my experience with estate owners was almost universally difficult. I was mistakenly lectured by none other than the then Duke of Argyll – when I politely corrected him, I received no apology for his rudeness and was ushered out of his office – while another major landowner tried to bar me from his estate after seeing 'Nature Conservancy Council' on my licence, despite my protestations that the agency I worked for had no association with the government. My own survey work soon began to show that the only areas showing an unexplained lack of peregrines were on Argyll's handful of shooting estates. These were the beginnings of three decades of professional conflict with such people and their 'servants', as the still extant 1832 Game (Scotland) Act describes their gamekeepers.

At this time I was 29 years old and had no direct knowledge of shooting or shooting estates. If I had been received with even a modicum of politeness, respect or understanding, it would perhaps have taken me even longer to find out what a hotbed of wildlife crime, aggression and corruption these places often are. The expression 'shooting yourself in the foot' springs to mind.

My battered old hire car broke down on the last day of my contract, 21 July 1981. The next day I hitched a lift to Dunoon and got a boat and train back home to Glasgow.

2

THE CONTRACT TRAIL

After my first heady taste of working with birds of prey, in Argyll, I was immediately unemployed again. This was to be expected. The number of people employed in bird conservation in Scotland in 1981 was minute. I could have no idea that we would see an explosion of conservation activity in the UK: that was still a few years away.

In my relatively blissful ignorance, out there in the hills, I was unaware of the drama and import of the passing of the 1981 Wildlife and Countryside Act, the UK government's response to the 1979 EU Birds Directive. The 1981 Act would, in later years, become my daily point of reference, the wording of certain sections as familiar as the words of a well-loved song and even less likely to be forgotten, in the heat of the moment, when I exchanged the stage for the witness box.

I went back to my old life of scratching a living through music. My wife, Jayshree, was finishing her studies in microbiology and was soon likely to be very employable in the new area of commercial medical microbiology. We lived fairly simply in our Glasgow West End flat.

In August, I set off with my friend Jim Gilbert, guitarist extraordinaire, on a busking and gigging tour of Holland and Rhineland Germany. By the time I got back, all the healthy exercise of the previous six months had been wiped out in one six-week adventure. Continental Europe, and Germany in particular, had all the respect for live music and musicians that the UK lacks: amazing hospitality from complete strangers, with only two nights' sleeping rough and the other 50 or so in friendly houses and flats, both in big cities and small towns.

The day-to-day struggle to earn money to eat and find a roof over our heads was so intense that I have only one memory of birdwatching in all that time: lying in bed one sunny morning in Heidelberg, in the house of a German couple who, as well as being live music fans, were a surgeon on a year's sabbatical leave and a restorer of mediaeval church carvings. Between the curtains, in the distance, I noticed a buzzard high above the valley wall, floating in a slow circle. A few minutes later, I looked again and saw a darker bird doing the same, then another and another. I finally realised that I was watching migrating honey buzzards, heading south for the winter. We, too, were soon heading south, hitching down the autobahn to Karlsruhe.

WEDNESDAY, 3 MARCH 1982

I was receiving a lecture from the rather severe young man in charge of RSPB vehicles at The Lodge, Sandy, Bedfordshire. This was my first visit to the famous address of the RSPB's UK Headquarters. I was looking at more wild bird conservationists than I had thought existed and was in awe of them all. Standing beside me was my partner in crime, Sandy Payne, a powerfully-built man with a big smile and a very large beard. We all had beards back then but Sandy outdid most of us.

1982 was the year of the first ever attempted full census of golden eagles in the UK, run jointly by the NCC and the RSPB. The respectful atmosphere changed, though, when our lecturer said '... and on no account take these vehicles off-road or up rough tracks!" Sandy and I exchanged knowing glances, trying not to laugh. We were thinking the same thing: that this bloke had not the slightest idea of what our jobs would entail. I had been given an area of Perthshire to survey, running west of Pitlochry across to Ballachulish in North Argyll. Sandy was my neighbour, with eastern Perthshire right across the centre of the Cairngorms to Deeside and the Ladder Hills. We would undoubtedly be driving up the odd rough track.

TUESDAY, 9 MARCH 1982

Tommacneil Cottage, Killiecrankie. I woke up early in my cold, damp cottage bedroom. Getting up and looking out of the window, the first thing I saw was an ermine stoat, running along the top of the low stone dyke that marked the bottom of my garden. Beyond the wall, a steep grassy slope led to the edge of the Killiecrankie Woods and, showing just above tree height, was the snow- covered summit of Ben Vrackie.

For the next few months I was able to watch this superb view change from winter wonderland to birdsong-filled summer sylvan paradise. I have seldom had a home that felt so close to nature. Roe deer were regular morning visitors to the garden, as were soaring buzzards and circling sparrowhawks. I saw bluebell woods and orchid meadows appear and disappear with the changing seasons.

On that first morning, though, it was simply time for breakfast before heading out for the start of my latest adventure.

As a near-lifelong vegetarian – as a very stubborn six-year-old, I developed an early dislike of the taste and texture of meat and, surprisingly, my mother went along with it – I have necessarily become interested in the individual eating habits of my fellow humans. Remember the timeline: I became vegetarian in 1957 and so, over the course of three decades, had to eat unending quantities of lettuce, tomato and boiled egg in cafés, restaurants and friends' houses. Thank God for Indian cuisine and modern choice.

In 1982, it was commonplace for grown men in Scotland to be unable to cook (I am sure it still is but bird conservation provides enough controversy in my life so I'll say no more). At the start of my second contract, I was still refining my 'fieldworker's diet'. My experiments with the evening meal involved instant mashed potato, packet soup, beans, cheese, milk, cake and custard. If I was feeling undernourished, I would occasionally buy a can of tinned fruit. Breakfast was cereal and milk. In Tommacneil cottage, I had a tiny kitchen with a Calor gas cooker but it was seldom used.

Whether indoors or in the car, I heated everything on a 'camping gaz' stove. I used as few plates, knives and forks as possible, as I always had to wash them immediately in the nearest burn to make my sleeping quarters (usually the car) as hygienic as possible.

Although very impressed by the food preparation and planning shown by Sandy on his visits to our shared cottage at Killiecrankie, I never followed his choices. He bought packets of dehydrated food, of the type favoured by mountain expeditionaries or military personnel, and produced quite tempting and, I was assured, healthy and balanced meals, also with the aid of a small portable stove. I could just have been lucky, or maybe it was a result of the incredible surge of positive energy which I always seemed to find when doing fieldwork in the Scottish hills, but I don't remember a day's illness throughout that whole incredible spring and summer.

What had changed by the end of that eagle contract were my daytime feeding habits. From taking a box of clumsily-cut cheese sandwiches and a can of juice in my metal-framed canvas pack in 1981, I had learned that all I needed was a packet of ginger snaps and an orange. Ginger snaps can't be eaten quickly but have sugar for energy; similarly, eating an orange takes time but is satisfying and good for you. In Scotland, of course, except during a spate after heavy rain, you would be very unlucky not to find a handy, clear, flowing Highland burn – the best water I've ever tasted.

9 March is Fieldwork Day 1 and it's time to go and hunt for eagles. The weather forecast isn't good. I try to search the crags of an upland area a few miles from the cottage. My notes from that day include 'snow, low cloud, strong winds, whiteout at 2..' This was the first and last time I ever got caught out in a blizzard. I was lucky: it struck when I was a few metres from an upturned boat at the side of a small loch and I was able to shelter behind it. Twenty eight years on, I can clearly recall thinking 'What have I let myself in for here? This is only my first day!' but, after a very long half

PATRICK WATT SANDEMAN

Sandeman was born in 1913 and grew up in Edinburgh. He had an 'interesting' war, being involved both in the British Expeditionary Force to France in 1939 and its subsequent desperate withdrawal across the Channel, and saw continuous action during and after the D-Day landings in June 1944.

His great passions in life were Scotland's golden eagles and the Gaelic language and poetry. On my first meeting with him in March 1982, I was regaled not only with stories of eagle eyries and Gaelic poems but also with a couple of tunes on the Highland bagpipes, a bowl of porridge and a large dram, all with huge enthusiasm and in the middle of the day.

Later in my career I would occasionally drop in on him in Killin when the porridge and drams continued. I still treasure the scribbled letters he would write, with details of some expedition to a local eagle eyrie, always ending with some Gaelic phrase. If I was lucky, I got the translation too.

One of my last meetings with Pat was when, to my astonishment, I met him ambling down a Perthshire mountainside on his way back from a remote eyrie. Wearing his trademark kilt and carrying a stick, his first words were 'Dave! What on earth are you doing here?' He was 86 years old. When I hear the line 'We will never see his like again', I always think of Pat. He died, aged 93, on 24 April 2006.

ient:sate:.

---

hour, the storm passed and I decided to stick to a lower altitude. Two hours later I had found my first, disused golden eagle nest.

Eagle monitoring in the Central Highlands of Scotland is utterly weather dependent. Over the next three decades I developed a strong dislike for the very common phenomena of low cloud and wet mist, sticking stubbornly to the upper slopes, where eagles normally build their nests and spend much of their time, hunting, displaying or merely roosting. This connection between golden eagles and our high wild places is, incidentally, every bit a result of human activity as it is a part of the bird's ecological needs. In areas such as Perthshire, the few breeding eagles which remain are the progeny of those which survived centuries of human persecution and disturbance, mainly by being difficult to reach. In many parts of the world, including the Hebrides and the Baltic states, golden eagles, when left in peace, will nest at all altitudes, right down to sea level.

Although my contract had begun on 1 March, a full week before I got into the field, much of my time had been taken up with very useful meetings with a series of 'eagle men', a mixture of professionals and 'amateurs' with some knowledge of the area I had to survey. This was a fascinating and, at times, humbling time for me, as I met some extraordinary individuals. The most extraordinary of all was Pat Sandeman.

Almost without exception, this previous generation of eagle enthusiasts were exceptionally helpful and generous with hospitality, time and, most importantly, with their hard-won information.

With nearly three decades of eagle monitoring behind me, I can fully understand the fierceness with which 'amateur' fieldworkers guard their bird information. Knowledge of the traditional home range or territory of a pair of eagles may be the result of decades of walking, watching, climbing and recording, often in the harshest terrain and in the harshest conditions possible on these islands. And that's not all. That work may have been carried out during the evenings and weekends, between a demanding job and inevitable family commitments. I have met quite a few eagle and peregrine 'widows' in my time and didn't always feel warmly welcomed when I arrived to take someone out on the hill. So when I had to deal with an official from a government agency, one of my own colleagues or, as often happened later, a police officer, demanding to know 'All the rare bird nest sites in the area.' They often got a negative reply. Unless the birds were under a genuine and immediate threat and passing that knowledge on would save them – sadly, that was rare – it was always up to the worker to say who could have access to such genuinely valuable and always hard-won data.

This short diary entry does not even begin to describe the excitement of those twenty minutes! My first active eagle nest, which I had found on my own, with the gigantic female flying a few feet above me down the narrow gully, quite literally blocking out the light. Like the vast majority of my fellow countrymen, I had never

WEDNESDAY, 24 MARCH 1982

'Walked up footpath (difficult to follow) into glen. Frogs spawning in pools and hollows in track … Turned off up river gully on north side of glen … started to see obvious bird of prey roosts. Then adult eagle flew off nest above me and headed off to north … beautiful gold head … scrambled over to other side for a direct view. Single egg (+2 feathers, large) … Left again very quickly … out of valley in 15 minutes or so.'

seen a wild eagle up close. It was a heart-stopping, awe-inspiring moment, most definitely the single most exciting encounter I had ever had with nature – and it will quite probably always remain so. I felt like I had seen a dinosaur or some mythical being: that there could be such a creature living wild in my own country was almost beyond belief. That may sound naïve or exaggerated to someone who wasn't there, but I wish that any young man or woman with the slightest empathy with the natural world could have an experience like that. It was, quite literally, life-changing.

Just one week later I had another life-changing experience of a very different kind. I make no apologies for placing these so close together – this is, after all, a book about wildlife crime. The fact that they happened within days of each other should convey a sense of the shock, bewilderment and then slow, deep anger which gripped me – and which grips me to this day.

MONDAY, 1 APRIL 1982

'Walked down track ...Walked up to area recommended by Bob Macmillan. Found nest immediately – large , 4–5 feet high, well-used on RH side lower, between small birch and rock ... recent looking branches and blueberry twigs with grass on top but no eggs ... Over to small crag to SW ... found dead adult golden eagle here ... half-eaten? ... Head and most feathers intact ...Took bird and feathers back in car to Killiecrankie.'

The body was taken to be analysed in Edinburgh. The result? Alphachloralose poisoning. As I now know only too well, this is the illegal poison of choice for gamekeepers and, back then, some shepherds. Its legal use was as a mouse poison (at 4% strength, no threat to birds) or as a licensed bird poison, still being used in the 1980s by 'vermin controllers' in towns and cities to kill 'pest' gulls and pigeons.

Despite the fact that placing poison in the open, to kill birds, had been outlawed in Scotland as far back as the 1912 Protection of Animals Act, it was still killing eagles in 1982. And it still is today.

I learned all this the hard way. No sooner had I discovered that these wonderful creatures were alive and nesting in the hills of my country than I found that there were people willing to break the law in order to destroy them. This bird had died within a hundred yards of an obvious nest, which it was building and where it was about to lay its eggs. It wasn't bringing food back to its young. There was snow on the ground and alphachloralose kills by hypothermia – even an eagle dies quickly in the cold. Eagles gorge on their food. It had died close to whatever bait had been left out. In short, someone had deliberately placed a bait close to the eagle's nest with the clear intent of killing one or, probably, both of the birds.

An investigation into the bird's death by the RSPB led to the discovery that the nest was located where three separate estates met. Letters asking for information were sent to them all but, not surprisingly, there were denials all round. There were no police Wildlife Officers back then and the Wildlife and Countryside Act would, in any case, not come into force until September 1982. Not that things are a whole lot better now: that home range remains unoccupied by breeding birds to this day.

Life carried on, as it does, and my eagle perambulations around Perthshire and into Argyll continued. By the time the contract finished in July, I had walked several hundred miles, climbed countless crags and was the fittest I ever expect to be in my entire life. I had even begun to walk like 'a mountain man', as instantly recognised by one of my wife's uncle's old friends, a Polish ex-mountain ranger who had escaped to Britain during World War Two. Apparently, continuous walking on narrow steep paths gives you a distinct, balanced gait. As I walked into his St Andrew's home, the old man smiled. 'Mountains!' he said.

Best of all, I took away memories of many occupied eagle eyries and was able to watch the growth of young eagles from tiny, just-hatched chicks to fully-feathered yelping juveniles. The sites chosen for eyries were, almost without exception, in areas of superb natural beauty. I can still recall sitting on huge nests, alongside eagle chicks as big as turkeys, and gazing out over wide empty glens. I knew how lucky I was. Sometimes I would be in the hills for three or four days at a time, totally alone except for wildlife. I watched foxes asleep on heather-topped blocks of rock, strewn down hillsides below my perch on a cliff, but never beneath an eyrie. I saw fox remains in several occupied nests. It's a stupid fox that sleeps in the open when a hunting eagle is about.

Again, the people I met were often exceptional characters. Eagle work back then was a largely secretive activity but I met a few forestry rangers, shepherds and stalkers who knew and loved their birds. Occasionally I accompanied them on their work in the hills, no doubt being covertly tested to see if I could keep up. This was before the era of quad bikes and the slopes of Argyll could be particularly tough.

The contrast between my week's work and my visits back to my Glasgow home were vivid. I can clearly recall the pleasure of playing my first chords on a guitar, sitting with my friends in a West End café, after days of hearing only the sound of pipits, skylarks and curlews on the slopes, the calling of peewits and the drumming of snipe outside my car at night, parked on a track down in the glen.

Once again, this paradise had to come to an end. I had learned a huge amount, though, about golden eagles and their environment and observed many other birds and animals as they went about their day-to-day lives. I had also carried on learning about how such countryside works: who owns it, who manages it, why people do what they do, be it living the hard life of a hill shepherd, with its own language and techniques, or living the life of a deer stalker or ranger. None of this learning went to waste in the years to come, when I was often called upon not only to look at the ways in which wildlife continued to be harried and killed while supposedly under protection, but also to try to understand the motives behind such illegal acts.

My growing love affair with golden eagles continued. After a winter working on geese on Islay for the NCC, I was delighted to get a call from Pete Ellis asking if I was available for a short contract on golden eagles in Lewis and Harris.

The 1982 Golden Eagle Survey had been a tremendous success, with huge areas of Scotland covered by hard-working contractors and 'amateur' workers. One exception, however, was the Western Isles where, after a heroic effort, the whole of the Uists had been covered, along with South Harris, but where coverage in North Harris and Lewis was patchy. It was thought that there might be a few more pairs to be found and Pete had managed to arrange a short – and very cheap – contract to find out.

In 1983, ornithologists were extremely thin on the ground on Lewis. In the middle of May, Pete Ellis accompanied me to Stornoway, where he introduced me to Nigel Buxton, the local NCC Area Officer. Nigel and his wife were to be lifesavers for me on what became a three-month endurance test, providing the odd meal and dram, not to mention amusing company.

(Nigel and I had a golden eagle v. ringed plover rivalry going the whole time). Back then, the biggest problem with going to sleep in a very welcome soft bed was the continuous racket from several calling corncrakes in the field outside. This was in Sand Street, in Stornoway itself.

Pete also introduced me to my accommodation and my transport for the next three months: a battered white Ford Escort van. Money was so tight that we couldn't afford to pay rent and hire a vehicle, so the van was the compromise. One glance into the back, through doors which never shut properly, told me that the last inhabitants had been live sheep.

At least it never broke down and, by careful arrangement of my belongings, I could sleep diagonally across the back, with my head against the passenger seat and my feet against a door hinge. Experience taught me very quickly that I would need to keep everything tidy and hygienic, washing dishes immediately, no matter how exhausted I might be.

The stars of this contract were undoubtedly the golden eagles which I found in profusion, nesting in a fantastic variety of sites, from huge remote corries, miles from any track, to gentle heather slopes within sight of peat cutters' huts where a flushed adult almost had to run across the heather to take off with deep, slow beats of its enormous wings. Nothing had prepared me for the sheer variety and density of wild birds on those moors: golden plovers, dunlins and snipe, along with the ubiquitous pipits and skylarks. On a sunny day on a sheltered hillside, I was surrounded by a beautiful symphony of bird song.

'Sheltered', though, might not be quite the right word. Lewis was without doubt the windiest place I had ever been and the almost continuous Atlantic breeze could be very cold. I clearly recall how disgruntled I felt at having to wear gloves at sea level in June. Fortunately, with three very physical Scottish fieldwork contracts behind me, I was prepared for the weather.

I had been told before I crossed the Minch that the people of Lewis, compared with other Hebridean islanders, were notoriously unfriendly to outsiders. That was not my experience. One particular encounter with a crofting household proves the point.

WEDNESDAY, 25 MAY 1983

I found myself looking helplessly across a narrow strait to a small island where, I had been assured, eagles had been known to nest in the recent past. I spotted a croft house close to the water, a few hundred yards along the unbridged sea channel. Tied up next to it was a small dinghy, with outboard engine and the ubiquitous pile of lobster pots. The door was opened by a youngish man with a strong local accent and a friendly face. I explained that I was carrying out a bird survey and wondered if I might get a lift in his boat across the channel? As luck would have it, he was about to go over to check his sheep.

We were across the channel in a few minutes and I arranged to meet the crofter again in a couple of hours. I soon discovered that the island had only one tiny crag and no seacliffs of any note, so that finding the old dried-out remains of the eyrie was very easy. It had not been in use for years and I wondered what had driven the pair to choose such a ridiculously accessible site. The attitude to golden eagles at that time on Lewis was difficult to predict. My experiences on the mainland in the previous year had reinforced my caution over even discussing eagles with people I didn't know, a policy which, sadly, I would still recommend to any incomer studying birds of prey in Scotland. As the contract progressed and I came across clear indications of disturbed and destroyed nests and, on a couple of occasions, openly-voiced hostility – once from a crofter worried about his lambs and once from a gamekeeper stupid enough to have put down pheasants in this almost treeless landscape – I began to understand what Peter Cunningham had told me.

Peter was a retired customs officer who had married into the local community. In 1983, he had just had the splendid *Birds of the Outer Hebrides* published and was the most well-known of the tiny number of naturalists living in the Outer Hebrides at that time. When we got to discussing eagles, he told me that he tended to avoid even talking about them with his relatives, as they were so disliked it would only lead to argument. I believe things have greatly improved in recent years, due to excellent liaison work between conservation bodies and the local community, and am pleased to say that the wealth of nature which I saw in 1983 and which was so generally unknown to the conservation community back then is now being fully recognised.

During my morning on the island, I took a rushed walk round, during which time I recorded seeing bonxies chasing terns, a raven, a pair of mergansers, wheatears, hooded crows, snipe, eider ducks, gannets, oystercatchers, various gulls, two wintering great northern divers and a blackbird, I met my 'water taxi' and was returned to the main shore. The crofter, John, then asked me if I would like a cup of tea. I, of course, accepted. (Note for anyone giving hospitality to a contract field biologist: never offer food or drink if it is in short supply, as it will all be eaten.)

We walked through the unlocked door and I was invited to take a seat in a warm kitchen where a kettle was put on. 'So where are you staying?' 'In the van,' I replied. 'What! That's terrible!' He obviously – pretty accurately, it has to be said – thought that I was living in dire poverty and discomfort and after giving me the friendly third degree, he loaded me up, with freshly-laid eggs and homemade oatcakes. (I got used to a full interrogation whenever I entered a house on the Western Isles; it wasn't nosiness, but a reflection of how close their own communities can be.) I still treasure that as one of most hospitable receptions I've ever had. There was a sting in the tail, though. As I was about to leave, a very old man came down the stairs and addressed me in Gaelic. 'Mr Dick is from Glaschu,' said John. 'I'm sorry, I don't speak Gaelic,' I said. 'What! You don't have the native language?' came the old man's reply. Many years later, I still go over the wisecrack reply I should have made; somewhere far back in my long Scottish ancestry, the old enmity between lowland and highland Scot still stirs. Fortunately, I was taken by surprise and could only smile an apology.

Every day was different and filled with the calls of golden plover, snipe and dunlin or the echoing screams of seabirds as I walked endless miles of moor and clifftop, searching for eagles. The great thing was, I was very often successful. The contrast with Perthshire could not have been greater. There, I would walk for miles over food-rich hills heaving with grouse and mountain hares, ideal eagle food, to find neglected or robbed eyries. As I moved down the islands, into the rocky mountains of South Lewis and North Harris where fast-flying waders and sheep carrion were the only abundant feeding, eagles were thriving. In case anyone thinks I am blinkered in my approach to eagles, I should point out that I found several occupied eyries containing dead grouse. As I walked these moors a live grouse was an extremely rare sight, but the eagles could obviously find them. Fortunately for the eagles, no-one was relying on these red grouse for their livelihood or profit.

My next boating expedition was a lot less comfortable than the last. I was living by the Ordnance Survey maps of the islands and scrutinised them each day, as I planned routes which would take me to likely eagle nest areas. One obvious target, with a kind of 'Here be dragons' allure, was the area of southeast Lewis known as Pairc. A huge expanse of hill and loch country, with no roads or even tracks of any size, I had never met anyone who had surveyed it on foot.

Tuesday, 14 June 1983

My early days spent monitoring birds came with a high degree of flexibility. No reporting back (perhaps once a week), no begging for permission to go into the hills, enough food, drink and equipment for a full day, carried on my back. So when I was passing the tiny cluster of houses on the west side of Loch Seaforth, known as Maraig, and saw two fishermen loading up a small boat, I made a quick decision to ask them for a lift across the loch. In a boat, it would be a five-minute crossing which I knew would save me hours of walking and place me right in the centre of Pairc.

With hindsight, I should have been more aware of the rather casual manner in which they agreed to take me over and pick me up again that evening. I should certainly have made more of the answer to my 'OK, thanks a lot … I'll see you tonight at around 7?' which was 'Aye … as long as the wind doesn't get up.'

Off I headed along the coast, as happy as ever to be out in the stunning Lewis scenery on a fine calm day. Two events stand out about that day's search for eagles. As the coastal strip narrowed – I had been dropped off at the only real flat area, next to a ruined croft – I had to resort to following a narrow animal track which hugged the increasingly steep hillside. Eventually, I found myself rounding a corner in what was just short of a cliff and about 150 feet above the waves. I remember thinking to myself, 'Well, this track was made by deer or goats and they were obviously going somewhere,' when the track stopped abruptly. All I could see in front of me was a landslide of scree. To add insult to injury, the carcass of a large red deer stag lay about 100 feet below me. I inched my way very carefully back round and down to the shore.

The second, rather more pleasant event was when, after a long detour up and along the high coastal ridge, I eventually located an occupied eagle nest on one side of a very steep gully. I had my back wedged into a crack on one side of the gully while admiring the sight of two large well-feathered eagle chicks sitting in their huge, inaccessible, overhung nest. They were only about 50 metres away when my view through the telescope was completely filled by an adult eagle landing beside them. My excitement can best be conveyed by repeating my field notes: 'Adult flew in while I was writing this!!!' I don't often put exclamation marks in what are essentially work notes. Throughout my career in bird conservation I have often been irritated by people saying, 'It must be lovely, birdwatching all day.' The reality has been that I have seldom been able to watch undisturbed wildlife for any length of time and I have always felt a bit envious of nest photographers with their hides, who can observe the home life of birds such as eagles for hours on end. This nest visit was no exception: although the eagle had failed to spot me, concealed as I was on the blind side of its nesting gully, there was no chance of such an alert and keen-sighted bird remaining unaware of my presence for long. To quote again from my notes: 'Carrying sprig of heather, turned round in nest, saw me 50 yards away and flew off again.' I got out of there fast.

I checked another likely eagle area inland, spotting clear signs of eagle occupation and resolving to go back another time, but was aware of my boatman's rendezvous on the west shore. As I came over the last ridge, the fisherman's words came back to me and my heart sank as I looked out over the sea loch, now a dull grey streaked with white, as a rising wind blew in from the Minch. No boat tonight, then.

I sat and waited for a couple of hours on the rocky shore but saw no movement from the other side. What should I do? Walking out was not an option; by the time I got any distance it would be dark and this unknown mountain landscape was not looking inviting for a midnight stroll. I walked up to the ruined croft and found it was already occupied. The local sheep had obviously been using it for shelter for some decades and had left their pungent evidence behind, to a depth of about two feet. I clambered up onto a platform of rotten planks, what had at one time been an upstairs room, and made myself as comfortable as I could. I had no sleeping bag but at least I had warm clothes. One bright spot was that my wife Jay had given me a large bag of home-made pakora and other spiced Gujerati food on her weekend visit a few days before. By complete chance, I had decided to throw it into my rucksack in my hasty packing at Maraig. At least I wouldn't go hungry.

I don't recall getting much sleep but I was young, and very fit after a few weeks of eagling. No harm was done, I came away just a bit chilled and with a few bruises from the floorboards. When I emerged in the early summer morning, it was to a fine day but with a strong breeze and, again, no sign of boating activity anywhere on the loch. I then made a decision which I don't know if I would have repeated later in life. My thoughts were, 'They know I'm over here, they can probably see me, they know Pairc and what a long walk out it would be … they'll come back for me at the same time tonight, won't they?' What made me trust to that, I'm not sure, but I'm very glad I did.

So, I had a whole day in Pairc. Only one thing for it: time to go and hunt for more eagles. I set off inland again, up and over steep ridges and across boggy glens. Even then I was probably thinking, 'I'm never going to be here again, I'm going to make the most of this.' The biggest enemy and all-round bugbear for a fieldworker is having to work against the clock. I hated it then and I still don't like it now. Working with eagles, in particular, is about a stubborn refusal to give up – what if the nest is in that very last gully? If I don't go over that ridge for a look, I'll be kicking myself every time I look at the map. On a good day they will have chosen the nest nearest the road, but on a bad day they will have found a new nest site in the last and most unlikely crag possible. This, though, was a good day. Two nests with chicks in and a third one with 'something white on ledge but distance too great – haze'.

I got back to my ruin at Kenmore (Ceann Mor) tired but optimistic after a marathon walking and eagling session. Seven o'clock and no boat, almost no food and the prospect of another cold, hard night and a full day's walk to follow. At last, at around 8.15 p.m., I saw the extremely welcome sight of a small boat heading out from Maraig and crossing the loch towards me. I almost leapt into the boat as it arrived. 'You'll have been wondering where we were?' said John. As a classic Highland understatement, I don't think I've ever heard better. I was too relieved to be annoyed and it certainly touched that black Glasgow humour which I have always relished and, I believe, inherited. My instinctive reaction was to laugh.

Lewis had one last laugh to come, however: halfway across, the outboard engine broke down so I shared rowing duties with John on the long trip back. I never did get back to Pairc, something I've always regretted, but I had a genuine wilderness experience that few could match in Scotland.

As I have mentioned before, close inspection of eagle nests was an expected and, indeed, crucial part of the 1982 census. We did occasionally come across a nice, big, freshly-built-up eagle nest with a conveniently-close high viewpoint and I was at times able to record nest contents, easily and accurately, through a telescope. What was far more common, though, was a single adult bird hanging about near a cliff which may contain several big stick nests. Early in the nesting season it can be very difficult to spot which, if any, nest is in use. Nests are often high up in a recessed, overhung ledge with no possibility of viewing from a similar height. Failed nests are notoriously difficult to monitor later in the season, when that year's addition to the top of a pile of sticks – which may vary from a few centimetres to more than two metres in height – has weathered down into an indistinguishable grey top.

There is often no alternative to a spot of rock scrambling – I won't dignify my efforts by calling them mountaineering. Years later, when I helped to design and take part in the RSPB's first climbing training course for fieldworkers, we appalled our professional trainers by describing the average eagle or peregrine site. Crags covered in vegetation and loose, wet rock are not the chosen habitat of expert climbers, who understandably avoid such places.

Although I had many hairy moments, one site in particular stands out in my mind. One of the few known nest areas was on cliffs above a sea loch. (I would like to thank the intrepid soul who 'gave' this site to my predecessors – the information here was certainly hard-won). I could see from my map that this was a big one – steep contours showing a straight drop from moor to sea level. I could see nothing of the cliff from above, due to its overhanging nature, so I walked a distance to the south where I could get access to the beach. Walking back to the expected spot, I wasn't too happy to see the front of a nest poking out of an immense cave-like hole, a good 100 feet up a near-vertical slope covered in woodrush. I had no climbing rope and wouldn't have known how to use one anyway. I psyched myself up and began a zig-zag ascent. Woodrush is a nasty plant to climb through – it can give good strong hand- and footholds but becomes lethally slippery when wet and, on a cliff, you never know when it will give way.

The nearer I got to the nest, the less interesting it was looking – all grey, with no discernible cup – but because of the recess, I could not tell if it was unoccupied. When I was a few metres below it, the woodrush ran out, but I could see a sloping ledge leading right to the foot of the nest. I started up the ledge to find that it sloped 'out the way' and the last two metres were covered very slowly, crawling on my stomach. Next, I had to climb the front of the nest itself – like woodrush, an eagle's nest can be very useful for climbing on but is unreliable. I pulled myself over the rim of the nest and found myself face to face with a half-grown eagle chick! Fantastic! As I pulled myself to safety beside the chick I noticed a dead bird at the side of the nest, a second, freshly-dead, eagle chick. I was having a very rare viewing of the result of the much discussed 'Cain and Abel' conflict which occasionally occurs in *Aquila* species.

After almost three months of such adventures and an unending daily list of wildlife encounters – eagles, otters, seals, skuas, ravens, merlins, greenshanks, all seen at close quarters and each one reinforcing my love for wild Scotland – I returned to a summer in the city of Glasgow. I had not once left the Western Isles in that time and it took me some days to readjust to crowds of people and exotic sights like double-decker buses and traffic lights.

In 1982, unemployment had again loomed ahead at the end of the Perthshire eagle contract but this time my work had been noticed and I was passed on by Pete Ellis to Dr Eric Bignal. I had met Eric during my peregrine contract in 1981; as the local Area Officer for the NCC, he was well aware of my presence and I had, in fact, accompanied him in his work boat on a couple of peregrine-related trips to islands.

The Wildlife and Countryside Act 1981 had now been given Royal Assent and was enacted in September 1982. At the time, it was the longest-debated piece of legislation ever to pass through the UK Parliament, an indication of how controversial it appeared to be to many MPs. One of the many immediate effects of this legislation related to barnacle geese. Under the 1954 Protection of Birds Act – the first modern UK-wide bird protection legislation, but most certainly not the first bird protection Act, since the 1880 Wild Birds Protection Act – there were County Protection Orders giving local protection, on paper at least, to many species including birds of prey and wildfowl. Barnacle geese had full protection, a fact I had to point out many times to those who referred to the 'good old days' when you could shoot anything. There was, though, one major exception.

Barnacle geese were given total legal protection, including on their two main wintering grounds in Scotland, the island of Islay and the Solway coast, from 1 December 1954. This protection was removed by an Order which took effect on November 1955 permitting barnacle geese to be shot in the months of December and January each year, west of the line of longitude that included the island of Islay. In 1978, this shooting season was extended to include the full wildfowling season of 1 September to 31 January, and to 20 February below the high water mark.

There were several reasons for this apparent anomaly. The main one was that the tiny Savalbard/Solway population had crashed to only 400 birds in the 1940s and was still very

Islay goose counters, December, 1983

fragile, while the Islay/Greenland population numbered perhaps 20,000, this figure including scattered groups wintering from the Western Isles down to the south of Ireland. Islay had the largest part of this flock due to its rich grass-based agriculture. Add to this a tradition of goose shooting on Islay and a very influential landowner – John Morrison, owner of Islay Estate, was MP for Salisbury, Chairman of the Conservatives' 1922 Committee in 1955 and later Lord Margadale – and the apparent anomaly is easier to explain.

The new era of the 1981 Act was a shock to this old system on Islay, where several estates, who owned exclusive shooting rights, had been hosting commercial goose-shooting parties from all over the world. Protection for the geese was not absolute, however, with an allowance under the Act, reflecting the European Birds Directive, for the granting of licences to kill for 'the purpose of preventing serious damage (to foodstuffs for livestock and crops)' if this could be shown to be taking place. The growing goose flock on Islay was a very visible presence on grass fields in the centre of the island, near their main sea loch roosts. By 1982, much of the livestock system of the island was based on the production of lambs and the first flush of grass, known as the 'early bite', was seen as essential. Unfortunately, barnacle geese do not migrate to their Greenland breeding cliffs until mid-April, well into the grass-growing season. The geese were learning to benefit from this bounty in order to build up reserves for their long flight and stressful start to breeding in the Arctic.

Almost every farm on Islay applied for a licence to shoot barnacle geese (it was still inconceivable then that the far rarer Greenland white-fronted goose would be a target for licences) and the Department of Agriculture granted them. The NCC – the government's statutory advisors on conservation – was concerned that the licensing system was very open to abuse. Conservation bodies such as the RSPB were also lobbying government on the issue, so the NCC decided to monitor the licensed shooting on Islay – and sent me to do it.

After more than 30 years of participating in, or even just observing, conservation politics, I would now see the storm coming. Back then, though, it was for a naturalist simply a very rare winter contract in a particularly pleasant part of the world.

I had only once before visited the island of Islay, on a long weekend during the winter of 1981 – 1982. I had been invited to join a group of birders (most of them were in fact 'twitchers', birdwatchers at the fanatical end of the scale) who were going there with the express intent of 'ticking' as many different bird species as possible. This led to two hilarious days of running round in two cars, communicating through a pair of very basic radios, in a competition to get a bigger list than the other group. I seem to recall one group's call-sign being 'Aquila' and the other one 'Dunnock', a clear insult at the time. This was my first real introduction to the bizarre world of competitive birdwatching: fun to observe but I've always preferred to hunt alone.

When I arrived on Islay in early October, Eric had arranged accommodation for me at Easter Ellister Farm. This was the home of Jane Dawson, the widow of Rod Dawson, one of the UK's early movers and shakers in the conservation movement. They had moved to Islay in 1974 with their collection of sea ducks including eiders, king eiders and harlequin ducks but, tragically, Rod died in 1977. I have since learned by experience that Scottish islands are a magnet for the energetic but unusual – some might say eccentric – within British society, and Jane is no exception.

I was welcomed in like a member of the family. As well as a huge menagerie of ducks, dogs and geese, there was a flock of very noisy guinea fowl, which woke me early every morning. I also recall Jane's two charming little girls, Lucy and Heather. I still smile at the memory of Lucy innocently asking me why I wasn't a pop star on television after I had been showing off to the family on my guitar.

My notebooks from that time are a mass of timings, numbers and place names – records of goose flocks on farms across the island. My main task was to record goose movements from their traditional roost site on Loch Gruinart, Loch Indaal and Laggan Bay. This meant getting up at first light for weeks at a time – fortunately, as these were the winter months, first light wasn't too early in the day. It was, however, often cold and wet. My field notebooks start in January 1983 with the poignant entry, 'Earlier NB waterlogged.'

This was an attempt to record the goose feeding behaviour, referred to by scientists as a 'time budget'. I used a canvas photographic hide to get close to the birds. I soon realised that this

With Nene goose, Slimbridge, 1983

30 JANUARY 1983

'Observe profiles, feeding behaviour etc, take NBs, torch, camera; in hide from 1050 to after 1400. Snowing, raining, wind – frozen! ... Back early to thaw out.'

was unlikely to be very useful, as it left me unable to follow individually-marked geese. Apart from slight variations in plumage between adult and juvenile geese, one barnacle goose looks remarkably similar to the next. One of my colleagues in later years used to refer to them as 'liquorice allsorts', a (possibly) affectionate allusion to their striking black and white appearance.

On another occasion, I had been lying on my stomach on a snowy hillside, overlooking a field containing a huge (3,000+) flock of barnacles, when I heard a strange series of croaking sounds from nearby. Looking up, I saw a pair of ravens circling no more than 20 metres above me. I realised that my lack of movement, as I counted and re-counted the shifting birds with my mechanical hand-clicker, had attracted these sharp-eyed carrion feeders. I left shortly after. Ravens are among my favourite species, wonderfully agile and evocative of wild places in Scotland, and I have often thought that at least I will provide them with a good meal, if I don't make it home!

I would not like anyone to think for a moment, though, that I was not enjoying myself. Once again, I had landed in a wildlife paradise. As I drove around the island each day, I had two cameras loaded and ready on the passenger seat – one with black-and-white film and the other with colour slides. I had used my unemployed years in the 1970s to learn how to handle a camera and, more importantly, had set up my own dark room back at my Glasgow flat. I returned from Islay with many rolls of film and have photos of geese, raptors, deer and landscapes which I treasure to this day.

The pictures in my mind become even clearer when I recall that, as I drove around in a changing variety of hired vehicles, I continually played Dick Gaughan's masterpiece 'Handful of Earth' on the tape machine. This combination of Scots and Irish folk songs was particularly apt for Islay, which has historical and geographical allegiances to both countries. As a musician, I soon fell in with other players and spent many a happy weekend afternoon playing in the back of Port Charlotte's pubs. The real highlight though, was the late-night sessions down in Portnahaven, the centre of Islay's *Gaeltacht*. Introduced to local society by Peter Macarthur, aka 'Peter Post', a talented singer and composer of comic songs, we would only stop singing in the early hours, when the drams had dried up. Some nights were held in the Portnahaven pub, created on the rural Irish model with no outside sign and consisting of a room with a few tables and chairs, peats in the fireplace and a hatch in the wall. A knock on the hatch brought the rather fierce landlady, asking what you wanted to drink. Most conversation was in Gaelic and everyone was expected to sing or recite. Allowances were made for my 'poor mouth', or lack of Gaelic. I communicated through music and only occasionally attempted to speak. This was a totally classless society, the only rules being an appreciation of music and good conversation. On one memorable night, I asked someone I had never met before, who had just finished a fine rendition of a Gaelic song, who he was. 'I'm ***** and I'm a superintendent of police in Glaschu,' was the conversation-stopping reply.

My favourite Islay memory is of saying goodbye at Peter's door, one of the beautiful horseshoe of cottages surrounding Portnahaven harbour, on a dead-still and frosty winter's night and hearing the great puffs of the breath of seals surfacing only a few yards away.

'On a night like this, you could count every star in the sky and not even care if you got it wrong,' as the local joke has it.

Not for the last time, I found the entry via music into the local culture to be very useful in my bird work. It was, for instance, a commonly-repeated line in landowning circles that the estates had protected the geese from poachers. When the chance came up, I asked some of my new, local singer friends what they thought about that? After a few knowing looks, one man's reply was 'Geese? Wouldn't touch them, everyone knows they taste fishy ... We've never bothered with geese here ... Now if it was a pheasant or a salmon, that would be a different story!' So that excuse, allowing the landowners to continue to 'manage' the goose shooting, was shown to be nonsense – or a cynical lie, for anyone in a belligerent mood. It was another crack in the crumbling edifice of any respect I still held for estate owners and managers.

The landowner line about poaching can still be seen in text books of the period, while the belief that barnacle geese taste 'fishy' is believed to come from observation of their habit of roosting on saltwater, whereas most goose species in Scotland roost on inland freshwater lochs.

My working hours, back in the centre of the island, included talking to the owners and tenants of the larger farms about any goose problems they might have been having. Their answers were very interesting and again opened my eyes to the extreme variations of attitude towards nature and farming which can be found even in such a small area. Some farmers told me that they had no problems with the geese, even when they were hosting quite large flocks. Some told me that they had very specific problems, at specific times of year, on specific fields. Others again had tried scaring the birds, with only temporary success. None of them had a good word to say about the estate shooting parties. Complaints varied from, 'We never see them, despite our having a licence to kill' to 'They just turn up on your fields, without any warning.'

One particularly friendly local farmer became exasperated with me when I asked him why, as he never appeared to have more than 20 geese on his farm at any one time (the farm lay many miles from the nearest roost), he had applied for a licence to kill? His reply was a classic of island obliqueness. 'See that byre roof over there?' He pointed. I looked at a broken-down farm building. 'Yes.' 'Well, I want the roof fixed!' The penny dropped: play ball with the estate over licences and they will look after you. No wonder most of the island had applied. Even after all these years, I will not identify the farm or the estate. I was learning that the relationship between estate and tenant can be a fraught one and I always avoided causing problems in that area if I could. Later, in my Investigations work, that tangled relationship often led to a wall of silence which broke down only when a pet or, just as bad, a working dog was poisoned. Anger would then overcome any fear of retribution and I would get a phone call.

The worst condemnation of shooting parties, however, came from my own observations, on several occasions, of geese being 'driven' off poor, unimproved grass and shot from behind walls as they attempted to land. Even when the birds were being shot on high-quality, improved grass, the effect was often to scare birds onto farms which otherwise had no problems. Shooting to kill seemed to make no difference over shooting to scare, as far as the surviving flocks were concerned. On several occasions, I saw geese return to feed on fields containing unretrieved goose corpses. I am aware that these are subjective comments, without the backing of large amounts of data, but no-one else was working on the problem at the time. It all looked like an unmanaged mess to me.

Even the counting of the goose flock was controversial. The geomorphology of Islay is particularly varied, as is the agriculture on top of it. Small fields of grass, hidden away behind hummocky rocks and rough grazing, are common. Every one has to be monitored to give an accurate count. By the time I got involved, Eric Bignal and David Stroud (on the island to study Greenland white-fronted geese for his PhD and today David Stroud MBE, Senior Ornithological Advisor to the Joint Nature Conservancy Council) had already designed a highly-efficient method of 'counting the island'. This involved several small teams of counters with set routes to be repeated, crucially, on a second day, to allow for changing weather and possible overlaps or omissions.

An accurate record of how many geese were wintering on Islay was becoming a very hot topic indeed on the island and beyond. It was not surprising, then, that some farmers were refusing to accept the official NCC figures, claiming that flocks had been missed, flocks that fed in the hidden corners of their own land. It was only after Eric actually took some farmers round on a count and showed them how thorough we were being that those complaints died down. (I am amused to see while writing this, in 2010, that the present Scottish Government, website explaining the Islay Goose Scheme states that 'Scottish Natural Heritage have only undertaken detailed annual counts of geese since 1992 …' Amused rather than annoyed, as I became inured in later years to the repeated claims of scientists and managers that until their new method was used to monitor, count or record birds, all previous information was useless.)

For me, these counts were a welcome break from routine – or as near to routine as that job ever got – and also an opportunity to catch up on off-island gossip with a small group of fellow bird enthusiasts. Due to my, by now extensive, knowledge of the island, however, I often spent most of the two days on later counts alone. The other counters were split into small groups, each of which included at least one experienced counter. The late afternoon of Friday, 22 April 1983 therefore found me driving slowly along a winding narrow road at the edge of the Gruinart Flats, a major goose-feeding area of level farm grassland and now mostly an RSPB reserve. Clicker in one hand, notching up groups of ten geese at the press of a thumb: '… ten geese, 50 geese, 30 geese, a hoopoe on the phone wire, 20 geese, 30… Bloody hell, a hoopoe!' I clearly recall my first casual recognition of this Scottish migrant rarity, followed by that proto-twitcher's accelerating heartbeat as you realise you are looking at something very unusual. The interesting point was my initial casual acceptance. A hoopoe is an unusual-looking bird, especially in the UK. About the size of a thrush but with black-and-white stripes across its back and tail, a long, downward-curving bill and an elongated head crest on top of a fawn-coloured back and head. The last time I had seen hoopoes, they had been grubbing about in the dust of a roadside park in Ahmedabad, in Gujerat State in India. They were a common bird during my first India trip and for a few seconds I hadn't registered the sight as anything unusual.

So what to do now, in the middle of a carefully-timed goose count? I understood enough about twitching etiquette to know that my name would be mud if I didn't pass on the sighting immediately. Unfortunately, this was years before the era of mobile phones and I was one of a tiny handful of birdwatchers living on Islay at the time. I dashed into the nearest farmhouse and asked to use the phone – I'm sure they must have imagined some terrible accident had taken place. The only person I could think of to call was Jane Dawson at Easter Ellister, who passed on the message to a couple of locals she thought might be interested. I rushed back to my car to carry on the count.

At the counters' meeting, in the Lochside Hotel in Bowmore that evening – it was by now completely dark outside – I casually mentioned that I had seen a hoopoe during my count. I had tossed a verbal grenade into the middle of the room. Two of the party were what I came to know as 'rabid twitchers' and they were not happy. 'Why didn't you come and tell us?' 'Gripped off by a bloody contract worker!' were two of the milder comments. I learned in a moment just what an affliction twitching really is: to be that upset at missing a wandering migrant, and not even a particularly rare one at that, struck me then as absurd and still does now. After they had calmed down, I told them that nothing would make me break off in the middle of a count and ruin a whole day, possibly even the entire two-day count. My 'affliction' was a sense of duty and responsibility to conservation, something which stayed with me during my later career. If you take on a job, you stick with it.

That's not to say, of course, that I don't relax – I have always made a clear division between work and play, and I know how to play, as my friends will attest! I've always felt a mixture of irritation and sorrow when I've met anyone – whether colleagues, police officers or twitchers – who just can't, ever, switch off. Again, I am very, very grateful for my ability to play the guitar and to be able to use that wonderful feeling of otherness that creating music can bring, both alone and with other musicians.

This is probably a good time to bring in my attitude towards competition or, more correctly, competitiveness. I am not a competitor. I don't like competition in any walk of life and I avoid it whenever I can. The only exception I make to that is in competing with myself. That could explain why I always did my best work on my own. I've shown that I can be a good team player but I do prefer to pick my own team.

Already, by 1983, I was forming my own opinion of how best to progress bird conservation in Scotland and it had little to do with birdwatching competitions or personal career improvement. I knew that the Scottish public had to see what was happening in their own country. My own experience as a lowland Scot, with a supposed good, all-round education, had still led to me being isolated from the real knowledge of why birds of prey – or geese or any other threatened bird species – live or die out there. That only came when I started walking the hills, seeing how precarious life can be for bird and man alike. It's about attitudes but it's also about individuals. Attitudes can be changed with a lot of hard work and by showing the facts in the right way, but some individuals will never listen and that's where the law comes in. I was learning to look at why some people don't listen. Money, profit and greed are great incentives to ignore or actively destroy wildlife and wild places. Just as powerful, however, are tradition, myths and old wives' tales. Add the two together and bingo – you've got a conservation problem. Add to that a mistrust of outsiders, understandable given the history of the Highlands and of Scotland in general, place all that on an island and bring in professional conservationists, and then you've really got yourself a conservation problem! I'm getting ahead of myself, though. As far as Islay was concerned, all that was still to come.

At this time, every farmer I met was keen to talk about the geese and their take on 'the goose problem'. Of course, no-one in power had really said 'No' to anyone yet. Some of the farmers wanted licences, so that geese were scared off their crops; all of the estates wanted licences, to continue hosting commercial shooting parties; and they had all been given licences by the Department of Agriculture for Scotland. As I've already hinted, attitudes varied across the island, depending mainly, but not exclusively, on how many geese were involved. The large-scale, centrally-based grass crop farmers were forceful about how much they were already spending on scaring and on compensating for losses to the geese. Some, a short distance away from the central farms, complained that the shooting in the centre of the island scared geese onto their farms. A couple of farmers even told me that they thought they got a better grass crop in the summer after the geese had been on those fields in the winter. All I could do was pass these opinions on in my reports.

My last day on the island – Saturday, 30 April – was an eventful one. A small party had been planned for that evening by my musical friends in Port Charlotte and Portnahaven and

I was due to drive onto the ferry the following morning. My wife Jayshree had come over to help me pack and enjoy the party and a leisurely drive back to Glasgow.

Pete Ellis, for whom I would once again start working, in Lewis, in a couple of weeks, had asked me to check out a peregrine nest site on a remote bit of the Islay coast. It was a beautiful, sunny weather, the kind of spring day that gives a taste of summer to come. It was hot and clear blue with stunning views of the cliff scenery. I walked across and around bogs and grassy heather, having left Jay at the car reading a book. 'I'll be back in a couple of hours ...' I said optimistically, knowing that such fieldwork can be as unpredictable as the Hebridean weather.

Although the Islay peregrine population at that time was fairly healthy – I had already visited a few traditional sites, which were all occupied – seacliff pairs can be notoriously difficult to locate. Quite apart from the viewing problems involved in trying to locate a bare ledge on what are often overhung precipices, the birds usually have a very wide choice of sites. They also have a bad habit, from the fieldworker's point of view, of flying quietly out to sea as a human approaches and it takes skill and experience to separate the adult peregrine from passing seabirds, which may be around in their hundreds at that time of year.

On this day my luck was in. I started finding 'kills' – the remains of birds the peregrines had eaten recently – at one particular clifftop area. An adult peregrine flew off almost immediately from under my feet, calling loudly, and as I scanned the cliff below, a second bird flew out from a crack in the face and joined its mate, their two harsh calls blending into that cacophony which speeds up the heartbeat of any peregrine worker. Success! An occupied territory with either eggs being laid, eggs already laid or laying imminent.

To get to the cliff edge, I had pulled myself up a steep heather-covered slope and I now started reversing down. As I carefully negotiated a mix of bare rock and leggy heather, backwards, and approached the bottom of the slope, I felt an odd sensation under my hand. Where I had been expecting a heather stem I had tried to grasp something that moved at my touch. It was a very odd feeling, but I had no time to reflect on it, as I felt a sharp stabbing pain on my forefinger, similar to a wasp sting. A moment's surprised shock came before I looked down to see a small, beautifully-marked adder, about a foot long, heading off into the heather.

I watched it glide away, sorry that I didn't have a camera at the ready. I looked at my finger. It was covered in a sticky-looking liquid around a small puncture wound. A snake bite. What do you do now? I was aware of adders in Scotland and even knew that Islay and Jura were well-known for them. I had never heard anyone who knew the countryside talk about them as a serious threat except, perhaps, to dogs. Malcolm, my childhood friend and now a vet on Arran, had told me that he regularly treated adder bites to dogs, usually with badly-swollen faces but even then not life threatening.

Some of this was going through my head but my main feeling was pleasure at having seen an adder, probably one of the earliest of the year brought out of its winter torpor by the first really hot day of spring. As I headed back to the car, I deliberately tried to keep an even pace – I remembered tales of 'hot country' snake bites and the advice that you should try to keep your blood circulation even, in case the venom spreads inside. Here's an interesting thing to tell Jay, I was thinking.

I got back to the car within about three quarters of an hour, by which time my finger had swollen visibly, in exactly the same way it might react to a wasp sting. I had been stung by wasps several times as a child, almost always due to my own stupidity – small boys were at war with wasps in my village childhood and could never resist poking a wasp 'bike' with sticks when we found them.

Jay's reaction was a surprise to me. When I proudly showed her my adder bite she was horrified. 'We must get to a doctor, fast!' I told her I thought it wasn't serious, I had been bitten nearly an hour ago and all I had was a swollen finger. She was adamant. 'Doctor. Now. Right now!' It was only later that I remembered her tales of growing up in a small village in Gujerat where cobras were common – indeed, she told me that they had a cobra which came to their house at the same time each year and for which, as respectful Hindus, they would leave a dish of milk. Cobras kill hundreds, if not thousands, of people in southeast Asia every year, mainly when they are harvesting crops.

So OK then, a doctor. I knew where the doctor's surgery was in Bowmore, the village in the centre of Islay, where I was staying at the time. A twenty minute drive later and we arrive at the doctor's surgery, which was also his house. It was shut, outside normal hours and on a Saturday. We asked around, to be told that he was playing golf but would be back in an hour or so. My finger remained swollen and stiff, as was part of my hand. I felt fine but increasingly uneasy about the evening's plans. 'Maybe we should just leave it?' 'No!' Jay was making sure I saw the doctor.

Eventually, a cheery middle-aged man arrived carrying a bag of golf clubs. 'What's the problem then?' I showed him my swollen finger. We agreed it didn't look serious, he asked my how I was feeling and took my blood pressure. 'It looks like you got only a small amount of venom.' I'm sure I avoided a more severe bite, as I was moving my hand when the adder struck, with one fang missing me entirely and leaving venom to lie harmlessly on top of my skin. 'First one of these I've seen, but I'm sure you'll be fine. Hang on, though, I'm sure I saw a circular about adder bites recently, I'll go and have a look.' He returned a couple of minutes later, looking serious. 'Yes, I thought so. Last year a young boy on the mainland died from a reaction to the venom so now I'm supposed to refer any bites to the Western Infirmary immediately.' 'The Western Infirmary? In Glasgow?' 'Yes, we'll have to organise an ambulance. What time is it? Oh dear, the last ferry's gone. Nothing for it, we'll have to get the air ambulance.'

At that point my world took a sudden shift. Even with this news, the bite didn't worry me in the slightest, but I was starting to get annoyed about this rapid change to all my plans. I had just spent most of the last six months on this beautiful slow-paced island, where everyone waved to you as you passed and people took time for a chat in the village shop. Now I was being whisked away – on an aeroplane, to the city – because I had a sore finger! Worst of all, I was going to miss my party. The doctor – and Jay – were immoveable. I was going on that plane, as soon as possible.

Phone calls were made and a short time later, I watched the tiny air ambulance land on the single runway next to the Big Strand. Holding a hastily-packed bag and saying goodbye to my wife, who now had to drive back to Glasgow alone, I stepped up into the plane and sat down next to a nurse. I had the first of many, many conversations about my sore finger. I felt like a complete fraud. This feeling wasn't helped when the pilot turned to us (this really was a small plane) and said, 'We're going to have to land at Campbeltown first, we've got a pregnant woman to airlift to Glasgow.' I don't remember much about the flight, except that the propeller engines were incredibly noisy and that it all went by very fast. As we approached Glasgow

Airport, the nurse said to me, 'You'd better get ready, you're a star, there's a load of journalists waiting to interview you with the ambulance!'

I'm pleased to say that my reaction to this news, in a time well before second-guessing the press became my almost daily job, was to tell her that I had no intention of speaking to journalists, who would only write up a 'snakes are horrible' story which would lead to more ignorant people killing adders. If I chose to grab hold of an adder by accident, it wasn't the snake's fault if it bit me.

I'm pleased to say – and many thanks again to the doctor, pilot and nurses involved – that I was whisked away to the Western Infirmary without being bothered. My next ordeal was a five day lie-in in the Western. All very nice, I'm sure, and I have no complaints about the service, but I was a very active young man back then and desperate to leave, sort my affairs out on Islay and get my life back. My daily routine – sitting up in bed with several monitors attached and reading anything I could find – was regularly interrupted by groups of medical students. Every few hours, a pack of trainee doctors would arrive and stand round my bed asking me the same questions. I'm sure they were all very disappointed when their 'rare snake bite case' turned out to be an obviously very healthy but grumpy young man, sitting up in bed and showing off a sore finger with, as the days passed by, almost no swelling.

Meanwhile, back at our West End flat, Jay was becoming increasingly irritated by phone calls and door-stepping by journalists, all wanting their 'snake bites man' story. I had explained that I didn't want an anti-snake story written and she readily agreed. As my days dragged by, she was left with just the one persistent tabloid journalist, who literally camped out at the door. Eventually her patience snapped and she let him in and made him a cup of tea. She told me later that the conversation went something like this: 'Right, my husband doesn't want an anti-snake story and I don't want one either. Where I come from, we worship snakes, they are a god called Nag. If you write a story which makes snakes look bad, I will be very, very angry and so will Nag!' 'OK ... thanks for the tea ... I'd better be leaving.'

She said he looked genuinely scared as she let him out.

A week later we were back on Islay to collect my things and have the much- delayed party. As I walked into the Lochindaal Hotel in Port Charlotte, carrying my guitar case, I was met with a chorus of 'What will you have, Dave – snakebite?'

An article did appear in a tabloid, a tiny piece describing me as a 'climber'. My main claim to fame amongst my friends was that my photo appeared next to the Page 3 girl.

The beginning of October 1983 saw me back on Islay. I was by now living close to the harbour at Bowmore, a beautiful village dominated by its round church at the top of Main Street, which slopes gently down to Loch Indaal. I was living in a small terraced building on a street made famous by the film *Whisky Galore*. This was a much more useful location for goose work, being centrally placed on the island.

By now, I was well acquainted with Islay and with the exception of a few isolated coastal areas, had walked or driven across much of it. Every day was still a new natural history adventure, though.

Earlier in the year, the local newspaper, The Ileach, had carried the shock front- page news that Islay Estate had sold off much of the Gruinart Flats area to the RSPB. Islay had, as I mentioned before, very few birdwatchers or naturalists with any profile, the exceptions being C. Gordon Booth, author of the excellent but now rather dated Birds in Islay, Dr Malcolm Ogilvie, then an official of the Wildfowl Trust, who had been coming to the island to study and count geese for many years, David Stroud, postgraduate researcher on whitefronts, Judy Warnes, researcher on red-billed chough, now married to David, and myself. The locals had no idea what this momentous change of land ownership would mean and there was, perhaps understandably, a good deal of suspicion of off-island 'birdy people'. Lord Margadale was widely known to have said that his land would only be sold to conservationists 'over his dead body'.

For me, there was little immediate effect. I had made myself known to the tenant farmers and kept away from the estate owners and managers. There was for me, though, a growing annoyance at the assumption that the NCC and RSPB were the same organisation. I was expected to know, in detail, what 'we' planned to do with the Flats. I had absolutely no idea.

One cold winter's night I heard a knock on the door and found a stranger asking if he could come in for a chat. He introduced himself as an ex-gamekeeper of Islay Estates, looking for work on the new Reserve. I poured him a dram and then explained that I didn't work for the RSPB and that I couldn't help him. We then had a friendly chat about his wildlife experiences. Two statements have remained with me. 'You know that bit of moor they've bought? There's no grouse on it and you know why? They shot them all! I told them not to but they didnae listen, daft b****s! This place is no use for grouse, it's too damn wet.' The other thing he told me was the location of an eagle nest, which I had never suspected – I checked it later and located a 'new' pair. Thank you again, whoever you were.

Judy and David Stroud with Hop the dog, Islay, 1982

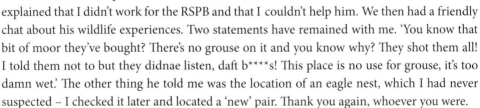

THURSDAY, 13 OCTOBER 1983

Notebook entry: 'Photoing scaup; pomarine skua flew past, very close, good view; two grey phalaropes on Lochindaal.'

I was sitting in my car, which was rocking gently in a Force 10 gale, sea-watching from one of the few high points above the inner sea loch. Loch Indaal is excellent for 'funnelling in' such birds of the open ocean during a strong south-westerly. Minutes before the skua turned up, I had been joined by a young man with a southern English accent who introduced himself as Richard Thaxton, the new temporary warden for the Gruinart Reserve. 'Anything about?' came the standard birder's greeting, just as the first of three 'poms' came hurtling past, just feet away from the windscreen. 'I think I'm going to like it here,' said Richard. This very early step in his career led on to greater things: for many years now he has been manager at Loch Garten, the RSPB's flagship osprey reserve near Aviemore, but I hope he still remembers that first day on Islay.

Life went on as usual – counting geese, listening to farmers' complaints, birdwatching and guitar playing on my days off. In November, there was a large increase in the number of shooting parties arriving on the island. I had to report two incidents of illegal shooting to the police, including one blatant shooting with a rifle of a barnacle goose, by a Frenchman, on the Gruinart Reserve. A farmer tried to give me a hard time over that latter incident. 'You can't report him, he's a guest of the Round Table'. I don't care if he's a Knight of the Round Table, I thought, but caution held me back. Little did I know that I was involved in the first encounter of what would be a 22-year saga. 'You can't do that, he's the head keeper of …/factor of …/ owner of …/Duke of …/ friend of …' Fill in the blanks! Funny how the law appears only to apply to lesser mortals in Scotland when merely wildlife is involved.

Then, in early December, I received a momentous phone call from Pete Ellis. 'Dave, I've just got the job as Shetland Officer. How would you like to take over from me?' 'What?' 'I think you should apply, you're easily the best qualified person I know.' I can't recall the rest of the conversation but I'm sure it went along the lines of 'Why me? I've never even thought about doing your job. Are you sure?' I said I would think about it.

In making my decision, I was well aware of the fact that Pete's job title was 'Species Protection and Investigations Officer, Scotland'. This wasn't just cops and robbers stuff. Pete was in charge of monitoring bird populations for the RSPB over the whole of Scotland. That really was tempting, as I was also aware that that would mean fieldwork all over Scotland. By now I was well hooked on working with birds of prey in particular and that would be the major part of my work. I decided to apply.

3

A NEW START

A clear frosty morning in December 1983 and I'm walking along the beautiful Georgian street that is Edinburgh's Regent Terrace. It offers a magnificent open view across to Arthur's Seat, the mountain in the middle of the city. Hearing a familiar noise, I looked up in time to see a long ragged 'V' of greylag geese, heading high over Calton Hill towards the Firth of Forth. I take it as a good sign.

'Who's on the panel?' 'Frank Hamilton, Roy Dennis and Richard Porter.'

Dear God. Three of the biggest names in UK bird conservation. 'You can't go in like that, you're wearing brown shoes, you need black ones! Quick, borrow mine.' Pete Ellis was more nervous than I was, if that was possible. Nope, I'd rather feel comfortable and be myself. I still don't own a suit. Old 1960s habits die hard.

I don't remember much about the interview, just that the questions about bird of prey populations seemed absurdly easy and that the panel of three seemed like nice blokes. I also don't recall who the other candidates were, or how many of them there might have been. I do, though, have a vague recollection of being called back in and told, 'It's unanimous, you've got the job!' with shaking of hands all round.

Fantastic! But hang on… what have I done? Panic seized me and didn't really leave me for several years.

I headed back to Islay to finish up my time there and hand over to my replacement. One rather surreal outing during that month was a flight to the mainland, organised by Pete Ellis, to attend the inaugural meeting of the South-west Raptor Study Group. Pete must have worked hard to get the RSPB to pay for that, as money was very tight back then, but it certainly paid off. Many of those attending that night, at Culzean Country Park, became colleagues and remain, I would like to think, friends to this day.

JANUARY 1984

A new year, a new city and a new life. For the first few weeks of my first full time job since 1977, I commuted by train from Glasgow to Edinburgh. I eventually moved into the flat above the office at 17 Regent Terrace, the flat which Pete Ellis and his wife Jan had occupied for some years before. This was very convenient for the office, of course, but perhaps too convenient.

We had what I later came to realise was a very unusual luxury: a month's handover time. Pete had no doubt explained to Frank Hamilton that this job was far too complex and important simply to be dropped into my lap without any explanation or guidance. After my relatively easy-going three years of fieldwork, I was swept up in a whirlwind of meetings, talks and travel. The whirlwind, of course, was relative – compared to what I was to face ten years later, it was a stroll in the park. But with new faces everywhere, new colleagues, new contacts and new ideas, I had a huge amount to learn.

Among the more alarming tasks was the giving of public talks. One of the first of these was to a Women's Guild group at a church hall in Dunfermline. As I sat with head bowed, mumbling along to long-forgotten hymns, I found myself wondering once again what I had let myself in for. Again, though, thanks to Pete, I was able to learn the arcane tricks of the trade: one slide per minute maximum and never leave a gory slide up for more than 30 seconds or you'll have them weeping and feeling sick. I came to enjoy giving talks to the public. At my lowest ebbs, feeling the sheer pressure of trying to keep going when it seemed the whole world was trying to stop me doing my job, I would go out to some village hall and be overwhelmed by the response. 'We're really glad you're out there, doing this for us,' was a common verbal pat on the back. Pity help any recalcitrant policeman or glib wildlife killer I'd meet the day after one of those talks. It was always about standing up for those who love wildlife and fighting the thugs and bullies who trampled on their values, values enshrined in our wildlife laws, although in 1984 you would have thought at times that the law simply didn't exist.

Pete left for Shetland. Day one saw me settle in to a room to myself (over the next 14 years at Regent Terrace, I had to move rooms seven times), a large desk and swivel chair, two filing cabinets, a Dictaphone, a telephone connected to a switchboard, a secretary in the next room and a large window through which to gaze. I'd made it to 32 years old without ever working in an office. 'So, if I want to write a letter, I speak into this, take the tape out and give it to you to type?' Isobel patiently explained such mysteries to me.

RSPB SHQ – Scottish Headquarters – was a very pleasant place to work. With only five executive staff (Director, Head of Reserves, Conservation Planning Officer, Education Officer and Species Protection Officer) and three secretaries, everyone was incredibly busy but we all found time, when back at the office, to have lunch together in an upstairs room and discuss our work with each other. That cross-pollination of experience and ideas was incredibly useful and productive and a world away from the sterile battery-farming 'work stations' in modern open-plan offices, with most people grabbing a lunchtime sandwich in front of their individual computer screens.

Pete had worked very, very hard in his five years as the first Species Protection Officer in Scotland. He had invented and then serviced a whole data recording system, based on card index files of course, as office computers were still in the realm of science fiction, as were mobile phones and digital cameras. This system included breeding bird details but also details of known or suspected wildlife criminals. I was soon to learn their value on both fronts and for my entire career, I both protected and enhanced such data and promoted its value. Most importantly, I used it. For the next 22 years, I watched people from many organisations, including the police and government departments, fight over the rights to such data, and then, if they got hold of it, fail to use it to anything like its real potential. I make no excuse for repeating what I wrote earlier: I always respected the fact that those who gave me information, be it the location of a rare bird's nest site or what the local gamekeeper was poisoning, had either worked hard or taken a personal risk to get it. Above all, they trusted me to guard and to use such information. It was also, of course, my job.

It is not my intention to go into any detail in this book on the internal workings of the RSPB, although I may occasionally allude to it, but I was always aware of the fact that the superb reputation of the Society as a whole was the reason why people phoned us in the first place. Years later, when police forces actually began to wake up to their responsibility to protect wildlife, some officers became frustrated by the fact that the public continued to phone the RSPB, instead of them, to report wildlife crime. I have no sympathy. If you want the public's trust, you have to earn it, and we did, the hard way.

It should not be surprising, to those who knew me before 1984 that I chose to take the Species Protection Officer route. After three intensive years of fieldwork, I knew a lot about peregrine falcons, golden eagles and geese, and had also made a lot of very important contacts amongst fellow fieldworkers, bird enthusiasts and bird professionals in different organisations. My plan was to get to know Scotland and its birds as well as I could and was encouraged in this by my Scottish manager, Frank Hamilton, and to meet as many key people as I could. It was a case of getting out there and doing what I could.

I won't lie. I had about as good a job description as I could have asked for anywhere. It suited me on a whole number of levels. As a lifelong birdwatcher and naturalist I could go and look at my favourite places and birds; I have always enjoyed travel and this work kept me on the move; I got to meet fascinating people and to live in places which I still feel are the most beautiful on earth, never mind in the UK.

In case anyone should be feeling jealous here, though, I should remind the reader that this was 1984. I was also working for a charity and one where we all still took the spending of members' money very seriously. Looking back, I know that we took that part far more seriously than did some of our pampered and occasionally pompous colleagues from HQ in Bedfordshire. A radio in a car was seen as a luxury. We were encouraged to stay overnight with staff or friends (those groups overlapped back then), for which no one paid or received a penny. The revolution in outdoor clothing and sleeping bags – I cannot begin to tell you how big a change a good modern sleeping bag made to my life! – was still to come and I recall often being cold and wet. The pay was ridiculously low, of course – I remember meeting NCC Nature Reserve Wardens with government salaries literally twice my own and who worked a fraction of my hours. Those factors were all just very minor irritations, though, as for the first time in my life, I had a full-time job and it was a damn good one.

There was almost zero provision of clothes or equipment so I bought and paid for my own cameras, telescope and outdoor clothes. Everything – every climbing rope, every rucksack, every sandwich and coffee, every litre of fuel –had, quite rightly, to be accounted for.

I had very little daily contact with colleagues at HQ at this time as I zig-zagged about Scotland, monitoring peregrine and golden eagle nests. I concentrated on areas I had known before, including Islay, Knapdale, Appin and Perthshire, but also managed to get round all the known peregrine home ranges, still referred to as territories back then, in Lothian and Borders. This latter area of work became a staple for many years. The main peregrine worker

Clutch of five peregrine eggs on nest scrape, Moffat area, 1985

for these sites was George Carse. Unfortunately, for both of us, he was ill that first season and I covered all his sites, while ignorant of their favoured locations and histories. Working from a dot on a map, no matter how accurately placed that dot might be, is only a small part of the story in bird monitoring. I wasted hours climbing up to the wrong ledges and meeting hostile gamekeepers, both of which I could have avoided if George had been around.

It was an idyllic time but certainly not an idle one. Once spring was well advanced, I started clocking up ridiculous hours on the hill and travelling huge distances. It was quite normal for me to be looking for ospreys at a loch in the Lothians in the morning and to be climbing into an eagle's nest in mid-Argyll in the afternoon. Although some of the raptor nests I was checking were undoubtedly under no real threat – most Argyll peregrines, for instance – I was already beginning to be steered towards troublespots. Without realising it, my happy days of successful ringing of chicks were almost over. As the 80s moved on, it became the norm for me to gaze into nests devoid of eggs or, worse, containing smashed eggs or shot chicks. It was some help later to recall the happy, successful days in beautiful untouched places, which may well have given me the strength of mind to continue dealing with all the horrors I was to witness in the future.

The Borders were a microcosm of all that peregrine monitoring can offer, from huge, untouched coastal cliffs with successful traditional eyries, recorded over hundreds of years, to the killing fields of managed grouse moors with peregrines attempting to breed and 'failing' year after year, as eggs and young were destroyed and adults shot, trapped and poisoned. I can recall George's astonishment when I told him that a pair of peregrines had bred on a grouse moor just south of Edinburgh in the late 1980s. 'The last time I saw birds breed there

GEORGE CARSE

A remarkable man, he was already well into his 60s when I first met him in 1984. I don't think that 'obsessed' would be too strong a word for George's relationship with peregrine falcons.

A shooting man in his younger days, he told me that he had first noticed peregrines when he watched one take a teal from just above the water on Loch Ryan at Stranraer. This was in 1945, at the end of the war, and George had been trying shoot ducks from the cockpit of a seaplane. He served in the RAF as a navigator, spending some time in bombers and then with coastal command. George's war reminiscences were unlike any I had ever heard – mostly unrepeatable but always vividly told and very funny.

He spent much of his spare time over the next 45 years looking at peregrines all over the hills of southern Scotland. This, of course included the bad years when pesticide poisoning by such agricultural products as DDT, Dieldrin and Aldrin had wiped out much of the UK's surviving top predatory birds. It must have taken a very stubborn man indeed to keep going with such poor reward, checking every likely cleuch and cliff over the vast expanse of the Southern Uplands. At one time the southeast population was down to seven pairs between Edinburgh and the A74 – in recent years this rose to 90+ pairs. We are again looking at a decline but nothing like what George had to suffer.

I learned a lot about peregrines from George, who realised that I was a 'stayer', despite the huge disadvantage of being a 'weegie' (a Glaswegian). George regularly stated his dislike of anyone who didn't share his Edinburgh background but in reality he could be a very charming man. He revelled in his supposed bigotry but was the first to laugh when you called him a silly old fool. I am proud of the fact that I was instrumental in getting George a President's Medal from the RSPB for a lifetime of service to peregrines.

George died, aged 90, on 13 October 2010.

was in 1945!' The other hazards they have to face are eggshell thieves, live egg, chick and adult thieves, pigeon fanciers (aka 'doo men') and disturbance from photographers., I had to contend with, or at least record, all of this and more in my first year as Species Protection Officer. By the time I left the RSPB at the end of 2006, the only real threat left was the direct killing and nest destruction on the grouse moors. I am aware that there is still the odd nest targeted by eggers, falcon thieves or 'doo men' but the birds face nothing like the problems we had in the 1980s. At the time of writing – 2010 – I have just read about a successful police-run guard on a notoriously-robbed peregrine site on the edge of Edinburgh. Well done – but where were the police back then, when we were losing perhaps a quarter of our nests to known falcon thieves and gamekeepers?

I may have wished I could spend my working life carrying out, or organising, fieldwork but the reality of the scale of law-breaking slowly became too obvious to ignore, thanks to an increase in information and informants. I have already mentioned the Raptor Study Groups (RSGs). In 1984 these consisted of the Highland RSG, North-east RSG, Central RSG, South-west RSG and South-east RSG. Even if they hadn't proved so useful for my work, I would have gravitated towards these people who shared my all-encompassing interest. I began to attend as many group meetings as possible and to follow up Pete Ellis' excellent work in identifying likely candidates for new groups. I may perhaps have overdone this, having been at one point (and in some cases for several years) chairman of South-west, South-east and Uists Raptor Groups.

The real trigger for setting up the Groups had been the very peregrine and golden eagle censuses on which I had been employed. I was one of a handful of full-time paid workers, in addition to many existing (and unpaid) raptor enthusiasts. The first two RSGs had been Highland and North-east, set up in 1980 by Roy Dennis and Adam Watson respectively in response to concerns about over-visiting of the same golden eagle eyries. This respect for the birds has remained the main ethic behind the groups and they carry out an essential role in monitoring their own fieldwork activities. Back in 1980s Deeside, passions ran high on this subject and the inaugural meeting of the North-east group did in fact end in a punch-up in the bar. I've never heard of anyone taking things that far since then, I'm pleased to say, but I've seen a few people get a rough ride verbally if group members disagree strongly with a suggested course of action. That tended to happen to government officials in particular.

Passions always run high on the subject of birds of prey and I used to say in my public talks that there are two types of people in Britain: those who want to stamp on every bird of prey they see and those who would like to take them home and cuddle them. I exaggerated for effect, of course, but wasn't too far off the mark. It is this very passion, both for and against, that has led to our protection laws. The 19th and early 20th centuries saw several species wiped out by people with a passionate hatred of birds of prey, as can be seen in any book about game shooting from the period, while today, a perceived threat, such as applications for licences to kill, can trigger a parliamentary debate.

Not all raptor enthusiasts were welcoming and here I have to single out the North-east group, which displayed an obvious mistrust of the RSPB. A fear of outside interference, similar to the one I had witnessed in Islay farmers, was apparent for a long time. Although I oversaw the growth and combining of the groups into the Scottish Raptor Study Group network, I never lost sight of the fact that these were individual volunteers who could and would just walk away if they didn't like what I was doing. More than once, I saw them face off attempts by the NCC and then SNH (Scottish Natural Heritage) to make asking landowners for access to land a compulsory requirement on their disturbance licences. They knew that they could simply not bother with licences at all, carry on as usual and cut off the flow of information on birds on which we relied. I fully understood that point of view and openly backed them up, sometimes as chairman of a Group. As I've said before, I'm not impressed by bullying, whether by a government agency or an individual. Twisting the law for political gain impresses me even less. It remains a fact that it is not a legal requirement to get a landowner's permission to monitor rare birds. Wild birds do not belong to the landowner in this country: a very important distinction is made in law between domestic and wild birds and animals.

In south Scotland I was welcomed with open arms. There, I came across a tradition of what might once have been called 'working-class naturalists'. The exemplar of that would be Dick Roxburgh. Dick was an ex-mine worker who had lived all his life in the village of Catrine, Ayrshire. His passion was peregrine falcons and like his contemporary, George Carse – with whom he shared a friendly rivalry, with me stuck in the middle – he was able to witness the decline and subsequent return of his favourite birds. I can still recall the excitement with which he showed me the first ground-nesting peregrine he had ever seen. In fact, the South-west Raptor Study Group was a happy crew altogether in those days. At the inaugural meeting, Gordon Riddle, kestrel worker par excellence, was haranguing all of us peregrine men about the fact that the newly-'returning' peregrines were reclaiming their old nest ledges from kestrels which had filled the gaps and killing them. Bernie Zonfrillo, an outspoken Glaswegian peregrine ringer, now a well-respected university researcher, drew a huge bellow of laughter when he replied, 'Come off it, Gordon, everyone knows kestrels are just members of the budgie family!' To be fair, we did all sympathise with Gordon but Bernie's macho line went down well.

Dick Roxburgh's biggest contribution to conservation in Scotland was not his own personal knowledge of birds but the fact that he worked so hard to share it. He built up a group of local men, enthusiastic to learn, and showed them 'the secrets of the peregrine'. These guys are now all stalwarts of the local RSGs – one of them gained an MBE for his work with birds, another is now a senior RSPB manager. It was a delight to me as a young man to again hear the accents and dialect of my North Ayrshire childhood, all those forgotten descriptive words and phrases: whaups [curlews], peesies [lapwing], puddocks [frogs] and mowdiehowkers [molecatchers].

When it became obvious that thieves supplying the illegal falcon trade were becoming a growing problem in the south-west, I was very keen to help out. The theme remains the same: if you want the public to work with you, particularly those people who have already worked hard, or taken risks, to get information, you have to earn their trust by standing up for them. And most importantly of all, you have to get out there and catch the thieves and bird killers. Knowing what you are talking about and having some street cred as a fieldworker does help, of course.

Similar problems were being experienced in Dumfries and Galloway (at that time, part of the South-west Raptor Study Group area), Fife, Stirlingshire and Perthshire (all lumped into Central RSG) and of course South-east. The Highlands were very much the patch of Roy Dennis and Roger Broad, RSPB staff with far more experience than I had. Little or no information was forthcoming from North-east and it was only much later on that I discovered that similar thefts had been going on within a localised area of that region.

By now I had a growing band of expert raptor workers willing to share detailed information with me. As a Species Protection Officer, that information was invaluable for understanding the status of rare birds – the main species being monitored then were golden eagles, peregrines and merlins – which allowed my colleagues to analyse any threats and allocate our meagre resources in the right places and in the right way.

This information was also showing me the extent and nature of wildlife crime against birds of prey. It was then, and remains today, by far the largest area of wildlife crime being committed in the Scottish countryside. I had no problem in seeing where my own priorities, as an Investigations Officer, lay.

Birds of prey were never my only concern, or indeed responsibility, no matter how pressing their threats might be – the UK has several hundred species of birds, either as breeding residents, summer or winter migrants or as casual visitors. Not all of this plethora of species are universally liked. Special interest groups within society may have their own reasons for wanting rid of some wild birds: car owners for the mess made by rooks and starlings, house owners for the mess made by house martins, sand quarries which find extraction blocked by sand martin colonies, salmon fishermen wanting rid of sawbill ducks and cormorants and seals, farmers wanting rid of rookeries, shepherds wanting rid of crows, gulls, ravens and even eagles. After that there are those individuals who like to shoot wild birds for 'sport' and who were, and are, extremely sensitive about any restriction on their hobby, or indeed any wildlife which gets in the way.

At this point I should mention that the RSPB's Royal Charter, what you might call its rules of engagement, very clearly states: 'The Society shall take no part in the question of the killing of game birds and legitimate sport of that character.' I took that very seriously. I always made this neutrality on shooting clear when I gave talks or when engaging with the press and media. At times this made my life difficult – it is a fact that the great majority of birdwatchers and, I am sure , RSPB members, are not shooters – and I had a steady stream of callers who wanted to complain about some legal ('legitimate sport') shooting activity. I had to advise them about legal shooting and 'pest' control as much as I gave advice about illegal activities, a fact that is never recognised by our very short-sighted critics in the shooting community.

Neutrality meant just that – we were as often criticised for not standing up for shooting on the grounds of habitat management or pest control, for example. Those people got the same response. It was quite literally not my job either to promote or disparage shooting.

The positive side of this was that I was able to concentrate fully on anything which was not legitimate without getting sidetracked. Given the fact that the RSPB was, even then, by far the biggest environmental organisation in the UK and, unlike many of the other lobbying groups, was actually unable to attack shooting organisations even if it wanted to, their stunning stupidity in repeatedly criticising the RSPB is quite unbelievable. Unbelievable, that is, until you begin to understand the scale of illegal killing of birds of prey and ruthless destruction of any bird or animal termed 'vermin', both then and, I'm afraid, to this day. By the mid 1980s I had already come to this conclusion and have found it reinforced with every passing year.

As already mentioned with respect to the Islay goose situation, the 1981 Act had some very interesting effects with regard to tightening up previous practices involving the killing of wild birds. Law-abiding members of the community changed some of these practices

I have always thought that the trite statement, 'Ignorance of the law is no excuse' is a bully's charter: with thousands of laws covering every aspect of our lives, no-one can be expected to know them all. Some areas of wildlife law can be complex – just consider the large numbers of bird, animal and plant species with differing levels of protection. However, many of those I came up against claimed very loudly to be professionals and experts on the countryside and their sudden ignorance when confronted by the RSPB and police didn't ring true. This was especially obvious by the time we get to the 1990s, when my own work in publicising crime incidents and court cases and that of professional organisations such as the National Farmers Union of Scotland, the Scottish Landowners Federation and the various Gamekeepers Organisations through their magazines and conferences, made these laws common knowledge.

One of the earliest groups to respond in a responsible manner were the UK's growing number of fish farms. In Scotland, freshwater trout farms were advised by the Department of

Agriculture for Scotland (DAFS) that they could apply for licences to kill fish-eating birds – herons and cormorants were the main targets – but that they would be inspected before any licence was granted. In a move that I now see as one of the more intelligent and successful partnerships, the Department involved the RSPB as bird experts to accompany their staff on these early inspections. I believe that there had been some concern expressed over the granting of such licences in the years prior to my employment.

And so in August 1984 I found myself travelling round Scotland with department officials looking at the siting and defences of around a dozen trout farms, from Galloway to Aberdeenshire. Amongst other benefits, this was my first friendly professional introduction to DAFS field staff, for whom I came to have a growing respect, later enhanced by working with them on many wildlife poisoning cases. Mostly, though, I learned about the workings of fish farms, including their economics.

At least one of the farms had been sited in a ludicrous situation, adjacent to a large heronry which I was able to discover had been established long before the fish farm, proving the usefulness of birdwatcher's records! Such indifference to wildlife, the belief that it is always disposable in the face of economic development, became a common theme in many of my cases.

The deciding factor, for no licences for herons were issued the following year, was that either no defences (stringing or netting over pools, steep banks and wire to keep birds away from pool edges) had been deployed or else they were not being used properly. Advice on these issues was given – free – and we asked a lot of questions about the costs of netting and levels of damage. On all occasions, the costs of defences turned out to be a very small fraction of the claimed annual fish losses. This information became very useful to me in my reports for Procurators Fiscal (and on one occasion, by request, directly to a sheriff) regarding cases involving fish farm bird killings in later years.

Two related issues arose here. Early attempts to get the farms to use brightly-coloured strings and netting led to local objections over their unsightly appearance – sometimes you just can't win! – while the problem of birds getting entangled in the almost invisible netting started to become serious when it involved members of the tiny migrating or locally-nesting osprey population. I am very pleased to say that where ospreys were concerned, fish farmers were universally helpful. In those days I would receive concerned phone calls if an osprey was caught or injured. I can only hope that attitude still prevails today, when the osprey population has grown and spread in such a welcome fashion.

Ospreys were very much on my mind in those early years. The Loch Garten story was well known to anyone interested in wildlife in Scotland. Numbers of breeding pairs had crept up during the 1950s, 1960s and 1970s, thanks to the efforts of conservationists and many dedicated local people, but they were still almost exclusively confined to the Highlands. In 1984, the total population was still less than 50 pairs. Roy Dennis, the RSPB's Highland Officer, had been heavily involved in the osprey story since the 1950s. I was shown successful artificial osprey nests built by Roy and was fired by his enthusiasm for spreading the population to southern Scotland. He rightly pointed out that the only limiting factor would be nest sites and food supply and that fish were plentiful in estuaries, lochs and rivers all over Scotland. I was hooked.

I started looking at all the records of migrating birds in Scotland, mainly recorded by keen birdwatchers and fish farmers. It was obvious that birds were using the main river valleys right across the south. By building nests on these flight lines, I should be able to 'catch' a pair of young birds heading north. Ospreys are ideal for this kind of benign manipulation. Young birds return from Africa and are seldom successful in their first nesting attempts, often due to the building of flimsy nests which can easily get damaged in Scotland's unpredictable summer weather. They also wander widely at this stage, seeking out good feeding areas. The real clincher, though, is that ospreys are a loosely colonial species, attracted by their own kind and particularly attracted to other osprey nests. On one occasion in the Borders, long before any nesting took place anywhere in that region, I was putting the finishing touches to an artificial nest at the top of large conifer when I looked up to see an osprey soaring above me!

Ospreys nest not in trees but on top of them, an unusual habit for a British breeding bird. They also tend to build nests in the tallest, most obvious trees, in a location where they have good all-round visibility. By now I've seen a good number of exceptions to those rules – small trees, trees lower than the surrounding forest edge – but back then, that's what I expected. I went tree hunting. One companion on those expeditions was Ray Hawley, the RSPB warden at Loch Ken in Galloway, an expert birdwatcher and a very amusing and informative companion. As well as using the rough migration routes, we had a few ground rules: not too obvious (egg thieves were very much on our mind, as well as casual disturbance and nuisance nest photographers), not near fish farms (there was no need to deliberately introduce a whole family of fish predators) and somewhere that the landowner wouldn't object to having the top lopped off a tree!

I had been given some good practical guidelines by Roy – you don't, for instance, actually need an old cartwheel for the base, as with the first early attempts in Scotland! We worked in the winter months, hoping to catch spring migrants and because the breeding season tended to be ridiculously busy with other matters. We'd find a tree, get permission and get our tools together: climbing harness and ropes, saws, string, spray paint. I eventually kept a nest building kit in an office cupboard. I always tried to use local materials – branches, grass and moss – as would an actual osprey. I also used my assistants, local RSPB staff or RSG members. Most of the nests I built were made by a team of two or three and they usually took between three and four hours to complete.

By the 90s, there were a growing band of nest builders in Scotland – particularly once Forestry Commission staff got into their stride – and we each had slightly different techniques. Conversations at bird conferences would have sounded particularly bizarre to any eavesdropper: 'So, climb the tree, attach yourself to the tree, chop off branches to form a tripod of stumps, lash on the large base branches, tie on the cross sticks, pile on smaller sticks, then dump a sack or two of deer grass and moss on the top. As a final touch, spray a little white paint around to imitate osprey's leavings. Job done.'

It sounds so easy. Getting to the remote sites could be a problem in itself. One of my first nests was on a Scots pine teetering on the edge of a cliff and swaying alarmingly in the January wind. I put up with rain, sleet and even snow. Treetops get all the weather but they can also be beautiful places, offering panoramic views and strange phenomena. Wild birds seemed to lose all fear of humans up there and I clearly recall on a treetop in Galloway hearing a whooshing sound as a flock of fieldfares descended on the trees all around me. On another occasion, a pair of crossbills, unconcerned, fed their nestlings in the neighbouring tree as I sawed and hammered away.

I must have built around 20 nests and helped build several more up to the early 1990s, from the west of Galloway to Berwickshire in the south and up to Stirlingshire and Perthshire further north. One particularly hilarious expedition, carried out with two colleagues, saw us carrying an inflatable boat over a ploughed field, over a barbed wire fence, through a reedbed, across a shallow loch, through tough willow bushes (tough enough to need a chainsaw) and onto a tree-covered island. That was before we started building the nest, in a gigantic Scots pine. By the time were finished it was dark and we carried out the return journey, rowing through flocks of roosting greylag and pink-footed geese, which merely paddled away on our very close approach.

I would like to say that all these nests were now fully occupied by nesting ospreys – several actually are – but my optimism was not matched by the birds and it is only now, over 25 years later, that the osprey expansion has begun in earnest in south Scotland. That said, this is a wonderfully successful technique overall. In the early 1990s, a third of all occupied osprey nests in Scotland were on artificial nests, including those at Loch Garten and Loch of the Lowes, flagship 'open sites' for the RSPB and SWT (Scottish Wildlife Trust) respectively.

I'm also pleased to have taught my techniques to others who continue to help the osprey population throughout the UK in this unusual manner. Lastly, this area of work brought me extra pleasure when I remembered my mother, now in her 91st year, giving me a hard time for my persistent climbing of trees as a young boy!

Friday, 6 December 1985

I'm in Northern Ireland. The RSPB had had a presence there for a long time but, as with Scotland at this time, that presence was small, although at the start of a major expansion.

Mainly due to the great success of the kestrel watch at Peterborough – a live-footage camera on a kestrel nest, beaming back pictures to an interpretation point manned by RSPB staff – out-posted staff were asked to be on the lookout for any such opportunities. A particularly keen staff member, Chris Murphy in Northern Ireland took this very much to heart and spent some valuable time assessing peregrine nest sites, mainly on the Antrim coast and close to Belfast. He reported his findings back to HQ, where it was decided by Richard Porter that I, as a peregrine expert, should fly across and have a look at Chris's ideas.

I had never been to Ireland before. My preconceptions of the place were based on the few very friendly Irish musicians I had met, the beautiful but almost incomprehensible Irish student nurses from Rottenrow Maternity Hospital in Glasgow who used to visit the Saltmarket folk pubs to listen to traditional music from home, and of course 'the Troubles', which were never off the news and which were in a rather lively phase at the time. It was a confusing mixture to say the least, so it was with some trepidation that I took the flight from Glasgow to Belfast Harbour airport in a rattly, aptly-named Shorts Skyvan.

Of course, I was just one of very many people at that time who had to learn first-hand that Ireland, north and south, is full of delightful, friendly, funny, bright, optimistic and, above all, hospitable people. My first B & B breakfast could have choked a horse, as they say. Getting people to stop talking to you was a problem. After this first visit, I always looked forward with eager anticipation to any Irish trip

That first day, Chris kept us hard at it – we visited eight or nine sites from Strangford Lough, south of Belfast, to the north coast of Antrim. We saw peregrines at almost all of these low-ground, coastal sites where the birds spend the winter on territory. The qualities I was looking for in the ideal open site were easy access to the public, close to an accessible source of human population (either locals or tourists), access to volunteers, access for camera equipment and, above all, somewhere where the birds themselves would not be put at risk. In those days of regular attacks by egg and chick thieves, confidentiality of information (what our detractors called 'secrecy') was all-important. I drummed my mantra into raptor workers and fellow staff alike: 'Once you've made a site public, you have a responsibility to protect it.' When you are dealing with a bird like the peregrine, which has traditional eyries, that responsibility is never-ending.

At most of the sites I met local people, birdwatchers and even government officials – everyone was very keen, to have 'their' nest chosen. Nothing, however, prepared me for our final site visit. 'OK, Dave, that's the lot,' said Chris, 'although there is one more. I'm not sure if it's what you're looking for? It's a bit up country... in a quarry... but it's got a primary school right beside it and we could maybe get the school involved?' Good thinking, Chris. In fact, very good thinking, and Chris was way ahead of his time here. It was some years before that kind of link-up was successfully made, culminating in the modern situation where red kite reintroductions in the Highlands and Gateshead have Adopt a Kite schemes by individual local schools.

Although fairly tired, I was up for it. We headed inland and after driving into gently rolling farmland for more than an hour– fairly untypical peregrine country at the time – we arrived on the outskirts of a small village. Chris parked the car at the side of the road and we were looking down and across a wooded dip towards the steep back wall of a small disused quarry when a man walked across and shook Chris's hand. 'Hello ****, this is Dave Dick from Scotland, we're here to look at the peregrine and talk over that idea we spoke about.' I introduced myself and we got into a pleasant discussion about the birds, the school and the possibilities of putting up a camera. Although the site was well off the beaten track, I was beginning to warm to it – I knew my friends in the Education Department would like it. However, my Investigations Officer instincts started to niggle so I turned to our companion. Thinking about pigeon fanciers, rogue falconers, egg thieves and the other usual roll call of enemies of the peregrine, I asked, 'Do you ever get any problems with folk interfering with the birds?' The man smiled. 'You see that wee cottage down there? Well, the man that lives there saw two lads with an airgun walking towards the peregrines. So he called up the boys. They fell down and hurt their knees badly on the way out'. Trying to stay calm I said, 'The boys?' 'Aye, sure, these are Republican peregrines – they've got green, white and orange roundels on each wing!' 'Right, so they're looked after, then?' 'Oh aye, no problem.'

The conversation tailed off soon after, we both thanked the man and then drove off. After we got round the first corner, I told Chris just what I thought of his wonderful idea. 'Repeat after me, the Royal Society for the Protection of Birds, you idiot! We'd end up with tit-for-tat peregrine killings!'

I'm sure I must have calmed down very quickly, though I was glad to get out of the area. We certainly sank a few pints of Guinness later. Thanks, again, Chris, for a very interesting visit.

4

FIRST CAPTURES

I have never harboured any secret desire to be a policeman. In fact, as a student and musician in the 1960s and 1970s, during my long-haired teenage years and into my early 20s, I had a culturally-normal mistrust of the police, no doubt reciprocated, given my appearance at the time. In fact, I had managed to avoid the police almost entirely up to the point where I became an RSPB Investigations Officer.

Some rather confused people – and among the worst offenders were the police themselves – objected to the very term 'officer' in my job title. All it meant was that I was an 'office holder' or 'official' of the RSPB with responsibility for investigating – finding out about, looking into, understanding – anything that my employer wanted investigating. In my case, I had to look at allegations of law breaking where wild birds were involved. Given the history of the RSPB, a charity which has been involved in trying to promote workable bird protection laws from its very inception in the late 19th century, I don't see anything odd about that. During my time with the RSPB, it was the organisation's very clear and often publicly-stated policy that it was up to the police to enforce wildlife laws and that we would do our utmost to help them. Like all my colleagues, I had no legal powers beyond those of any civilian and certainly no desire to change that. I promoted that policy as hard as I could but I did expect the police to do their job at least as well as I did mine.

One of the commonest statements I heard, particularly after giving a talk and particularly from birdwatchers, was, 'I don't know how you do your job, having to deal with all those nasty people.' After a few years, I learned how to express very clearly how I felt about the job. 'I'm glad to hear you don't like these 'nasty people'. The difference between you and me is that I get to do something about it!'

At first, though, I didn't get to do much about it at all. Although my experiences as a contract fieldworker had given me hints as to the crimes taking place against wild birds, my own experience was relatively narrow. I'd found a couple of poisoned birds, I'd checked a few robbed nests, I'd reported some people to the police for shooting protected geese, but not until I sat behind my desk in Edinburgh and started answering the phone did the reality kick in. There were a lot of bad people out there and I was expected to help stop them.

The clearest way I can show my progress to becoming a fully-fledged RSPB Investigations Officer is by describing actual cases. To get to the stage where anything could be described as a 'case', however, was in itself a matter of hard trial and error. So here are a few tips for dealing with the public on wildlife crime – and don't worry, none of this will be of comfort to the enemy!

To start with, you must have a clear idea of what you need to learn from a caller before you take any calls. The best way to do this is to have a template with the essential questions laid out. Who is calling? How can I get back to you? What are you reporting? What is the exact location of the offence? Who did it? When did it happen? Was there a vehicle involved? Can you describe it? What type of bird is involved? Are you sure? That list is simple enough to write down but it the scope for problems is huge.

1. The wrong species of bird. At certain times of year, various wildfowl species can be legitimately shot. Many members of the public don't realise that. I had to devise simple questions to test a caller's identification abilities if I thought they were unsure. This, of course, has to be done with tact, as some people get very annoyed when they are queried in any way and all callers are stressed already by the fact that they are reporting an alleged crime.

2. Vehicles. I was very seldom given a correct car number. First instincts, for many people, are to recall the colour, make or type, without realising how little use that usually was. When I did get a correct vehicle number, it was often a vehicle previously reported by us and then unwisely given out by someone else to a section of the public. Such information loops could be avoided by carefully checking whether they had actually seen it themselves.

3. Timing. At first I would take a mass of details before being told that the incident had happened the previous year … Even worse was when a caller would talk on endlessly before explaining that they had witnessed a nest robbery minutes before they had called. It was then a matter of getting them off the phone as quickly as possible.

4. Who did it? Commonly, someone would report an allegation against a named person and only much later in the conversation admit that they hadn't a clue who was responsible. Or they would leave it to the very end of a conversation to say it was their next door neighbour after you had asked a lot of questions about a culprit.

5. What had they seen? Many times, after a few questions, it was obvious that the caller had mistakenly thought a crime was being committed due to a misunderstanding. Someone might simply have been carrying out a routine farming operation, for example.

6. Location. Always my top priority. Very few callers were able to give a grid reference, so verbal descriptions became very important. After you've driven a hundred miles and walked in the rain for two hours, only to find nothing at a vague location, and then done it again the next time, you learn to make very sure that you have all the details possible. Apart from the time-wasting aspect, if the incident is on ground controlled by a suspect, there is a high chance that you will be spotted and any follow-up will be an even bigger waste of time.

7. Lastly, although this should always be asked first, try to get contact details from the caller. That way, if you have slipped up on any of the above, you will get a second chance by calling back. If the caller wishes to be anonymous, of course, then don't push it – but they will never call back.

I learned that lot the hard way, and passed it on to a series of secretaries, assistants and front office receptionists over the following 20 years. God help any of them if they forgot to ask for contact details or a location.

Remember that I am talking about the 1980s, when no one else was doing this work. It's also worth repeating – more than once, as it seems either to have been conveniently forgotten or never to have been asked by critics of our work – that we saved the police thousands and thousands of pounds and a great deal of embarrassing mistakes by filtering out 'mistake calls', never mind the cost in time and resources spent on field visits, checking on everything from alleged robbed nests to dead birds lying on mountainsides. We seem to have gone backwards on such matters recently – but more of that later.

In 1984, I had three sets of bosses (the term 'line managers' had yet to be invented): in Scotland, Frank Hamilton and from HQ, Richard Porter, head of the Species Protection Department and Peter Robinson, head of the Investigations Section. When I got my first good tip-off about an egg thief, in Scotland, I naturally asked Peter for advice and help.

Scottish egg thieves were – and are – a rare breed. By the 1980s, the widespread culture of schoolboy egg collecting was in terminal decline. I should also make it very, very clear that when I refer to egg thieves in this book, I am referring to grown adults taking entire clutches. Children taking wild birds' eggs is most definitely an issue for education not for prosecution, a fact I occasionally had to point out to police officers, who regularly wanted me to drive 100 miles to identify a pile of single eggs thrown into a shoebox with a handful of sawdust. That was once word of my successes began to spread.

For some reason the tradition of adult egg thieving continued in certain hotspots in England, while it had either died out or been non-existent in most of Scotland. The other startlingly obvious fact is that, in 25 years of bird work, I never even heard of a female egg thief. This, ladies, is one area where you can most definitely laugh at men, or at least shake your heads in disbelief at their stupidity. Having had plenty of time to think about such matters and having been asked about it a hundred times by press and media, I believe that this goes beyond the commonly male-oriented habit of making collections. There are, after all, many female collectors of items such as china ornaments and furniture. I believe that the reason that there are no female egg thieves goes beyond collection mania or male bonding (egg thieves often operate in close knit groups or secretive cells, similar, I am assured by police officers, to paedophile or even terrorist networks). It is because the very core of what these eggshell collectors are about is taking living eggs from a mother bird, piercing that living egg and flushing the contents down the sink. When you look at the stark reality of egg collecting, then its true horror is revealed. When you add to that the fact that it is the rarest eggs which are most highly prized, then the disgust of the thinking public towards this now-illegal activity is perfectly understandable. These people are killing live birds.

We had a saying in the Investigations Section: 'No one likes an egger'. There was no lobby trying to cause friction between the RSPB and the police when it came to this crime. Even gamekeepers, very occasionally, helped us catch egg thieves. If it wasn't for their illegal killing of birds of prey on estates, I'm sure they would have helped us catch a lot more. Women, as I have just explained, are particularly unable to understand an egger's activities and the commonest tip-offs we got were from wives and girlfriends. No doubt the fact that the egg thief headed off with his mates every evening and weekend in spring and summer to follow their obsessive hobby – leaving wife or girlfriend at home – didn't help. When the husband or boyfriend got locked up in Scotland or Wales and then had the family car confiscated, or got a £1,000 fine, then that didn't do much for relationships either.

Thursday, 17 May 1984

Along with Peter Robinson I had visited Saltcoats police station on the Ayrshire coast the day before and organised a search warrant based on the detailed information I had received, to add to local knowledge held by the police. At just before 9 a.m., we arrived at a house in Saltcoats, accompanied by a Sgt Blake. An elderly man came to the door and the policeman explained why we were there. The elderly man, who turned out to be the grandfather of the suspect, was more than a little hostile and kept up a steady stream of chat with the sergeant. Eventually, he admitted that his grandson was upstairs, in his bedroom. I could see that Peter was getting more agitated as time ticked by.

'We'd better get up there,' he said.

We followed the policeman up the stairs and walked into a small bedroom. The policeman asked the suspect if he had any birds' eggs. The suspect handed over a shoebox from the top of a wardrobe. In it, Peter found a small number of single blown eggs mixed in with sawdust. 'Is that all you've got?' said the policeman, who up to this point had been presenting an open, friendly attitude. 'Yes,' answered the suspect. I then noticed an egg partly concealed by a curtain on a windowsill and pointed it out to the sergeant. It was the first of dozens of such finds I would make during house searches, often simply by taking a long, slow look round while a suspect was talking to the police and occasionally, when directed to look at something by an officer. He pulled back the curtains to find half a dozen small, whole and unblown bird eggs laid out along the windowsill. The man had obviously been busy while his grandfather kept us occupied downstairs.

The sergeant's demeanour changed. He was beginning to see what he was dealing with. 'Any more eggs?' 'Aye, there's some under the bed.' I dragged out a couple of wooden boxes and opened them up on the floor. They contained the best part of 500 eggshells, laid out in clutches on cotton wool. I immediately saw four peregrine eggs amongst them. Things had suddenly got serious and the egg thief had gone very quiet. The grandfather's head had gone down too. As we started to leave the room, carrying the egg boxes, Sgt Blake pulled back the bedcovers to reveal four lapwing eggs neatly grouped with their pointed ends together, for all the world, like an actual nest. 'Trying to hatch them out, were we, sir?' Sgt Blake was enjoying himself.

We took the eggs back to Saltcoats and laid them out for evidential and publicity photos (see cover photo). I watched as Peter sped through the process of identifying the eggs. It took me some years to get anywhere as good as he was at what is a highly skilled job. With the exception of egg thieves themselves (and not all of them, by any means) and some museum curators, there are only a handful of people with the experience to be able to go through a collection of UK birds' eggs to the standard required by a court of law. They are all RSPB Investigators. This was my first collection. Over the next 22 years, I would have to identify tens of thousands of eggs, the only way to learn in this bizarre parlour game.

And when I say 'tens of thousands of eggs', remember that that means tens of thousands of dead birds. 'What a great job you've got, birdwatching all day!' was a common jibe from policemen but I never heard it after I'd spent three days painstakingly identifying thousands of eggshells in a police cell, usually the only available space for working if I wasn't allowed to sign for eggs and take them back to my office.

Peter had brought a UV lamp with him. Back then, peregrine workers like myself routinely marked any peregrine eggs in nests we could access. We marked eggs with individual numbers which were recorded on our government licence returns and we kept a copy in our own files. Experiments with hen's eggs had shown this to be a safe procedure. The idea, of course, was that if eggs were retrieved from suspected thieves, we could show a court the exact location of the nest and the date we were there. It is common practice for egg thieves to lie about where eggs come from: claims of the source being captive birds or their being 100 years old are routine.

Along with my colleagues and RSG workers, we must have marked hundreds of clutches back then but I'm aware of only a handful of successful cases. The criminal community soon caught on to what we were doing and obtained chemicals with which to remove the UV marks. I want to make the point as clearly as I can that it doesn't work – unless you are very, very lucky.

My luck was really in that day and Peter's light revealed the marks made by a fellow raptor worker – Ian Hopkins, the 'bird man' on the Isle of Bute – on our one seized clutch of peregrine eggs. We soon got a statement from Ian that he had marked these eggs on Bute in the spring of 1982, two years before. It turned out that the egg thief was a professional diver and fisherman who had been taking eggs from locations such as Arran, Bute and Islay as well as from local inland Ayrshire sites.

I was already on a steep learning curve with this rare capture: how to conduct a search, how to obtain a warrant with the police, how to identify eggs. The biggest lesson of all, though, was yet to come. Peter had said he thought the man would get fined a few hundred pounds. During the first week of August, just over two months after the search and seizure of the eggs, I was sent a cutting from the *Ayrshire Post*: 'On Thursday, 2 August, at Kilmarnock Sheriff Court, Saltcoats man Stuart Hindmarsh fined £2,000 for taking and possessing wild birds' eggs'. At first I was delighted. It had been my first egging case and £2,000 was a colossal fine in 1984. Then I realised I had missed the boat entirely in terms of publicity. One small local newspaper article does not have much of a deterrent effect.

Looking back now, the Hindmarsh case seems extremely unusual because of the swiftness with which it got to court. In later times, even the most cut and dried cases dragged on for a least a year, sometimes longer, to the extent that the time bar on wildlife cases (in simple terms, the length of time within which a case has to reach the prosecutor or the court) has had to be extended. This case taught me that I had to allocate time to following the progress of any court case very carefully. This often meant repeated phone calls to the Procurator Fiscal's Office or Sheriff Court. Even so, I had the great frustration of seeing some cases slip through without proper notification and with no resulting publicity – my job, after all, was bird conservation, not the punishment of offenders. This work is all about deterrence and to me, a court case without a certain amount of publicity was a complete waste of my time. Even worse, I occasionally saw a case dropped because it had gone out of time due to the failure of a police report to reach a Fiscal's desk, or a Fiscal failing to get a case to court on time. The effect that had on witnesses and colleagues is easy to imagine. At times there were rumours of deliberate chicanery but I tended towards the cock-up theory – or did, at least, during these early, apolitical years.

POLICE STATIONS IN THE 1980S

A typical visit by yours truly to a typical police station in Scotland , whether in the country or the city, would go as follows. Having located the building – in those pre-Tom-Tom or Googlemap days, I always looked for the aerial mast – I would walk up to the reception area.

'Hello,' said the uniformed constable. 'How can I help you?' 'Hi, my name is Dave Dick I work for the RSPB' 'Is that the cruelty?' 'No, we're a bird conservation organisation.' 'Oh... (slightly hesitant)... 'how can I help you? 'A dead buzzard has been found poisoned, it was lying beside a rabbit bait and I'd like to discuss getting a warrant to carry out a search.' 'Right... (long pause) ... can't you do that yourself?' 'Er... no, I've no powers, it's a police job, I just help advise you... as an expert.' 'Right... hang on... I'll just go and get the sergeant.'

If I was very lucky, I would get a sergeant who liked wildlife and who was keen to help. Sometimes we even got the search warrant – easily done then, by swearing out the information in front of a local Justice of the Peace. More likely though, was the hesitant repeat of all the above questions, followed by 'Well, I can't just get one like that, I'll have to run it past the Inspector. Can you come back tomorrow?' It took me some time to realise that no one in the station knew anything about the 1981 Act, and why should they? They had had about half an hour's worth of tuition on it at Tulliallan Police Training College, if they were recent recruits.

If I was very unlucky, and I was on several occasions, I would be asked directly who I thought was responsible. When I gave the name of the local gamekeeper, I was told, 'Oh Jimmy ****, he's a nice bloke, it won't be him,' and that was the end of that case. If anyone thinks I am exaggerating (those readers with a long-term countryside background, will know I am not), I give you the following story. When trying to follow up a blatant case of peregrine persecution (traps and shooting, eyewitness evidence) in the Borders in May 1986, I was told by a policeman in the first police office I visited to go to the next village office because his colleagues were too friendly with that keeper. Good man, that. As I hope this book will show, I was continually meeting helpful, professional policemen but unfortunately, they never had any clout.

I went into Crawford police station, now long closed, in April 1990, looking for help after finding poisoned egg baits on the Leadhills Estate in South Lanarkshire. The constable said, 'I know all about that wildlife stuff,' and proudly pointed to a poster version of the law, pinned up, yellowing and curled at the edges, on his wall. It was a copy of the 1954 Protection of Birds Act, repealed and replaced by the 1981 Act nearly ten years before! After explaining the situation to him, he let me keep it as a souvenir. It stayed up on my office wall for years, I've still got it.

I thought things could only get better.

WEDNESDAY, 20 JUNE 1984

With my first egger investigation successfully under my belt, I was still well aware that I was a complete beginner. I had very little knowledge of police procedure, court procedure and, even more important for my expert witness role, I had much to learn about that weird practice known as egg collecting. When I received my next good tip-off regarding an illegal collection, I again asked Peter Robinson at HQ for help.

After the usual lengthy but necessary explanations to the local police (this time at Kilbirnie police office in Ayrshire, not far from my home village of Uplawmoor), a warrant was obtained. This was an unusual and, to my mind, rather disturbing case. The allegation was that a local schoolteacher had amassed a substantial egg collection, occasionally using his own pupils to take eggs during school field trips. An appalling lapse in his 'duty of care', I would suggest.

We arrived with the police and after a heated discussion on the doorstep, the man admitted he had an egg collection in the house. In the bedroom that he shared with his wife, we found a proper egg cabinet, with carefully arranged clutches of birds' eggs. Some of the eggs were quite rare, with specialities such as corncrake, showing that the collector had travelled extensively in Scotland, at least. We also found collecting boxes, climbing ropes and climbing irons (specially constructed metal leg braces with spikes, which allow a climber to walk up a tree trunk) which I came to know as parts of an active egg thief's kit. Importantly, we did not find any diaries or other data relating to the eggs.

The egg thief continued to be verbally abusive until Peter took him aside and explained his rather precarious position. The conversation went something like this: 'Right now, you are a schoolteacher but what do you think will happen to your job when it comes out in court that you've been encouraging schoolchildren to break the law for you? We can see that you are an active collector and many of the eggs appear to have been taken recently but without data, this would be a very public argument. If you sign over these eggs to the RSPB, that will be the end of it.' The schoolteacher saw the light. I'm sure he was close to tears as we carried off his precious hoard.

The police were happy: a successful outing with very little paperwork at the end of it. As I write this, I'm still in two minds about the outcome. Yes, it would have been very difficult to get a prosecution but given that he had been warping the minds of those kids and implicating them in his crimes, it still bothers me that he walked away, albeit with the real stinger of losing his whole collection. This was at the time that the educational fight to stop children taking birds' eggs was still very much a live issue.

Peter was pleased. He was the veteran of many attempts at prosecutions over egg collections in England and knew that a wearing and wasteful court case had been avoided. I still had those hard lessons to come in the wholly unprepared Scottish court system.

As we sat at a table in the nearby Lochwinnoch RSPB Centre, starting to sort out the eggs by species (the collection was handed over to the Royal Museum of Scotland in Edinburgh), a phone call came in to Reception. Joan, the receptionist – a local woman, who had worked at the Centre since it opened in 1978 and who was later to be awarded an MBE for her efforts – called me over. 'You won't believe this one. It's a wumman from Easterhoose and she's shopping her neighbours for killing burds!' This was indeed worthy of comment – Easterhouse at the time was probably the most notorious housing estate in Glasgow. It was not the sort of place where you would expect the locals to contact the RSPB – or the police, for that matter. 'Let me talk to her.'

I took the phone and introduced myself. 'Listen, ahm no' the sort ay person tae grass oan anywan but it's rotten whit thur daeing... thuv goat some hawks in a boax, I didnae mind that but noo thur killing sparras wi' a catapult and chopping them up wi' a bread knife tae feed thum... and thur daeing it in front ae the weans!' I got the location from her, thanked her and put the phone down.

'Peter, how would like to see something interesting? We could drop by on our way back to Edinburgh.'

A couple of hours later, after watching Peter do his magic on the egg identification, we turn off the M8, on the east edge of the city, and enter a different world. A maze of streets, many with signs removed and a lot of glass and rubble across the road. We were soon lost and I was not looking forward to asking for directions. By a great stroke of luck, we spotted a 'jam sandwich', the local slang for a marked police car – white, red and white) and flagged it down. Traffic police from the M8 cruising around the estate for some reason. I walked over and explained what we were up to. 'Nae problem son, just follow us,' and they sped off. I just had time to jump into our car and dash off after them as they rounded the first corner.

A couple of minutes later, I pulled up behind the patrol car to see the policemen, in full uniform, walking quickly into a close. By the time Peter and I catch up, they have already rung the bell and been answered by a teenage boy. 'Right, you've goat burds you shouldnae have... gie thum tae these guys.' 'Aw comeoan...?' 'Ye cannae keep thum, where urr they?' 'Thurr upsterrs...' and the boy headed up the steep stairs followed by both policemen and ourselves. I then watched in fascination as the boy climbed out a bedroom window and onto the standard balcony I could see attached to every house in the block. These places were so badly designed that the only access to the balcony was by an awkward head-first scramble. The boy handed a large box, containing two bedraggled half-grown kestrel chicks, through the window to the policeman, who then handed it to me.

'Don't dae it again!' said the policeman before turning round and heading back down the stairs, followed by his colleague. I looked at the boy. All I could think of to say was, 'Right, we'll get them looked after,' before leaving with Peter. We met the policemen at the mouth of the close. 'You'll no' be wanting any paperwork then?' 'Er... no...' and they jumped in the petrol car and disappeared.

With the kestrel chicks safely in the back of the car and the egg collection in the boot, Peter turned to me and said, 'I didn't understand a bloody word of that!' 'That's why you employed me,' I replied with a smile. Peter was a Londoner.

A detour to Eaglesham and my first visit to the legendary – and now sadly deceased – Carol Scott. She was a lifesaver for me and the Scottish SPCA, one of those essential individuals who had both the expertise and the energy to look after injured and mistreated wild birds. Her main expertise was in birds of prey. The kestrels were in safe hands and would go back to the wild, if at all possible.

Easterhouse had a bad reputation from well before this episode. One of several 1950s and 1960s new housing estates, built to re-house Glasgow's slum tenement dwellers after their demolition post-war. It suffered from the same problems of short-sighted planning as Castlemilk and Drumchapel, most importantly a lack of amenities. It was also a considerable distance by public transport from the centre of Glasgow, where such amenities had been adjacent to the old tenements.

My first experience of Easterhouse was in fact an entirely positive one. In 1978 I played at the first ever Easterhouse Festival with the young Eddi Reader and Angus Aird. We went with great trepidation. The very idea of there being a Festival at all in such a notorious place seemed bizarre – this was 12 years before the 1990 Glasgow City of Culture radically changed attitudes in the city. We were stunned, delighted and overwhelmed by the friendship and hospitality we were given. These were good people and I still recall the after-gig party in an organiser's house, a high point in my long memory of great, late-night music sessions.

The early 1980s were for many reasons an exciting time to be involved in raptor work. Much of the survey and monitoring work we were doing was breaking new ground and it felt like exploration. Every new day was an adventure, taking me into remote parts of Scotland (well, remote to a southern lowland Scot like myself, anyway) with the strong possibility of seeing some of the most stunning wild birds and animals Scotland could offer. I never got used to it and I certainly never got bored with it. Time and again my line managers would tell me to slow down and spend more time at home, but I cannot stress enough what a privilege it was to do that job. I loved every minute of it.

Health and safety was a personal responsibility, not a diktat from some remote office. It was the terrifyingly embarrassing scenario of having to be rescued that kept us safe and careful, rather than the threat of disciplinary action. The very idea that you would face criticism for having an accident, rather than sympathy, was unthinkable – this was more akin to a family than a work team.

For the last 25 years, late March has always been a favourite time of year for me. Into the mountain areas of upland Scotland, with perfect days of gazing across landscapes of a dazzling variety of shades of brown, from light buff grass to chocolate patches of heather, greys of lichen on rock, to the black fringes of leafless birch and finally the washed-out green of close-cropped grass to the deep dark conifers in valley bottoms with a dusting of snow on the higher tops. Using scope and bins to pin down the nests of eagles from across a glen ('where will they have chosen this year?') when even a blizzard just feels right – wet, uncomfortable, even dangerous, but real.

By the time I started work as an RSPB Investigations Officer in 1984, I had become aware – it would have been difficult not to – of the fact that egg collectors were alive and well and robbing Scottish raptor nests. The extent of the problem with regard to eagle nests was, though, little known. Except for a handful of notorious cases at a very small number of sites, limited information had been collated. Over the next 15 years we gathered a much better idea of how much damage was and is being done to the whole population by man's interference, thanks to a combination of successful cases producing volumes of data, some self-published books from a few vainglorious and vengeful thieves and – most important of all – the hard work of a largely unpaid volunteer force of eagle enthusiasts.

At some point in 1984 or early 1985, I was at RSPB HQ in Bedfordshire when a colleague showed me some diaries, recently seized from two egg thieves. In amongst the usual, long but ultimately pathetic records of their crimes ('It was a red letter day as I stood on the nest of the eagle, holding the ultimate prize, for which I had striven throughout many expeditions ...') I noticed a recurring name: 'Glen M., c/2 GE' – a golden eagle nest containing two eggs.

A certain glen in Central Scotland had been on the edge of my study area in 1982. I recalled a discussion at that time with the man who monitored the birds in that area. 'They always fail when they nest in Glen M. but are usually successful when they nest in Glen K. We don't know why, maybe it's the way the nests are facing, or some other natural problem.' I accepted this as gospel at the time. I was 'the boy' and this was an eagle man of the old school. However, after two seasons of really intense fieldwork, tracking down sites in a variety of habitats, I was pretty sure that Glens M. and K. should easily have been large enough and food-rich enough for two pairs.

From the egger's diaries, I could see that Glen M. had been getting a pasting. Every year, for several years, one or other of these thieves (they either worked together or took turn about) would remove all the eggs. This pair had not raised young for a very long time. (Incidentally, when we set up a round-the-clock watch on the nest in 1986, they reared two chicks, a certain sign of a healthy home range.)

So I decided to do something about it. A relatively new idea at the time was to mark rare bird eggs in the nest with either visible, or invisible but retrievable, markings. This caught on in a big way as far as peregrine protection went and led to many of us spending a lot of our field seasons risking life and limb, hanging off ropes each April as we crouched on small rock ledges in remote places, a pair of peregrines screaming round our heads, desperately trying to write decipherable letters and numbers on anything up to five eggs (on one memorable occasion – the eggs were later stolen) and get out fast, to cut down disturbance. The welfare of the birds always came first.

For anyone who thinks this marking system would be a good one to revive, a word of caution. The idea with peregrines was that the Department of Environment Inspectors, who had the power to enter and inspect captive breeding peregrine facilities, would examine eggs for markings. The bird breeders, however, convinced the Government Inspectorate not to inspect eggs because they claimed that this would disturb the peregrines and possibly cause them to fail. We found this out years later, blissfully unaware that all our hard work had been wasted by gullible office workers. We suspected that many of these early breeding stations were bogus and found ourselves fully vindicated in the 1990s, when DNA fingerprinting of supposed captive-bred birds helped to close down whole networks of live egg and chick thieves and supposed breeders of peregrines and goshawks. Several people went to jail, but I still wonder how many we could have caught earlier if the government inspections had been more robust?

Eggshell thieves, as I've already mentioned, soon realised what was going on and managed to find chemicals to remove even the invisible marks, although they usually left a distinctive blurring across the egg. In a career of more than 20 years of helping seize and identify eggs – both onsite, in transit and, most often, out of collections in houses – I can recall only two occasions when I retrieved marked eggs (one being my first ever egg case, detailed above). In 1985, however, this was a new and exciting technique for catching egg thieves. There was only one problem: you had to get into the nests.

Between March 1981 and July 1983, I free-climbed into dozens of peregrine and golden eagle cliff nests. These varied from surprisingly easy (you could 'take your granny in') to a sea-cliff eagle nest so terrifying that the second time I climbed it, to ring a chick, I photographed the last pitch below the nest, to remind myself never to be so stupid again. That was what we all did back then and we were rightly proud of our abilities. I was very fit and had become a self-taught climber.

In the spring of 1984, it was pointed out to me that I could get into a lot more nests if I learned to use ropes and I was well aware that the opposition were doing so. By a stroke of good luck, I had John Davies working two doors down from my office, the secretary of the Scottish Ornithologists Club and a technically proficient rope man, having been involved in monitoring sea birds on cliffs for several years. John quite literally taught me the ropes and was no doubt delighted to be able to see peregrines close up while working as my trainer and 'top man'.

A year later, I was in the dangerous position of thinking I knew what I was doing in abseiling and had been practising over winter on the steep back wall of my office. The following account is, I freely admit, a description of my own stupidity and incompetence in climbing solo but it should also be remembered that in 1984 and 1985 I was the single-handed RSPB Investigations Officer for the whole of Scotland, with no assistant and no back-up. My companion that day was an ex-police officer and fellow Investigations Officer from HQ, Karen Bradbury, with no bird fieldwork experience. I felt lucky just to have a driver.

A man behind every bush? Ah dinnae think sae!

23 MARCH 1985

A day I am unlikely ever to forget. I'm walking up a track into Glen M. with a single 9 mm nylon rope and various carabiners and other bits of climbing kit in my rucksack. The weather was ideal, clear and cold. As I got to the area of valley floor below the known nesting area, I started scanning the crags above me until I spotted the brown top of a recently built-up eagle nest. There was no- one around but sheep and deer, so I started the hard pull up the steepening valley side until I got to below an isolated crag, about 60 feet from top to bottom. Two-thirds of the way up the crag and to one side, I could make out the large stick nest with a heather top but, as yet, could see no sign of a bird.

I was already working out my route to the nest and was glad I had brought the rope. The nest was on a large recessed ledge with an overhanging rock and well beyond my abilities as a free climber. Above the overhang, however, was a rowan tree jutting out over the crag. As I scrambled up the slope to one side of the crag, I got level with the nest and had the always-wonderful sight of an adult golden eagle staring straight at me as it sat tight. With that apparent air of grace and dignity that I have so often observed, she stepped off the front of her nest, dropped downwards for a second, then soared up and away to the north.

The clock was ticking. I carried on with my scramble up until I arrived above the overhang. Looking over with great care, I could make out two large eggs, finely marked with red brown spots, nestling in their cup of deer grass and woodrush. It was a sight to make an egg thief drool. But I had no time to waste. The rowan tree was growing out of the turf of the top of the overhang, a healthy young tree, which I judged would easily support my weight, protected from the nibbling mouths of sheep and deer by its precarious position. Out with the rope, sling round the tree, attach metal figure-of-eight to sling and rope, struggle into harness, attach figure-of-eight to harness and prussic loop to rope. Lean back to test the rope and belay point and try not to think of the drop below me.

I have never thought of myself as a particularly brave person and even at the height of my climbing career, I was always afraid of heights. I think a fear of height is an eminently sensible trait in a human being. So instead of behaving like a commando in a film and jumping off into the void, I slowly let myself slide over the edge of the overhang on my stomach trying to find some rock to push against. Unfortunately, I didn't find any such rock. My feet were dangling in mid-air and as I slid off the turf, my main rope was pushed up by the grass until it locked in position at the top of the figure-of-eight. Nylon rope stretches, particularly thin, 9 mm nylon rope. Within another second, I was a couple of feet below the overhang with my rope hopelessly jammed. (I found out years later, during a rather belated rope training course, that this is known as a Lark's Foot, caused by pushing the rope the wrong way through the figure-of-eight – the trainer was delighted to find an idiot who had experienced this and called all his colleagues over to hear about it.)

If I had known how bad this was, I would immediately have become seriously worried but I was in my usual state of suppressed terror on a rope and wasn't yet looking at this abseil as being very different from any of the others. I began to try to pull myself back up the rope but found that I couldn't get a grip on the ground above me. I tried pulling the rope from beneath me and making a loop for my foot to stand up on – the rope just stretched even further, downwards. All of this time, I was slowly spinning round. As my arms got tired, I rested for a while and focussed on the valley across and beneath me. Even at a time like this, it looked beautiful. I looked down and saw the eggs beneath me. What a bloody shame, I thought, here I am trying to save these from thieves and I could end up causing the bird to desert them. I was still hearing the ticking clock.

Again and again I tried to pull myself up but it was hopeless. I may have strong wrists from years of guitar playing but I've never had strong arms. It's amazing how quickly you become exhausted when you try to hold up your own body weight just using your arms.

Well, the only way was down, but how could I do that? I wondered if maybe I could slide down the rope, but was stuck in my harness, which was attached to the jammed figure-of-eight. I had somehow to get out of the harness.

At this point the possibility of not making it began to slide into my thoughts. Fear like that is a physical thing: you can feel your stomach tighten and your heart speed up. 'If I get stuck up here, no one will find me for hours. It will be dark before Karen even raises the alarm, which means I'm unlikely to be found until the morning, which means hypothermia. I'm at least 1,200 feet up a Scottish mountain and it's still winter up here. It could snow ...'

So rest for a while... just dangle and spin... bloody shame to go like this... just 34 and I don't even have any children... if I get down, I'm going to seriously think about that...

I don't know how long I was on the rope, probably the best part of two hours. I tried pulling myself up again a few times. Then reality got through and I knew that my only chance was to get out of the harness. I undid the buckles, with the idea of turning upside down and sliding out of the harness, while holding onto the rope. So far, so good. The harness down to my knees, I'm turning over... it's sliding down my lower legs... it's sliding off my feet... it's...

stuck on my boot!... I'm upside down, wriggling, spinning around, 60 feet above the nearest ground. I would say that was the worst moment. I knew that if I could get free, I would need some control but I also knew that it was very unlikely I would be able to hang on. I also knew that if I couldn't get free, I could never straighten up, so I would be left there hanging upside down until the inevitable end.

So I kicked hard. My boot came free and I plummeted head first for 20 feet, bounced off the outer edge of the nest and dropped the best part of 40 feet, landing on my back on a grassy slope. I must have turned round at least once in the air. I couldn't breathe but don't remember trying very hard. I was stunned as much by the speed of the fall as by the actual thump of hitting the ground.

I moved my fingers and then my arms, I moved my toes and then my legs. I turned my head to the side and back again. I very slowly tried standing up. This took a while, as my arms were too weak to push with. I sat down again. Everything was working. 'You lucky bastard...'

After a few minutes, something approaching normality kicked in again. I looked up at the crag, where I could see my rope hanging down to the nest ledge. Keep moving. Scramble back up to the top. Don't look down. Don't look down! Pull up the rope and harness, stuff the gear in any old way, put on the rucksack, wobble back down the slope, somehow climb the deer fence and drop down the other side, stumble across the glen and out to the watershed. Looking back at the nest with my bins, I see the female eagle fly back to the ledge, poke about for a few seconds and settle down on her eggs. Fantastic.

The light was fading when I got to the roadside, where Karen was sitting waiting in the car at the rendezvous point. 'Where the hell have you been?' My reply was not very sympathetic.

A week later the eggs were stolen.

Stealing rare birds' eggs is easy. OK, you can make it difficult for yourself – you can choose the eggs of a bird which nests only on protected nature reserves. You can choose birds which conceal their nests very carefully. You can choose birds which only nest at the top of tall trees or high up on perilous crags.

Some egg thieves do specialise in those species and boast about their exploits when showing their collections to a small trusted group of fellow criminals. Some egg thieves have even published accounts of their crimes, usually adopting the 'in the good old days' stance, or have a third party write their story for them. It is always presented as a struggle between them and nature, the prize obtained through a mixture of cunning and enormous physical effort.

The diaries of egg thieves – and I certainly found that most persistent egg thieves wrote diaries – are in turn enlightening, sickening or puzzling, always pathetic and often laughable. Where the (black) humour comes in is in their common use of the language of Victorian and Edwardian naturalists when describing some hunt for the eggs of a rare bird. They have often been reading the published diaries of such people in order to learn nest-finding techniques. They then go one step further and actually imagine themselves in their footsteps. 'A chill wind blew across the Scotch moor and I struggled on for hours until I came upon the thrilling sight of the mother plover dragging its supposed broken wing... It tried to lure me from its nest but I knew better... After only two or three minutes of frantic search I spied my prize, a clutch of four dark blotched eggs on a golden background. As I held them in my hand, I knew this was a blue riband day, one I would never forget... 'Unfortunately, the effect was often spoiled by the inclusion of some really awful spelling mistakes.

Over the years, I watched a long succession of police officers react in the way I did to these diaries, with an added sense of incredulity that any criminal, facing fines of thousands of pounds if caught, and eventually with the real threat of imprisonment, would be so stupid as to write down details of their crimes.

The reality in Scotland was that very, very few egg thieves we caught were even competent naturalists. Most could tell you the average clutch size of many wild birds, they could describe the bird's nest structure, its likely position in a tree or on a moor or cliff, they could tell you in some detail the tiny differences in shape, or colouring, of individual species' eggs – but ask them about the bird's migration, its feeding habits or even its winter plumage and they were floundering.

When it came to finding the location of rare birds' nests, most of these criminals had to rely on second-hand information. Drop them in golden eagle territory – the wide open spaces of northwest Scotland – and they would quite literally be lost. So how did they find, say, the nest of a golden eagle? They begged, borrowed or stole information from other egg thieves. After that, as I said, stealing rare birds' eggs is easy.

It was commonplace for these people to travel in groups, usually of two or three but occasionally as many as five. Usually an older experienced egg thief, such as Colin Watson, in his 40s, would take younger men, in their 20s, on trips up to Scotland to steal eggs. Part of the deal was that the younger men would supply the transport in exchange for being shown where the rare bird's nests were located. If they managed to take several clutches, the younger men would get a share, particularly if they had actually taken the eggs from the nest.

WEDNESDAY, 27 MARCH 1985

Well before we had collected enough data to carry out detailed analysis – from actual incidents of thefts, or attempted thefts and from diary and egg collection records – we knew that the area of northwest Argyll known as the Morvern Peninsula was a hotspot for the theft of golden eagle eggs. Local eagle watchers had reported the disappearance of eggs early in incubation. Many bird species have relatively fixed dates for egg laying every year, the result of environmental and ecological factors such as temperature and food supply. Golden eagles are no exception and generally in Scotland lay their eggs between the middle of March and early April. An eggshell collector will ideally want to take eggs soon after they are laid: 'fresh' eggs, to use their terminology. Even within these parameters, there will be variations in dates of eagle egg theft, due to knowledge of a particular early-laying eagle, weather conditions affecting travel, the preferences of a particular egg thief and the personal circumstances of the thief or thieves – is it a holiday weekend, will the wife let him take the car?

Bearing all of the above in mind, it was not surprising that a group of RSPB staff should be watching the area of Morvern at the end of March 1985. In charge was Peter Robinson, who had travelled up on what had become for him an annual visit to the Highlands. Peter was already very experienced in hunting egg thieves, having worked for the RSPB's Investigation section since its inception in 1974.

I was the local man, the only Scot in the team, with two seasons of full-time work on golden eagles behind me. I had been the Scottish Investigation's Officer for just over one year. We had kept a close eye on the accessible eagle nests, with no sign of trouble, and a few days were spent watching the few roads in the area for suspicious vehicles. Back then, any vehicle with English number plates stood out, and we looked for groups of men travelling together at odd times of the day. This was also in the era when travelling thieves still used their own vehicles – all that changed later, with the confiscation of wildlife criminals' vehicles by Scottish Sheriff Courts. I'm pleased to say that Scotland led the way in vehicle confiscation and in imposing heavy sentences on egg thieves.

We decided to pull out of the area and try elsewhere, so after a last check on our easiest eagle nest, we drove east in two cars. After crossing on the Corran ferry at Ardgour, we drove in the winter sun across the Ballachulish Bridge and eventually into the stunning scenery of Glencoe. I was in the second car, feeling quite relaxed, when suddenly we spotted Peter standing beside his parked car and waving at us from a lay-by. We pulled in behind him, thinking that he must have had a puncture. 'Did you see those three guys back there? It's Watson, he was looking up at something through binoculars! They're in a blue Escort.'

A quick scramble and we turned our cars round and head back down the glen. No sign of the blue Escort. We then drove all the way back towards the Corran ferry, still with no sight of the car – until we turn off the Fort William road towards the jetty in time to see the ferry, a blue Escort in the middle, pulling away sideways into the strong current of the Corran Narrows. This is a very short crossing and within five minutes, we could see the vehicles driving up onto the road in front of the Ardgour Hotel, up onto the road screened by a wall on each side of the entrance to the jetty.

With my telescope perched on the top of our car, I had a window of perhaps ten seconds to adjust focus and read the numberplate. 'WNH 899 S,' I called out to my companions. 'Got it!'

The RSPB, of course, have no legal powers to stop someone they suspect is about to take rare birds' eggs. Or, for that matter, for any other reason – the police are the authority when it comes to applying wildlife laws. In England, before there was any structured police response to wildlife crime, such as the Wildlife Liaison Officer network, and before the formation of such bodies as the Partnership for Action against Wildlife Crime (PAWC), the RSPB could and did take out private prosecutions against wildlife criminals, working closely with English police forces. They had a relatively high profile there, but in Scotland in 1985, the RSPB was unknown to most police officers.

We now had to wait for the next ferry, drive across Morvern to the police station at Strontian and inform the slightly bemused police officer there that he had a notorious egg thief loose on his patch. Despite many hours patrolling the area over the next few days, the car was never seen again, but neither did any eagle eggs disappear from known nests. Perhaps Watson had seen us and been scared off, perhaps he never found any nests with eggs – we will never know. This was a very good dry run for me and had the hugely beneficial effect of alerting the local police to the problem, which led to a number of captures and prosecutions in following years.

That was not the end of the matter, though. The car number was traced to an address in Sheffield, later searched by the RSPB and police. Eggs were found and one of the two young men with Watson was charged. He later absconded to Australia.

MONDAY, 17 JUNE 1985

For some time I had been hearing about a man living and working near Stranraer who, it was alleged, had been combining his work as a 'goose guide' – taking out commercial shooting parties from local hotels – with taxidermy. On the face of it, both were entirely legal occupations but the allegations included information suggesting that the bird species being shot and stuffed sometimes included rare, protected species. There were also rumours of poaching.

I took my notes on what I knew about the man – a Mr Pickersgill, now long deceased – to Stranraer police office. The desk sergeant listened to what I had to say and, with hindsight, I realise that the most interesting part of my story to him was probably the alleged poach-

CAR NUMBERS

As mentioned, a car with English plates was unusual in such an area in the pre-tourist season in the 1980s. This made life easier for us when watching roads for egg thieves – certain areas in England came up time and again in relation to known offenders. I can still recall many of the suffixes relating to particular towns and counties. In the old system, the last two letters of the three letter grouping were what mattered. This was also before the era of personalised number plates. The police now have electronic Vehicle Recognition Systems on many major routes, which make a vast difference when they are actually used to combat wildlife criminals.

Static area watches for egg thieves were our normal practice in the 1980s, a more relaxed time. The entire team could take a couple of weeks out to concentrate on a target area. I recall with pleasure my days in the beautiful oakwoods of the Welsh Borders, drafted in to help colleagues watch for egg thieves who were after the nests of the then extremely rare red kite. In 1985, there were 45 known nests with ten known nest robberies! Those days could be long and physically arduous but my memories are of sunny afternoons watching eagles, kites and ospreys, conveniently blotting out memories of cold, rain and midgies and of crawling out of a sleeping bag before dawn.

ing activities. It seemed that the police were already aware of the shooting parties. I therefore found myself at the address, an isolated farmhouse in the beautiful, rolling farmland in the north part of the Rhinns peninsula. The place was deserted. While walking around the steading looking for signs of life, we found an outdoor aviary containing two very lively young ravens. There is a history in the UK of people keeping ravens as pets – the ravens at the Tower of London being the most famous example – but it has never been very common and, even for me, this was an unusual sight. Looking closer, I noted that both birds had had their wings clipped – their flight feathers roughly hacked through. They were also both wearing large aluminium split rings, leg rings which could be placed on a full-sized bird, with letters and numbers printed on them. I knew enough about licensed bird ringing to realise that these were home-made rings and not part of any legitimate wild bird ringing scheme. There was no sign of parent birds and it should be remembered that captive breeding of wild birds in Scotland was in its infancy in 1985. There were a few species of finches captured for cross-breeding with canaries – both legitimately and not – but the captive breeding of birds of prey, later to cause such problems to legislators, government licensing, welfare organisations and conservation, was still not widely practised anywhere in the UK.

TUESDAY, 5 MAY 1981

Oban Sheriff Court. My first boss, Pete Ellis, thought it might be interesting for me to see a court case involving alleged wild birds of prey. I was working on peregrines in Argyll at the time and this was my first attendance at a trial in a Scottish court. A man named Brodie had set up a 'Wildlife Centre' near Ardfern in mid-Argyll. Paying customers got to see some remarkable examples of Scottish wildlife at close quarters, including short-eared owls and herons. Many of these birds were displayed as chicks. Pete had received information that much of Mr Brodie's collection had been 'borrowed' from the wild. A large number of birds were seized when the police raided the Centre and Brodie claimed the birds were all captive bred, leading to the Oban trial. Star witness for the prosecution was one Leonard Durman-Walters, a well-known face in the then tiny UK world of falconry and an expert the very new science of captive breeding of birds of prey. Lennie, as he was universally known, was an incongruous figure in that rural Scottish court, a small, dapper man, with a strong Cockney accent. When asked, by the Procurator Fiscal what he thought about Brodie's captive breeding claims, he said to the court, 'I think Mr Brodie has a glittering career ahead of him at Cornell University!' He was met with laughter until he expanded on that answer (The technique of artificial insemination of birds of prey was only used at that time by Cornell University.) Result? A £150 fine and confiscation of the birds. This was tried under the Protection of Birds Act 1954 and was a significant case at the time, despite what looks to us now as a ludicrously low fine.

We left without meeting anyone but returned later in the day, armed with two more police officers and a search warrant. This time we were in luck. Just as we arrived, Mr Pickersgill drove up behind us. He didn't look pleased. The police officer in charge explained who we were and showed him the warrant, which explained the reason for our search. We entered the house, where I soon spotted a stuffed buzzard. A wider search revealed a number of bird and animal cage traps of various sizes. The real excitement began, however, when we looked into some large chest freezers. On the instructions of the police, I began to remove and identify a large number of bird and animal corpses.

I soon spotted an otter and a Greenland white-fronted goose, both rare and both very much protected. It was becoming obvious that this was turning into a large- scale job. The sergeant called up Stranraer and asked them to send a large van to carry away all the seized items. By this time Pickersgill had gone quiet, no doubt realising he was now in serious trouble.

The van arrived and we loaded, with a great deal of effort, the freezers into the van. One last job remained. 'Now, Mr Pickersgill – about the ravens in the shed?' 'But they're my pets!' The docile suspect now turned into a very angry and threatening man. As I carried out the inevitably rather clumsy job of catching up two live and very wild ravens, he kept up a stream of abuse until I had put them safely into carrying boxes and placed them in the van. The next minute I saw him walking towards me, violence on his mind. I looked at the two policemen standing beside me, expecting them to intervene, but they hadn't moved. 'I'll wait in the car,' I said and moved quickly away. I still wonder whether they would have allowed him to assault me before intervening – after all, an arrest for thumping someone would have been far more in their line than some obscure conservation charge. Of course there was no power of arrest under the 1981 Act. That was still many years away, no matter how serious the conservation crimes.

I watched the police finish their business before we drove in convoy back to Stranraer police office. Now my job really began, just one of many long days and nights spent in the essential task of carefully identifying and cataloguing, without which proper charges and reports could not be made by the police and myself. Although I was to complete many such jobs working in police interview rooms and empty cells, I had on this occasion the relative luxury of using the extensive floor of an outside garage. Soon that floor was covered with dead, frozen birds (including owls, finches, guillemots, warblers, grebes, ducks, geese, swans and even a single robin) and animals (otters, hedgehogs, weasels and adders). There were also quantities of foxes, deer, grey squirrels, magpies, ferrets and game birds which could easily be separated from the obvious, protected, species.

Hearing footsteps approach from the police station, I looked up to see a friendly, bearded face above an immaculate dinner suit. 'Well Mr Dick, you've had an interesting day!' This was my first meeting with Frank Walkingshaw, the local Procurator Fiscal. Being aware of the search warrant, he had asked the police to keep him informed and when the sergeant described the garage full of frozen corpses, he had left a formal dinner to see it for himself.

I came to enjoy such meetings with Frank, with whom I had the pleasure of working on several high-profile cases. He had a great interest in the countryside and became so relaxed with me that he would sit and describe his latest pheasant shoot with obvious pleasure and not a trace of irony. Those were the days when Fiscals were delighted to see a bird expert such as myself and would actively encourage me to send detailed background reports on cases. Most important for such cases were the regular case conferences which we had in the days (or sometimes hours) before a trial. True partnerships were forged, before that term became so tarnished in this context. There was a mutual respect for each other's knowledge – conservation and the countryside on one hand and the law and court procedure on the other.

On 30 April 1986, Pickersgill was fined a total of £950 – a respectably high fine at the time – for possession of protected birds and offering them for sale.

After my first two years of this all-embracing job, which was physically and mentally exhausting, particularly between the months of March and August, I was given the tremendous boost of being able to employ an assistant. In those early days, I needed to harass my managers continually until they saw the obvious – that there was far, far more important work to be done than could possibly be carried out by one person. I had spotted Iain Macleod's potential as soon as I met him, when he was working as the annually-employed contract warden for the RSPB reserve at Balranald on North Uist. A giant of a young man, well over six feet tall but with a gentle manner and a very good people person, as he has shown throughout his successful later career with the New Hampshire Audubon Society. He is now a senior manager in that organisation. Although I may not give them a large mention in these stories – it is far easier to recall details when I was the sole investigator – I unreservedly acknowledge the excellent work and companionship of my three assistants, Iain Macleod, Stuart Benn and Keith Morton, during most of the period covered by this book. I'm sure they all agree that the work was more important than the individual. We all cared.

I was sitting at my desk, trying to keep up with the multiple tasks of recording peregrine nest records from my field notebooks, occasionally marking the office maps with site information and fielding the usual series of phone calls from colleagues, police, other conservation bodies and, of course, the general public. It was, in other words, a normal day at RSPB Scottish Headquarters. A day of Dictaphones, typed yellow memos and colour slides. Digital was then just a type of clock.

The phone rang again. 'Dave here'…'Hi, it's Graham. Got an interesting one for you. I'm in Leeds. The Post Office have opened an undelivered box and it's full of peregrine eggs…blown.'

The best ones always seem to come totally by surprise. This was one of them, although I didn't know it at the time. An egg collector (a thief) had tried to send blown peregrine eggs to another egg collector (another thief) but had, to his great misfortune, got the address wrong. It was very lucky for us that this mishap occurred in a large city – anywhere smaller and the local postman would have got the box delivered, no problem. One wrong street number, however, and the parcel ended up with the Post Office Investigations Branch, which, incidentally, is the oldest criminal investigations authority in the world, formed in 1793.

The next piece of good luck (or bad, depending on where you were sitting) was that the box opener was an RSPB member and, more importantly, knew a peregrine egg when he saw one. He immediately phoned RSPB HQ in Sandy, which explains why Graham Elliott, RSPB Investigations Officer, was calling me from the Leeds Central Post Office.

'Why I'm phoning you, Dave, is that there's a Paisley postmark on the wrapping… (rustle rustle)… and on the inside, there's an address of a company at somewhere called… White… Inch… the paper's been turned inside out and reused. Does that mean anything to you?' I said I thought it did, but that I would need to do some research and get back to him.

'Well, don't take too long, we reckon we've got enough for a warrant here. There's an egger living in the street on the posted address and his house number is the exact reverse of the one given. What a plonker!'

'OK, I'll phone you back asap.'

When I took over as Investigations Officer in January 1984, there were so few records that I was able to read through all the main case files, well before this incident. I remembered that an egg collector in the Paisley area had been identified and searched by Roy Dennis (RSPB Highland Officer) a few years before. Large-scale egg thieves were highly unusual in Scotland, even then, and this seemed more than a coincidence.

I checked the Yellow Pages for Glasgow against the address for a wallpaper company written on the inside of the eggbox wrapper and got a Glasgow phone number. I knew that Whiteinch is very close to Paisley, having grown up about ten miles from there.

What to do now? There were no police Wildlife Officers back then and the idea of passing this on to CID in Paisley or Glasgow was laughable – I knew that, I'd tried it before. So I picked up the phone and dialled the number.

'Hello. *** Wallpaper Company here,' said an unmistakably female Glasgow accent. 'How can I help you?' 'Can I speak to R*** W*** please?' There came a long pause. 'There's a Mrs R*** W*** works here?' 'Oh, sorry, my mistake, sorry to bother you…'

Gotcha! I made a short lap of honour round my own desk before picking up the phone to Leeds.

Strathclyde Police received all the above information from the RSPB and the POIB and a search warrant was obtained for W.'s house in Paisley. A huge collection of more than

CASE LAW

In Scotland, with the exception of literally two or three cases in a century, all criminal prosecutions at Sheriff Court level are brought by the Crown through the Procurator Fiscal system. Basically, all crimes are prosecuted by the public prosecutor – by contrast, in England, private prosecutions are commonly brought by organisations and individuals.

A good example of the use of the English system to further the aims of bird conservation was the practice of the RSPB, until the late 1980s, of bringing cases against alleged wildlife criminals in order to test the new Wildlife and Countryside Act 1981. Any new Act is open to interpretation by lawyers, both prosecuting and defending, no matter how thorough the legal draughtsmen and elected representatives may have been during its passage through Parliament.

In this fashion, the RSPB took on and paid for cases which were likely to throw up defences based on a lack of case law – basically, loopholes in the law. These cases were then appealed by the RSPB, leading to the creation of case law through High Court decisions. Those decisions have since been used in many cases to successfully prosecute individuals and, importantly, they have caused some offenders to plead guilty at an early stage, saving courts time and money.

English High Court decisions are not binding in Scots law, although they can be taken into account. It is not, in practice, a useful strategy for a Procurator Fiscal to quote English legal precedent to a Scottish sheriff. In Scotland, therefore, there is a massive extra barrier to get past in order to get case law – the local Procurator Fiscal and the Crown Office. Whereas the RSPB was able to take cases purely to promote its conservation objectives through the successful application of law – with the full backing of its membership – Fiscals and the Crown Office are constantly watching the linked problems of court time and public spending. In order for conservation to advance through the application of law in Scotland, it had to compete with other criminal cases and issues.

In reality, up to and including the present day, Fiscals are very unlikely to take on any wildlife case which is likely to fail through a lack of case law, where there is likely to be time consuming legal argument during a trial. The effect of this is to restrict the law to being applied to obvious and blatant offences under one or two areas of any Act. This of course negates much of the legislative process and certainly does not reflect the intentions of our elected representatives in creating these laws.

So what we now see, in a growing number of cases, is a well-prepared report put forward by trained and committed wildlife police officers ending up as a small number of bland 'guilty' charges in front of a sheriff. In making his decisions, the sheriff has no real knowledge of the case, as he is not allowed to hear any evidence with any relation to the dropped charges, only those which can seem almost randomly picked from the police report.

Such charges of course, are in no way random: they are those which are acceptable to both prosecutor and defence lawyer. Acceptable to the Crown, as avoiding a costly trial, acceptable to the defence, as being the least damaging to the reputation of his client and hopefully incurring the lowest level of punishment from the sheriff.

In order to give the reader the fullest picture of what is and has been preventing the successful prosecution of the proven large-scale estate-based wildlife crime. I should point out that the above situation falls perfectly in favour of those who seek to take the pressure off these particular wildlife criminals, by continually attempting to downgrade the status of such crimes. This is being done in the press and media at wildlife conferences, in lobbying Parliament and the police service and by some individuals working within the justice system itself.

We will know when wildlife crime is being taken seriously. It will be when we start to see the number of Crown Appeals rise from their present static position.

Having described some of the cases in which I was heavily involved, including meeting criminals face-to-face, I might reasonably be thought to have become hardened and cynical towards my fellow human beings. Far from it. For many years I remained, if not exactly naïve, then fairly trusting. That trust, however, was being undermined from early on. I clearly recall one incident in particular among a series of turning points in my dealings with the public.

3,000 eggs was seized from W. and I spent several weeks back in Edinburgh, identifying and cataloguing them. After three days at Paisley Sheriff Court in October 1987, during which time I spent many hours in the witness box giving evidence as to the identity of the eggs, the trial was abandoned. The sheriff accepted the defence argument: that there was insufficient evidence that any of the eggs had been *recently* taken. A local builder and friend of W*** – who some years later was himself found during a police search to be in possession of a stuffed buzzard and a small egg collection – gave evidence that the bulk of the collection was his and that he had given them to W*** some years before. This was not corroborated by any written data or other witness, it was nothing but the word of a self-confessed egg thief. It was illegal to take wild birds' eggs after 1954 but only illegal to be in possession of those taken since 1981. This has now been resolved, as recent legislation (Nature Conservation Scotland Act 2004) makes it illegal to possess wild birds' eggs taken post-1954.

It was one of my earliest frustrating court outcomes but was by no means the last. Each such case, however, was a stepping stone for those which came later. Continuity was, and is, very important if those involved in the enforcement of such legislation are to avoid making the same mistakes over and over again.

MONDAY, 5 NOVEMBER 1984

Mauchline, Ayrshire, Guy Fawkes night, around 7.30 p.m., and I'm standing at the door of a council house on a main road. All around are the sound of rockets and bangers exploding in the frosty night air. Beside me is a large policeman – all policeman are large when standing beside me and are often a comforting presence – holding a search warrant.

A few days before, the occupier of the house, whom I shall call Tam, had met a birdwatcher in the Ayrshire countryside. They had got talking and the subject of birds of prey came up. Tam regaled his new friend with a tale of having shot two peregrines near a named (and real) peregrine nest. He added the detail that he had had them stuffed and kept them at home.

The birdwatcher phoned me up and related Tam's gruesome tale, including his home address. After some background checks, which showed that Tam was a locally well-known pigeon fancier with an equally well-known dislike of peregrines, I contacted the local police. Luckily (it was all just luck back then), I got a helpful sergeant and here I was, on my first self-led search.

The door was opened by the 'lady' of the house, whom I will call Jean. She looked surprised, which was understandable, but it was immediately obvious that the policeman knew the family well. It was first name terms all round.

'This is Mr Dick from the RSPB. We've been told that Tam's got a couple of stuffed birds he shouldn't have.' 'Stuffed burds!.. Stuffed burds!.. What'll we get next?' 'Aye, Jean, I thought it sounded daft… but we have to investigate any report we're given. So, where's Tam?' 'Oh, he's down the pub.' 'Well, we'd really like a word with him, Mr Dick's come all the way from Edinburgh.' 'Oh well, you'd better come in then.'

We all filed into the house and sat down on the couch. The TV was on loud and we had to shout above the noise, a situation I became used to over the years but a very far cry from the household I had grown up in. 'Will you have a cup of tea?' 'Aye, fine.' 'Biscuit?' 'Lovely!'

We then had a 20-minute wait, which would have been more bearable if it wasn't for the fact that *Coronation Street* was on the telly (I've never understood what all the fuss was about) and every conversation was a series of shouts. One extra worry for me was the shotgun casually propped up in a corner of the small sitting room – again, not something I was used to at home, or indeed in any of the houses I'd ever lived in, up to that point.

At last, we all heard the front door opening and got up as Tam came into the room.

'Aye, what's going on here then?' 'Well Tam, I know it sounds daft, but we've been told you've got stuffed birds you shouldn't have…' 'Aye, they're out in the shed. Didn't Jean get them for you?'

To say I was surprised doesn't begin to cover it. The room went very quiet (outside, Guy Fawkes was still being roasted, loudly). Jean's head went down. 'I'll just fetch it…' and she left the room. She returned quickly, holding a stuffed immature peregrine falcon, certainly the worst mount I have ever seen. I later used a photo of this travesty as a joke to lighten the atmosphere during slide talks. I would describe it as 'the Quasimodo of Peregrines'. Tam or one of his pals had obviously had a first stab at taxidermy and missed.

I wasn't laughing at the time, though. My shock at finding out that this pleasant little lady had just sat and told me a bare-faced lie was turning to anger as I viewed the mangled remains of what had once been a magnificent live bird of prey. When Tam started wittering on about 'These brutes, killing all the wee burds in the hedgerows,' I didn't even try to hide my contempt. 'With a lifetime as a birdwatcher and a degree in ecology, I think I'm in a better position than the likes of you to look after the wee birds in the hedgerows!' Fortunately, the police constable saw the way things were going and we were soon outside the door, with him holding the stuffed peregrine. 'Mr Dick will get the bird looked at and we will get back to you. And by the way, do something about that shotgun!'

I can honestly say that this was only one of two occasions where I openly lost my temper with a member of the public during 25 years as a professional conservationist. The other time was on the phone to a 'raptor rehabilitator' who had patched up a buzzard after it had been pole-trapped a second time and wouldn't tell me – or anyone else - which estate was involved. He got a flea in his ear and the police at his door.

I'd like to say that this alleged raptor killer was dragged through the courts but an X-ray examination failed to provide any proof of an illegal cause of death. Although the Wildlife and Countryside Act clearly stated that mere possession of a dead peregrine was an absolute offence (the RSPB, in May 1988, *Robinson* v. *Everett*, had this enshrined in English law by way of an appeal in the High Court of Justice) no Procurator Fiscal in Scotland, as I repeatedly found out, would prosecute unless a protected bird or animal was shown to have been unlawfully killed. This was to me an early example of the obvious gap between the real world of the justice system and the imagined, optimistic world of legislators.

The more alert reader will have noticed, of course, that the original report was of two stuffed peregrines, and Tam himself referred to 'them' when he arrived home. A second bird was never produced by Jean and neither I nor the policeman noticed. Another of many loose ends from a long career…

WEDNESDAY, 7 MAY 1986

On a rare day in the office, in the middle of the breeding season, a young raptor worker arrived first thing, carrying a Fenn trap. Fenn traps, which take the name of their inventor, are spring traps, not unlike a large rat trap in appearance, and were one of the few spring traps recognised by the government and listed in the Spring Trap Approval Order at that time. Used in their thousands in the UK for the legal trapping of rats, stoats, weasels, mink and grey squirrels, they must be used under cover. They are the main type of trap used by gamekeepers and others, as an illegal pole trap, a generic term.

He had a very interesting story for me. The day before, while out with a fellow enthusiast looking for nesting merlins in the Pentland Hills, the pair had approached the top of a small rock face. On looking over the rock, they were surprised to see a man sitting smoking, with a shotgun on his lap. The man was wearing the traditional tweed suit of a gamekeeper and carried a game bag. They were even more surprised when the man, instead of challenging them, as would have been the norm on a grouse moor, got up quickly and walked away.

Intrigued by this and also carrying on what would have been a normal search for nesting birds, they walked round to the place where the man had been sitting. The rock was split by a large ledge and in a hollow section of ledge was a nest scrape, containing what they immediately recognised as four peregrine eggs. Immediately adjacent to the eggs was a set Fenn trap. Fortunately, they spotted the trap and knew what it was, or one of them might have become its next victim. Its intended target was an adult peregrine returning to its eggs. They sprung the trap, removed it and left the area in a hurry, in case a peregrine was still capable of returning and resuming incubation.

The trap was now lying on my desk. I knew enough by then to know that it had been unwise of the raptor workers to take it. By removing evidence, they would make the police less likely to become involved, despite the fact that there were two corroborating witnesses willing to give statements, so there would be no problem in law. But remember that this is 1986, before the days of wildlife police, and when I was already beginning to come across two main types of response from police officers when faced with a report of wild bird crime. The first was to try to pass the whole case back to me – which was often very useful, as will be shown later – while the second was to attempt an investigation on their own, only coming back to me when they came unstuck. If they were to take the latter course, they would expect everything to be as untouched as possible.

I wrote down as much detail as I could, including the fact that this man was likely to be the new gamekeeper, the previous one having left the year before, then went out looking for a policeman to help me. As it was within easy striking distance of my office, I drove to the police office nearest to the incident. Again my luck was in – the young constable (no, they didn't all look young then: I was still only 34) who came to the door listened carefully to my tale and plea for help, eventually stopped me and said, 'I would strongly advise you to take this to the next station – the sergeant here is best friends with that gamekeeper. Just tell whoever you get that there's no one here today!' Again, whoever you are, thank you.

I drove a few miles to the next manned police station and again repeated my tale to the on-duty constable. He listened politely before saying that he knew very little about this area of law, so could I handle this on my own? We then agreed that I should go up to the area, take photographs, see what the situation was at the nest and report back. He also asked if I could ob-tain a statement from both witnesses (which I did that night) as they both lived in Edinburgh.

In 1986, I had little or no casework experience – and neither did Procurators Fiscal, defence agents and the Scottish police. We all had to learn from actual cases what the limits and limitations imposed by the little-used laws involved. From my point of view, I had to assess the chances of a successful prosecution where it appeared to me that a crime or series of crimes had been committed. Battle was about to be joined between the spirit and the letter of the law on wildlife crime – and I was the rather unwitting catalyst.

I had no hesitation in walking onto the estate involved. After all, I had been asked to do so by a police officer, but I was also well aware, after several years of fieldwork and a lifetime as a Scot, of my right to walk where I pleased on open land in my own country. In later years I was repeatedly assured by Procurators Fiscal, police officers and even sheriffs that as a civilian I had the same right to roam as anyone else. That advice – if not the law – changed only much later, when a coterie of landowners and gamekeepers' representatives managed to bring influence to bear on certain authorities, no doubt in response to the increasing number of RSPB-led cases against them.

As I walked across a steep hillside on my way up to the moorland crag, I noticed a large walk-in crow cage trap, unset, with its door open. I was familiar with these legal traps, having seen some in action during earlier work in upland Scotland. As I got closer, I was surprised to see three white hen's eggs on the ground near the trap. They had been placed together, looking for all the world like a normal wild bird's nest, except that no normal ground-nesting wild bird in Scotland lays white eggs, as they would immediately be seen by flying predators such as crows. (Raptors such as short-eared owls are the exception, as they are able to defend their nests.) And of course that is exactly why the eggs had been put there. On closer inspection – done with great care, as this was the era of strychnine and Phosdrin, deadly poisons both – I saw that each egg had a small puncture mark in its shell, a classic sign of eggs as poisoned bait, having been injected with poison by syringe.

I photographed the eggs, then carefully wrapped them up in paper tissue and put them in my rucksack. As I headed towards the peregrine nest a further two kilometres up the hill, I started thinking about the sort of person I was dealing with. He had available a legitimate crow trap but instead chose to ignore it and placed poisoned eggs, potentially capable of killing any bird or animal or pet or child attracted to them, on an open hillside within sight of a village.

I arrived at the small rock – it's astonishing what peregrines will nest on, if the food supply is good and human disturbance is low – and found the three cold damp eggs on their ledge. No sign of adult peregrines. On lifting an egg, I could see that it had not been turned for some time. These eggs were dead. Again I took photos and wrapped the eggs up and put them in my rucksack.

I retraced my steps and on the way back down found another clutch of punctured hen's eggs, placed beside a sheep track on the open hill. This time I saw that one egg had 22/3/86 written on it, in ink. Again they were photographed, again carefully wrapped and taken. I also noticed a number of dead lambs lying on the hillside. I could see none of the obvious signs of crow or fox predation on these – their eyes were intact and no puncture wounds were visible. They had probably succumbed to one of the normal reasons for hill lamb mortality in Scotland: respiratory disease, hypothermia or just poor mothering by ewes.

When the eggs were scientifically analysed, they were found to contain alphachloralose, a narcotic rodenticide which was to become extremely familiar to me as I dealt with dozens of cases of its illegal use on shooting estates and farms throughout Scotland. It had been illegal to use in the open since the 1912 Protection of Animals Scotland Act, illegal to use against rats yet in 1986 was still used by local authorities, under supposedly strict one-off licensed conditions, to kill gulls and pigeons.

So what did we have here? An illegal set trap beside a peregrine nest (with no evidence as to who set it); a man sitting with a gun within a few feet of the nest (possible disturbance

Chloralose egg baits next to crow cage, Pentland Hills, 1986

but no evidence of birds being in the area when he was; and it wasn't known if the eggs were deserted); an attempt to kill peregrines by shooting (ditto); placing poison in the open, attempting to poison birds (again, no evidence as to who put the eggs there or when).

All the evidence, including the statements I obtained from the two witnesses, was presented to the police, who in turn sent a report to the Procurator Fiscal.

Back in those halcyon days it was not a surprise when I was contacted by the Fiscal, resulting in a sit-down with him and the relevant police officer. The conversation was rather depressing, as he outlined, perfectly correctly, the reasons that a court case would not succeed. And not because of any of the spurious technicalities now beloved of certain Scottish defence agents – such as my not having contacted the landowner before investigating his own staff – but because of a lack of direct evidence against one individual.

I look back at such a case now and see all the missed possibilities, but remember that these were indeed early days. There were no trained police, no trained Procurator Fiscals, no liaison with DAFS field staff to follow up pesticide abuse and no experience of searching gamekeepers. Things were so primitive, that there was still an open lobby for the use of alphachloralose to kill crows, but all that was about to change and I would like to think that my own work played a large part in that.

And this Fiscal wasn't defeated. He could clearly see what had been happening on this estate and he didn't like it. To my astonishment, he ordered me to go with the police officer to visit the landowner and personally convey the Fiscal's displeasure.

The uniquely Scottish official known as Procurator Fiscal has enormous power. From their beginnings as a kind of tax collector for the Crown, they have been able to demand that any citizen should investigate a crime on their behalf. The fact that, in almost all cases in Scotland, they use the police as their agents is merely a convention, not a law. One old-style Fiscal for whom I had enormous respect, Frank Walkingshaw at Stranraer (now, sadly, deceased) started his lecture to a UK Police Wildlife Officers' Conference in England with the words, 'I am a Procurator Fiscal and where I come from, I am God!'

Soon after that meeting I found myself standing in front of the landowner in the library of his large country house, repeating the Fiscal's words and adding a few of my own. When he attempted to deny any involvement either in peregrine persecution or poisoning, I answered that the Fiscal wasn't debating what had happened, he was telling him that it must stop. I may sound very brave here but having a uniformed constable present was a big help. I could see that we were getting nowhere, so I changed the subject to the state of his grouse moor. He relaxed visibly and then went on to say that things were so bad, was it any wonder that he had to resort to extreme measures against vermin? A little more pushing and a reminder that he wasn't going to be prosecuted and he basically confessed that his keeper had been responsible, with his encouragement. Before leaving, I made it very clear that I didn't expect to have to come back.

Procurators Fiscal can and often do issue written warnings instead of initiating court proceedings. I much preferred this method but, sadly, it was unique in my career. I never did have to go back but it was some years before a peregrine used that site successfully. I am pleased to acknowledge the respect which the RSPB and I myself were granted by the Fiscal service but I am utterly convinced that a conviction against the gamekeeper would have done more to stop future killing. However, that would only have been possible if more evidence had been collected by way of a DAFS/RSPB/police search.

MONDAY, 2 MAY 1988

6 p.m. on a beautiful May evening in Highland Perthshire. It had been a bright sunny day which I had had every opportunity to enjoy, as I had been doing the rounds with Keith Brockie and Stewart Thompson, checking several osprey nests in the area. Keith was and is a dedicated naturalist and a superb wildlife artist, and I remember at the time feeling very privileged, even with my own extensive fieldwork experience, to be shown 'his' sites. Keith had already spent several years studying and protecting this group of nesting ospreys but sadly an equally dedicated group of egg thieves had being doing the same and at least one nest had been robbed of its eggs the year before.

Stewart Thompson was an unpaid helper, a student on a year's work experience with the RSPB. One of the most hilarious field companions I have met, with a rough-and-ready sense of humour, no doubt sharpened by several years working as a coalminer in his native Doncaster. An unusual background, perhaps, but just one of the huge variety of hardworking and willing nest protectors I saw throughout Scotland in our prolonged war against egg thieves.

Although Keith and a couple of other raptor workers had already spent many frustrating hours trying to catch the egg thieves, it was decided in 1988 to try a more ambitious plan. Keith, along with the local RSPB officer Ken Shaw, had been in contact with the two estates on which the birds were nesting. Contact had been made with the relevant land managers and we had permission to use some buildings nearby as our night-time base.

Unfortunately for someone, the estate factor of the larger shooting estate had forgotten to tell his gamekeeper about our presence on the ground. It was, therefore, with a strange mixture of anger and amusement that Keith and I found ourselves looking at two hens' eggs, neatly capped and laid out on top of a grassy tussock in the middle of a small bog. This was within site of our temporary HQ.

We were both very experienced in the subject of illegal poison baits – you didn't work on birds of prey in the Scottish uplands in the 1980s for very long without coming across something like this. We knew immediately that we were looking at poisoned eggs laid out for crows – a well-used trick was to use egg baits close to water, where the crows would eat and drink.

The eggs were photographed, then carefully transported to the Department of Agriculture toxicology lab in Edinburgh, where it was established that they, too, contained the poison alphachloralose. This narcotic rodenticide, which kills by a hypothermic reaction, has several nicknames in the gamekeeping world – sugar, salt, powder, dope – and alpha was still, in 1988, the most widely-used illegal method of poisoning wildlife in Scotland.

For all of us protecting the ospreys, this presented a quandary. These were the days before any meaningful schemes or protocols had been set up by the police or the Department of Agriculture to deal with any sort of wildlife crime in Perthshire, or anywhere else in Scotland for that matter. That would have to wait a few years yet. Doing nothing was not an option. We were all aware of the effect of poison on the food chain and both Keith and I had seen eagles poisoned, either directly by eating meat baits or by secondary poisoning, eating the victims of poisoned eggs like the ones that we had found. It was decided that the best course of action was to approach the estate factor as soon as possible and get him to have the estate cleaned up.

When Keith Brockie, Ken Shaw and I met the factor in his office, he was not a happy man. After a brief apology and assurances that it would not happen again, he did himself no favours by going on the attack. 'We have too many peregrine falcons here, they are decimating the grouse, why can't you take some of them away for us?' was not quite the wildlife-friendly attitude we had hoped for. We stayed calm, however, and explained to him that his suggestion, as well as being impossible under domestic and European legislation, would be totally impractical: these birds are a natural part of the environment and would merely keep coming back from outside to fill the gap.

By the time we finally left, he had perked up. His parting shot – 'Well, we didn't have any of these fancy chemicals in my day, we just used strychnine!' – was not a joke.

MONDAY, 5 DECEMBER 1988

A long, long pause had followed the sheriff's gentle question to the man in the dock. 'What kind of fish were you expecting to catch, Mr Young?' Douglas Young, the accused, stared in front, then, at last, said, 'I'm not an expert on fish, your Honour.' Stifled laughter from the normally stolid usher and attendant Tayside police officers broke through the solemnity of the proceedings for a moment before the sheriff indicated, with a silent wave, that the Fiscal should carry on with his examination of the witness.

Court Room No. 1 of Perth Sheriff Court, on that December morning, was a seriously impressive place. It still is. With an astonishingly high ceiling, through which shafts of light pierced the dusty air, the first thing that the usual day's custodies would see was the imposing figure of the sheriff, sitting on his bench a good ten feet above them. As he was escorted by a uniformed policeman, up through the hole in the floor, the hapless accused must often have wished he had gone home early before that eighth pint of heavy turned him into a fighting machine.

But this wasn't a usual day. A couple of urgent cases had been dealt with and dates set for further hearings in agreement with relieved defence solicitors, who nevertheless were hanging about, as if waiting for the main act.

After a short adjournment to his rooms, Sheriff McInnes returned to his bench and, after the usher's stern cry, 'Court!', all present stood up and then sat down in unison, leaving Robert Brown, the Procurator Fiscal, to open the prosecution case. Four men sat in the front bench – Colin Watson, Marcus Betteridge, Barry Sheavils and Douglas Young – and listened as the Fiscal described the events leading up to, and following, an unsuccessful attempt to rob the eyrie of a golden eagle in highland Perthshire.

5.20 P.M., MONDAY, 28 MARCH 1988

We could hardly believe our eyes. Through the fading light, about half a kilometre away and 150 m. below us, three figures had appeared on the lip of the track leading up from the main glen. As the men trudged along the track past the old abandoned shielings, I was beginning to make out the features of the taller leader of the group. 'I'm sure that's Colin Watson!' I whispered to Andy as we crouched in the snow. 'Let's get into the burn gully, fast!' Scuttling across the soft snow of the steep hillside, we were soon concealed in the only cover possible, a small gully channelling a trickling stream past curving walls of overhanging snow, snow which had to be hastily scraped away with wet gloves to create a temporary shelter and viewing position.

Rising out of the gloom above us was a broken line of crags, a fringe of birch at each end and an occasional hardy rowan tree's curving stem reaching up to the sky from a crack in the black rock. A very sharp eye would also have noticed the light brown top to a metre-high pile of sticks at the centre left of the crags, from where the even sharper eye of an adult female eagle was watching the intruders to her territory. Minutes before I spotted the men approaching along the track, I had been pointing out to Andy the built up eagle's nest and advising a quick retreat, to allow the bird to remain on her eggs. By this time a veteran of six seasons of eagle monitoring, I was unlikely to miss such an obvious occupied nest. Besides, I had been here before.

Far below, the three men were an odd sight in that place. Oddest of all was the short stocky figure of Barry Sheavils, clad in a bright yellow oilskin more suited to the deck of a North Sea trawler. The three men reached an old sheep fank – a rough circle of low stone wall – below and slightly to the left of us. They were opposite the centre of the nest crag. One of the men pulled out the aerial of a large walkie-talkie radio.

Above them, and now well concealed, Andy and I were discussing our options. No one involved in bird conservation would want to be responsible for the loss of golden eagle eggs, but we were experienced investigators, who knew that the gang below were fully capable of coming back and robbing the remote site at will if they were merely chased off, by two civilians. We also knew that the law can be a very tough taskmaster and evidence has to be watertight for a conviction, even if a situation like this was blindingly obvious at the time. We decided to sit and watch a little longer, while keeping a close eye on the bird sitting on its nest.

One of the men left the fank and started to walk up the slope. I could clearly see now that it was Colin Watson, a notoriously persistent but hapless egg thief with several convictions (and several more to come, in the years ahead. It was a heart condition, then a fall from a York-shire tree which eventually stopped Watson, not the belatedly-introduced prison sentences). He moved slowly but steadily upwards, before circling round the east end of the line of crags and disappearing behind a fringe of overhanging birch trees. Then, to our astonishment and relief, he reappeared above a narrow cleft and threw down a rope, past what I knew to be a disused eagle nest. He clipped the rope through a carabiner, already attached to a sling worn on his upper thighs and stepped off the clifftop. 'My God, he's using commando style!' said Andy, 'I bet that hurts!' 'Aye, and he's going to the wrong nest too!' I was laughing quietly, because I could see that this attempt would use all the available daylight. Sure enough, by the time we saw Watson return to the cliff-top, empty-handed, it was getting difficult to make out his tall figure.

Watson rejoined his companions, no doubt complaining that the birds had been robbed by someone else, and they trudged along the floor of the hanging valley. A sickly yellow light was showing from below the clouds at the valley entrance and snow flurries had started up again.

'Now we've got a problem,' said Andy. 'How do we get to the road before them and get their vehicle number for the police? And even if we do, they won't have any eggs on them.' 'No, but we've got two witnesses to an attempted theft, Section 18,' I replied, beginning to straighten up and brush wet snow off my backside 'and there's the equipment, that's another section 18.' 'Oh yes,' said Andy, smiling broadly, looking up at the crag now shrouded in darkness, 'and she's still sitting!' *(See note opposite).

As the three men reached the lip of the upper valley, a battered old Land Rover appeared and a uniformed police officer stepped out. After appearing to chat to the egg thieves, he opened the back door and they all climbed in. At the side of the vehicle, and out of sight to those inside, he looked over in our direction and waved a gloved hand before stepping into the passenger seat. Grant the shepherd put his Land Rover into low gear and it trundled out of sight along the steep winding path down to his steading.

Earlier the same day, on passing the farm steading in the main glen, I had noticed a group of men working with sheep penned in the yard. I walked over and introduced myself to Grant Macdonald, who had identified himself as the local shepherd and stalker. I told him that we were expecting trouble from egg thieves, who were after the birds up the hill and that we were going up to see if all was well and plan some way of guarding the nest. I also gave him a quick rundown on how to tell egg thieves from ordinary hillwalkers and who to call (Pitlochry police station) if he saw anything suspicious. Grant was obviously very busy and I got what I had come to expect in the way of slightly offhand replies – why should I expect any more from a busy working man? As it turned out, he had remembered every word and carried out my suggestions to the letter. Not for the last time, I was pleasantly surprised by the help I got – often from shepherds – when eagles were involved.

Within twenty minutes of our conversation, the egg thieves had walked past the steading on the same track. Grant told me later, 'I couldn't believe it! I thought you guys were magic!'

This was one of my first cases working with Andy Jones, a new Investigations Officer based at the Lodge and later to become the head of the Investigations Unit.

At the end of the one-day trial, Watson was fined £2,000 and the other three were fined £1,300 each. They were respectable fines at the time but we were right to be under no illusion that this would stop these people.

By the time I eventually began to give training talks and lectures to police officers, wildlife rangers and countryside user groups, experience had taught me that 1980s egg thieves were, as a rule, very ill-equipped for the hill. The use of poor-quality footwear and other clothing was the norm, even to the extent of ignoring the obvious ploy of wearing dark or camouflage clothing. Similarly, their climbing gear – ropes, slings, harnesses – was almost always of a standard that would have had a mountain safety trainer openly weeping. This case shows the importance of such inside knowledge.

It would be a dangerous assumption nowadays. From the 1990s, egg thieves and nest disturbers began to purchase clothing, climbing gear and optical equipment from the same new outdoor shops frequented by legitimate fieldworkers.

* Under Section 18(1) and 18(2) of the Wildlife and Countryside Act 1981, 'Any person who attempts to commit an offence under the foregoing provisions of this Part shall be guilty of an offence and shall be punishable in like manner as for the said offence' and 'Any person who for the purposes of committing an offence… has in his possession anything capable of being used for committing the offence…'

By 1989 my staff level remained constant although the personnel had changed. I had been joined by Stuart Benn, brand new Assistant Investigations Officer and a fellow Glaswegian. Some of the truly enjoyable moments of my professional life were when the opposition, usually people with close connections to wildlife criminals, would complain in the press or media, after some high profile case or crime report, that 'the RSPB has a man behind every bush'. I found this by turns hilarious and hugely complimentary.

Only a complete idiot would ever imagine that one person could solve and deal with all wild bird crime in Scotland, even back in 1984, when we were still seriously underestimating, or at least seriously in the dark about how much was going on. There were those with a touching faith in the power of the new 1981 Act, which came into force in September 1982, thinking that by its very existence, somehow, wildlife criminals would stop their depredations. I see this attitude still in 2010, despite what is now massive evidence to the contrary. I was never one of those deluded optimists.

So my strategy, such as it was, was to try to make sure that the wildlife law we had was used all over Scotland – to at least give the impression that, wherever you were poisoning that eagle, shooting that harrier, stealing that peregrine chick or lifting its eggs, you might be being watched and you might get caught.

It is a truism that wildlife law enforcement is about people as much as, or even more than, about wildlife. Having said that, I have been surprised at how few wildlife crimes were ever reported to me, or anyone else I knew, in the populous Central Belt of Scotland. Glasgow, in particular, would seem to be a wildlife crime-free zone. Now, I come from a long line of Glaswegians, going back to the early 19th century, so I believe I am in a position to say that I find this odd. There are some bad people in Glasgow. Perhaps they've just found other outlets for their badness. The following story shows that I did, very occasionally, get to work with 'my ain folk'.

JANUARY 1989

Dr Neville Cartwright is a top scientist and an observant man. So when he was forced to hang about the fish and poultry shop, waiting for his wife Kathleen to purchase their dinner from the queue at the counter, he couldn't help but notice the young man plucking a bird at the back of the shop.

As the secretary of the local members group of the RSPB and an experienced birdwatcher, Neville thought there was something unusual about the feathers growing into a pile at the lad's feet. So he walked over and politely asked him what kind of duck it was. 'It's naw a duck, it's a barnacle goose!' 'But aren't they protected?' 'Aye, but this wans frum Islay, ye can get a licence to shoot them.' On the way out of the shop, Neville noticed a black lump in the window, with a sticker on it proclaiming 'Wild Goose - £9'.

After leaving the shop, Neville phoned me direct. 'Not quite right, Neville. You can shoot a barnacle goose for crop protection on Islay, but you can't sell it, or any other wild goose for that matter. I'll get right on to it.'

FRIDAY, 20 JANUARY 1989

Being already very experienced in the art of losing cases because 'the bleeding obvious' had been neglected, I knew that I had to obtain evidence of sale. So with Stuart Benn by my side and a Dictaphone in my pocket, I travelled to Glasgow. From my local knowledge, I knew that the shop was one of a chain in the area, so we first went to the Anniesland Cross branch. The conversation with the female shopkeeper – a splendid example of, perhaps, an overeager and none too bright salesperson – went roughly as follows: 'Do you have a goose?' 'A goose?' 'Yes, a goose...' 'A goose?' 'Aye, a goose!' 'Whaddya wannt wun o' them fur?' 'Well, for dinner... you know...' 'Och, you don't want a goose, they're all full o' grease, you wannt a turkey!' 'You don't sell geese, then?' 'Naw, we're all out o' them...' 'Your other shop does...' 'Does it? Naw, you wannt a turkey, geese are full o' grease...' 'How much are they anyway?' 'Do you know the price of them, it would make yi die!''About £9?' 'Don't kid yersell!' 'Someone said about £9...' 'If they're selling them for that, it wid be wanns they want rid of! We were selling them fur 16 quid.' 'OK, thanks anyway...'

Next stop, the original shop in Byres Road, where things went much more smoothly. Black lump in window with sticker, sold to me for £9 with a till receipt. No head, no legs. In court I could already hear the defence agent: 'So, Mr Dick, what kind of bird is this exactly that my client has been charged with selling?'

Next stop, the Applied Ornithology Unit of Glasgow University, a few hundred yards (metres came later) from Byres Road. Dr Pat Monaghan and Bernie Zonfrillo, two well-known figures in the bird world, weighed and examined the bird. 'If it's a goose, it's a barnacle, it fits the weight and length parameters closer than any other species.' That'll do me, I thought.

That, as usual, was the easy part. Now it was time to get the police involved. The nearest police office was the dreaded Partick police station, famed in song and story (literally, in Glasgow), an imposing old stone building down towards the River Clyde on the dodgy side of Dumbarton Road. I knew exactly the reception I was likely to get when I went in and asked for help in apprehending a wild goose seller on Byres Road, and I wasn't disappointed. Disbelief, followed by a repetition of the relevant sections of the Act from me, followed by a showing of my copy of the 1981 Act to the desk sergeant, who took it away to study, followed by a very long wait.

Perhaps an hour later, two very brisk and cheery young men in suits came out of a door at the side of the main bar. 'Mr Dick? We're CID, we're going to get a warrant for the shop. Have you got a car?' Now there was a surprise!

A few minutes later and I'm driving up Byres Road with the CID beside me. I'd already learned that the best way to get policemen to relax and work with me was to show an interest in their normal work. so I always asked them what things were like around wherever we were at the time – Bettyhill, Stornoway, Stranraer, Kirkcaldy. The difference here was that I had lived close to Byres Road for over 12 years, my first girlfriend had lived within two minutes of the fish shop, and as a schoolboy, a Strathclyde University student or even as a blues guitarist in Glasgow, the very idea of talking to Partick CID would have made me run in the opposite direction.

But here goes. 'So what's it like around here, then? Busy?' Short pause before Suit Number One says, 'Busy? Busy? See, if Terry Waite ever turns up, he'll be passing dodgy cheques in Byres Road!' Cue roars of laughter, which I join in. I'm definitely in my home town and the ice is broken.

The next half hour is a hail of goose jokes, broken only by the surreal and serious business of the swearing out of a search warrant in front of a J.P., a retired businessman of some sort, living in an upmarket tower block off Great Western Road.

It is only as we are actually entering the shop and another two CID have miraculously appeared that one of them says, 'Keep your eyes open for fush.' All is revealed: wild geese might be good for a laugh but it's salmon poaching that really gets their interest.

Finally, we are in a large walk-in freezer room at the back of the shop, several dead greylag geese hanging from hooks, plucked to reveal black dots about the size of a pencil end randomly distributed across their flesh. 'You don't get many farmyard geese being slaughtered with a shotgun – these are wild, aren't they?' I say to the shop manager, with a policeman standing beside him. The policeman smiles back at me.

Although some species of grey geese can legally be shot during the open season in Scotland, the selling of all dead wild geese is forbidden. The shop manager pled guilty to selling wild geese and was fined £30 at Glasgow Sheriff Court on 26 April 1989. It was a good result at the time but, sadly, would still be a good result now.

SPECIES V. HABITAT: CONSERVATION SCHISM IN THE 1980S

One particular area of debate which came to a head during my formative years as an Investigations Officer was over the importance of species protection vs habitat protection. Although the plight of wild birds in the UK was being addressed both by the purchase and management of reserves and by the protection of individual species through the passing and enforcement of legislation, attempts to protect widespread, undesignated habitat were only just beginning.

In particular, the 1981 Act allowed for, indeed insisted upon, the creation of SSSIs (Sites of Special Scientific Interest). In terms of wild bird protection this was a revolution, once again brought about by the EC Birds Directive, which the UK government was legally obliged to follow. I strongly believe, from what I have seen over the last 30 years, that with the continuing dead hand of traditional landowners and managers in our countryside, we would have lost a huge amount of (dreadful word!) biodiversity that has been saved through such European Directives. Not that the designation or indeed protection of SSSIs has been smooth or indeed, in some areas, complete or effective.

The RSPB was well ahead of the game on the habitat issue and, of course, had long before realised that without its habitat in a healthy and stable condition, no bird species could survive, no matter how well individuals were protected. With growing alarm and agitation, though, I saw that view allowed to flourish to the extent that it almost completely overwhelmed more straightforward species protection resources.

The spectacular growth of bird conservation in the 1950s, 1960s and 1970s, with the RSPB in the vanguard, was due to the convergence of a number of well-recognised phenomena: the devastating effects of pesticides such as DDT, the growing exploitation of birds in general due to a boom in the world economy and huge improvements in travel but, above all, by the explosion of interest created by new television stars such as David Attenborough and Sir Peter Scott. Hard work by those promoting membership of RSPB, through encouraging the feeding of garden birds, visiting reserves or watching wildlife films in local halls, led to a massive increase in public interest.

Now add the Loch Garten effect – a direct cops-and-robbers tale, a story of decades of fighting against egg thieves – along with the efforts of local groups of volunteers working to protect the nests of peregrine falcons from egg and chick thieves as they struggled back after the pesticide era. The RSPB and others, quite understandably, encouraged an already softened-up press and media to give species protection stories as much coverage as possible. This included, by the way, now long-forgotten bird of prey persecution campaigns such as the first Map of Shame, published by the RSPB in the 1960s to name and shame estates where pole traps, outlawed by a 1904 Act, were still being used. Nearly 50 years later, some keepers are still being caught illegally using spring traps in the open.

Those involved in habitat protection soon found that the press were not so interested in their issues, no matter how important they were to conservation. As a veteran user of the media I fully understand this: a good photo of a bird, egg, nest or trap will fill a page of a newspaper but no photo editor wants a picture of a reedbed, bog, loch or wood.

This would have remained a small internecine issue if it hadn't been for the fact that certain individuals involved in habitat protection used their case to empire build within conservation. Add to the undoubted importance of habitat protection the fact that it can mainly be carried out without direct physical confrontation, through meetings with lawyers, MPs or MSPs and other bureaucrats, unlike the messy confrontational involvement of fieldwork, criminals, police and the criminal courts which species investigative and enforcement work involves, and it is easy to see which side won out in the yuppified business management decade of the 1980s.

These arguments carried on throughout my career. I never tired of telling those involved with habitat protection, reserves or research, that one man with a bottle of poison, a gun or a trap could remove thousands of pounds' worth of their work in the twinkling of an eye. To me, it's always been the most obvious no-brainer: you need both efficient species and habitat

protection if you are to conserve wild birds in Scotland or, indeed, anywhere else. And if conservationists don't do it, no-one else will.

5

FALCON THEFT

While Scotland's reputation as a wildlife haven and wildlife tourism destination was growing during the latter years of the 20th century, it was also attracting unwanted attention from a group of specialist wildlife thieves. The big attraction was our population of peregrine falcons although golden eagles were also a target for a short while.

As I've already mentioned in relation to the Argyll wildlife collection case, the early 1980s were a very interesting time for the small world of British falconry. ('Falconry' is a term restricted to those who actually fly falcons at game, while 'austringers' fly hawks.) Prior to the huge boom in raptor keeping, brought about by the advances in artificial insemination techniques, very few people kept peregrines and goshawks or even buzzards and kestrels in the UK. It was even rarer to own a golden eagle or a merlin.

Despite the widespread success in the late 1960s of the book *A Kestrel for a Knave* and the subsequent film *Kes*, falconry remained a mainly elitist sport. Practised by enthusiasts who had the time and money it needed, there were few applications for the tight quotas of licences to take wild chicks from nests. In Scotland, these were administered by the Scottish Home and Health Department of the Scottish Office in Edinburgh. Links with the RSPB and the NCC were close, through a body known as the Advisory Committee on the Protection of Birds in Scotland, set up under section 11 of the 1954 Protection of Birds Act. It was even possible, at one time, to get a licence to take a golden eagle chick for falconry.

It should not be thought that there was no pressure from falconry, through nest robbing, on peregrine and eagle populations in those early days. As I have already explained, the effects of widespread use of organochlorine pesticides had been catastrophic in some areas. In the late 1970s, for example, the population of peregrines in southeast Scotland had crashed to around half a dozen breeding pairs. At its height in the late 20th century, this population had risen to over 90 pairs. Despite this, they were still under attack from chick thieves. In 1984, my new colleagues regaled me with tales of 24-hour watches on remote hillsides and of entire communities guarding 'their' peregrines. Little did we know that that was just a taster of what was about to occur.

Before modern captive breeding techniques became accessible, falconers obviously had to take wild birds. Many old books contain details of the robbing of eyries to obtain peregrine chicks, often from cliff nests which have been known for this reason for centuries. I recall visiting a regularly-robbed cliff in the Borders, which, George Carse informed me, had supplied birds for Mary, Queen of Scots. In latter decades it had been supplying a gang of thieves with drug-dealing convictions from the shabbier parts of Newcastle.

In the pre-Protection Acts days, Scottish falconers would take and train eyasses (nestlings) from wild nests, use them for a few seasons until they escaped or were simply found wanting as hunters and were released. The most prized birds were passage birds, young peregrines of the year which had already learned to fly. These had to be trapped, using nets and live traps.

I learnt much of the above from legitimate professional falconers. As the thefts began to build up throughout the 1980s, such knowledge was valuable in understanding not only the *modus operandi* or M.O. – to use the term beloved by crime investigators! – of falcon thieves but also their motivation, or that of the end users of the birds. The robbers themselves were always driven purely by money. These were professional criminals who could make very easy money this way and found themselves in no danger of being jailed, as conservation legislation was so weak.

Sadly, the legitimate side of falconry was very slow to accept what had become obvious to those of us in the front line: that more and more peregrine nests were being robbed in Scotland to satisfy the growing demand of a rapidly expanding hobby. This led to considerable unnecessary and divisive conflict between organisations which should

Karen Bradbury (RSPB Investigator) and seized captive eagle

have been working together to catch the criminals. As I have said with regard to shooting, the RSPB was the one conservation body with an openly-stated neutral position on the killing of game, whether with a shotgun or with a falcon.

The logic which was being applied by the falconry world was that surely no one needed to steal peregrines, when increases in captive breeding were drastically reducing the price of legitimate captive birds? This surprised us too, for some time, until we heard the criminals boasting of selling 'pure-bred, wild stock, Scottish birds'. It appeared that those falconers with enough money – initially in the Gulf States but also in Germany, Austria, Belgium and Holland – were indulging their fantasies of flying 'the best falcons in the world'. These were the people who were paying ridiculous prices – thousands of pounds, dollars or Deutschmarks – at a time when you could buy a captive bird in the UK for £350 to £500. It should always be remembered, though, that those high prices were for birds which had already been through several pairs of criminals hands and which, having been smuggled across several borders, arrived at their destination fully grown, fully trained and fully acclimatised to the heat.

If anyone still doubts this, they should consider the case of Jeffrey Lendrum, caught smuggling live peregrine eggs to Dubai and convicted as I write in August 2010. This comes at a time when such countries have had temperature-controlled breeding aviaries for years. The only explanation is that they are desperate for peregrines with a proven UK bloodline.

The context in which the following Scottish case histories are told encompasses all of the above: an expanding world market, poorly understood at first by those suffering the consequences and trying to prevent conservation damage, and also poorly understood by many within falconry. This lack of understanding was often, I believe, due to criminals within their own ranks, feeding in disinformation, in what is again a close similarity with the UK shooting community.

MONDAY, 16 JUNE 1986

It's early afternoon and a police patrol car in the Dumfries-shire town of Annan notices two Newcastle-registered cars, a Saab and a Ford Granada, driving through the centre and heading east. Although they have no record of the cars, something about them attracts the attention of the policemen and they radio the details, including the fact that they were full of young men, to their HQ in Dumfries.

A short while later the cars are spotted by an unmarked CID car, which tries to follow them. The CID officers later told me that they had had a recent tip-off about a gang of thieves coming to Stranraer to raid a supermarket. They thought they were dealing with conventional criminals but began to wonder what was going on when the vehicles headed up into the Galloway Hills. They finally lost the car amongst the maze of forest tracks and small roads west of New Galloway and headed back to Dumfries.

The next sighting of the cars, some hours after the CID lost them, found them heading towards Dumfries from the Galloway direction on the main A75 trunk road. When they drove through Dumfries, they made the idiotic mistake of shouting and waving at female pedestrians, not only attracting attention but also giving the police the perfect excuse to stop them.

When I spoke to the arresting officer, after a call for help and a dash down to the police office from Edinburgh, he was still a bit stunned by what had happened. By now it was 1 a.m. 'My colleague was talking to the occupants and I opened the boot and saw three pairs of eyes staring back at me! I got a real shock and slammed the lid back down!'

In the boot of the Saab were three very large, fully-feathered live peregrine chicks.

At this time, and for some while after, three of the men, all found in the Ford Granada, claimed they knew nothing about the Saab, the two men in the Saab or, of course, the peregrines in the boot. I was present at the search of the Granada and spotted some 'chick fluff' on one of its seats (chick fluff, or down, is a common sight around fledging time when many raptors moult it out as their feathers grow in. It is also very sticky, clinging to any surface, including an intruder's clothes). I also recognized the names of three of the men. One was the head of the already notorious 'Geordie' gang of peregrine thieves, along with two of his more active henchmen. Under a back seat in the Granada, we also found a keychain with a picture of a goshawk and falconry jesses on it. The local Procurator Fiscal was contacted and granted a warrant for their overnight arrest based on these links. As always, I was aware of the lack of a power of arrest under the 1981 Act, a thorn in our side for years to come. During their confinement, the police were able to carry out further checks on the men and discovered that another of them had given a false name. He was also, in fact, a known criminal and was then charged with an attempt to pervert the course of justice: a serious charge, with possible serious consequences in terms of a jail sentence.

So, all in all, it was rather a good, unexpected capture. My job really started then, though. I had to take photographs and officially identify the birds and give a statement about peregrines and peregrine theft. I learned in later years to save all that for later, when back in my own office, but things were moving fast on this one. Now for the part that all too often gets second billing in such cases – we've got five criminals banged up and retrieved three peregrine chicks, but what will we do with them?

After talking to the CID men and making several middle-of-the-night calls to Raptor Group contacts, we got a likely nest location for the robbery, someone to show us the way and a local forest ranger to help. Also, essential to the case, I obtained permission from the Stranraer Fiscal – my old friend Mr Walkingshaw, in whose Stranraer jurisdiction the theft had taken place – to release into the wild what was, in fact, the main evidence. It was always my priority to get live birds back into nature as soon as humanly possible. Over many cases, the provision of corroborated (witnessed) photographs of live birds and a statement from me, detailing their fate, was accepted by sheriffs as fully adequate to allow for a prosecution to proceed.

The next morning found a bleary-eyed couple of RSPB Investigators (I had Iain Macleod with me on this one) approaching a crag high in the Galloway Hills. With us were Dick Roxburgh, the grand old man of the Southwest Scotland Raptor Group, and Frank McGhie, the Forestry Commission Ranger (and an amateur falconer). To our great relief and pleasure we found not only a recently-occupied, empty peregrine nest but adults still in attendance. After a nest is robbed – a sight I saw all too often – peregrines will usually drift away to another, presumably less traumatic, part of their home range. If birds are still calling at a site, it's usually a sign of a very recent robbery. With great care, we replaced the chicks on the nest ledge (these were very large chicks, known as 'leapers' in peregrine monitoring terminology) and walked away down the hill. As we went, we kept looking back until we spotted an adult land close to the chicks. Success! Frank monitored the birds until they were safely fledged a few days later.

That same day, the five men appeared in court and pled 'not guilty' to charges of taking and possession of peregrine chicks. I contacted Frank Walkingshaw and was able to supply him with details of the mens' previous convictions. That last statement may seem strange, particularly to any policeman, but the fact was that for the greater part of my involvement in this work, record keeping and retrieval by courts and the police was woefully inadequate when it came to Summary (lower court) cases such as wildlife. By 1986, RSPB Investigations Section already had a sophisticated record keeping system on offenders which, as the decade wore on, was accessed on many occasions by the police and Fiscals. It was, of course, all completely legitimate and something of which we were rightly proud. At this point, I doff my hat to the long line of hardworking collaters who ran this system, from the remarkable Penny Tedder on. Its accuracy and comprehensiveness was essential and woe betide any Investigator (including myself) who forgot to send in case details, no matter how hard pressed they were.

The results of a failure by police and courts to access this information, or of trying to avoid involving us, were all too apparent. You can imagine my anger at seeing convicted individuals described by their defence agents as 'never having been in trouble – this was a one-off crime' when you know they have been caught and fined for the same type of offence in some far-off English magistrates court. I had to endure that more than once and would be very surprised if it didn't happen still, even in (or possibly because of) today's all-singing-and-dancing computer culture.

As so often happens, all five accused entered guilty pleas at a later hearing. Sentencing took place on Monday, 22 December 1986. All five received fines of £2,000 and one man received a jail sentence of three months (already served) for giving a false name. A grand total of £10,000 in fines, far and away the largest ever given in a wildlife case in the UK at that point. Three of the gang appealed against sentence and on Thursday, 17 December 1987, they had their fines cut to £1000, £500 and £500).

These large fines of course, did nothing to slow down the increasing rate of nest robberies. The prices allegedly being paid for peregrines (there was very little real inside information at that time) combined with the fact that the chances of being caught were very low and that a fine would be the worst penalty a court could impose.

Every 'peregrine spring' was the same, with a sprinkling of new pairs as the population continued to recover from the pesticide crash. April tended to be an optimistic month, with reports coming in from all over Scotland of birds sitting. Then would come the inevitable phone calls and letters from raptor workers carrying out later checks: 'nest empty, no sign of eggshell, footprints above the cliff, etc…' As the RSG network grew in size and efficiency, we started to become aware of the robbery hotspots and the true extent of the problem. In Southeast Scotland, Moffatdale and Tweedsmuir; in Southwest Scotland, the Solway Coast of Wigtownshire and the entire Ayrshire population; in Central Scotland, the hills around Loch Earn and Loch Tay; the edges of the A9 from Fife to Inverness. Very specific patterns emerged, as with eggshell thefts. There were 'traditional' robbery sites and many, although not all, were the smaller, easily climbable crags.

At the same time, persecution of peregrines was also continuing on grouse moors, but the methods used there were different and often quite blatant – the shooting of adults, the laying of spring traps on nest ledges, poisoning and smashing of eggs. We did occasionally hear of gamekeepers being approached by falcon thieves and being offered money, either to take chicks and pass them on or to turn a blind eye when the thieves were at work. One keeper contacted me through a third party after receiving just such a phone call, worried that he would be implicated.

This was a frustrating time for me – on the one hand, we had a higher profile than ever, due to a growing number of prosecutions, particularly of egg shell thieves, but on the other, I had a growing number of angry and upset raptor workers. For the first time, I was seeing the size of the wildlife crime problem, just on the wild bird side of things, and realising how pathetically inadequate was the conservation and justice system response. Ironically, as

I write, when eggshell theft and widespread falcon theft are rarities, the might of modern 'virtual conservation' is still aimed at these phantom thieves while estate-based persecution, the politically difficult but very real threat, is either ignored or conveniently sidelined by the authorities.

SUNDAY, 8 APRIL 1990

On Saturday, 7 April, Charlie Hall, an RSG member, was monitoring one of his peregrine sites, southeast of Stranraer. He found the nest where all appeared well, with two freshly-laid eggs and a pair of healthy, vocal peregrines in attendance. He also noticed an unusual vehicle, a German-registered VW camper van, parked nearby. He took the number and carried on with his bird work. This alertness was soon to pay off. Returning to the nest the same evening, he found it had been robbed and raised the alarm, giving the police the German vehicle number.

At 4.30 p.m. on the following day, a Sunday, I received a phone call at home, from the Duty Sergeant at Stranraer police office. Could I come and help? 'We've just caught two German nationals red-handed, in the act of stealing peregrine eggs.' I can't recall if the police got my number from the local Fiscal, a local birdwatcher or from one of the police I had worked with in the past. All of these were possibilities as I gave out my card to anyone I could think of, with the words, 'Don't hesitate to call, day or night.' I was greatly angered to read the following statement in a recent book written by a retired police officer: '...time can be wasted by a person waiting to report a crime to an agency...' (the RSPB) '...that works 9-to-5, Monday to Friday.' For over 20 years I was on call 24 hours a day, seven days a week, a fact that was known and used by police officers, Fiscals and a host of civilian raptor group members. Time and again, I saw cases damaged by a lack of response when incidents were first reported to the police. That situation had changed little, due to apathy or a lack of organisation, by the time I left the job in 2006. The man concerned would not enjoy a conversation with my adult daughter, who complains that I was never at home as she was growing up.

Stranraer, I had already found out the hard way, was one of the more remote parts of Scotland as regards travel from an Edinburgh office or home – a three-and-a-half hour drive, on a variety of roads, from motorway to a long twisting, narrow coastal route. I jumped in my car (by then I had a vehicle available at all times between March and August), collected photographic and climbing gear from my office and set off. I had had a few hours' rest after traveling back from a search for illegal traps in Cowal, followed by a lecture to a birdwatchers' group in the same area the night before.

Arriving at Stranraer at around 8.30 p.m., I was met by police officers very keen for me to identify eggs found concealed in an incubator within the VW camper van belonging to the two German men. What I saw astonished me: a complex home-made system consisting of an incubator box, thermally sealed and containing a thermostat alarm, all wired up to the vehicle's battery. The incubator contained nine peregrine eggs. I was also shown a plastic bucket with a lid, containing egg cartons and packing and another thermostat alarm. The bucket had been found with the German men when they were caught near a peregrine nest.

Where had the eggs come from? A series of phone calls within the RSG network through-out the evening and some rapid checking of local sites had produced only Charlie's certain robbery. Once again, the close working relationship with Frank Walkingshaw, the local Fiscal, paid off and I was able to get permission to take two of the eggs to return to Charlie's nest.

Monday morning, early, and I'm handed two peregrine eggs by the Stranraer police. By 11 a.m., I've abseiled into the nest, on a low Solway coast cliff and replaced the live eggs where they belonged. Adult peregrines were still in the area. The remaining eggs were kept in the Germans' incubator, which was being looked after by Sgt Ken Bruce, Dumfries and Galloway's first police Wildlife Liaison Officer (WLO). A birdwatcher, with a special interest in buzzards and bird ringing, Ken was a great asset in those early days. Unfortunately, later WLOs in that force appear to have been picked more for their interest in fieldsports than for their knowledge of wildlife.

Kausen's and Baly's seized equipment, Stranraer, 1990.

The two Germans, Peter Baly and Leo Kausen, young men from Cologne with an interest in falconry and who gave their employment as cobblers, were brought to Stranraer Sheriff Court from custody the following day and pled guilty to charges of taking and possession of peregrine eggs. Their defence agent, speaking on their behalf, said that Baly had not realised that taking peregrine eggs was illegal in Scotland and that the eggs were for their own use (the two men had earlier told the arresting officer that the eggs were for consumption!) The Fiscal asked for sentencing to be postponed until Wednesday, two days later, and the sheriff agreed. After explaining to the defence that this was a serious matter, with a possible £18,000 fine, he refused bail as the men were 'of no fixed abode' and asked for social background reports.

By 1990, we were well aware that there were many German nationals involved in international falcon theft and smuggling. My colleagues in England had made good contacts with German customs and police officials. When Baly's name was mentioned, alarm bells immediately started ringing. I was told that he had previously been caught in Iceland while stealing live gyr falcon (*Falco rusticolus*) eggs, had been fined the equivalent of £8,200 but had absconded on a German freighter without paying the fine. The refusal of the freighter captain to hand over his passenger had caused a minor diplomatic incident. I passed all this information to the Fiscal, so that there would be no protestations of innocence, again, at sentencing.

I talked on the phone to Helmut Brücher, a German falcon theft expert with official links to Customs and police, who said he would arrange for searches of the two men's homes and premises. Helmut helped us out on many occasions back then and I was delighted to be able to return some favours by arranging for him to talk at a police Wildlife Liaison Officers' conference in the UK and showing him round some of our birding hotspots, including peregrine crags. He had helped retrieve chicks stolen from some of these very nests.

At some point it entered my mind that the Icelanders, having some unfinished business with Mr Baly, would love to get their hands on him again. I imagined how we Scots would feel if it was the other way round. How, though, to find out about extradition and Icelandic legal matters? Who did I know in Iceland? Then I had a brainwave: Magnus Magnusson. Probably the world's most famous Icelander, Magnus was a well-known supporter of conservation in Scotland and was, in fact, made President of the RSPB in 1995. Through a series of increasingly unreal phone calls, I spoke to the RSPB hierarchy, Magnus himself, the head of the Icelandic Parliament and the editor of Iceland's most prestigious newspaper. The Icelanders seemed very excited by the whole idea, which generated considerable publicity, in both Iceland and Scotland (after the Stranraer sentencing, of course). Sadly, I was eventually told that the Iceland offences had gone out of time, so that extradition would have been pointless. It was, though, an interesting dry run.

WEDNESDAY, 11 APRIL 1990

We all arrived for Kausen's and Baly's sentencing. Mr Walkingshaw outlined the events of the previous Sunday, when the police, already alerted by Charlie, had done an excellent job in locating the vehicle and then the two men, who had tried to run off along cliffs and a rocky shore close to a peregrine nest site to the west of Stranraer. After describing the equipment found on the men and in the vehicle, the Fiscal went on to describe the background to peregrine theft, using the information I had been able to supply. He said that German nationals had been caught raiding falcon nests from Spain to Turkey. He also described the finding, the day before, by the German authorities, of three 'breeding machines' (incubators) in Baly's flat and a price list for falcons and eagles.

In summing up, he calculated that all their equipment (including the vehicle, incubators, climbing ropes and the eggs) were worth a total of £45,000. He asked for forfeiture of all of this and added the fact that the men had been uncooperative with the police when first interviewed.

The sheriff then asked the social worker that had interviewed them about their means. Baly had admitted the Iceland affair. He was 28 years old and worked with Kausen, who was the same age. They shared an interest in falconry. He claimed he taken the eggs to hatch, then fly the birds himself.

Next came the defence agent's plea in mitigation: in my own experience, these always include the fact that 'my client loves wildlife', no matter how awful the offences. This could be the hardest part of a case for me, when I had to listen to a string of obvious second-hand lies and blatant red herrings, with no regard to facts or evidence. Such mitigation can only be challenged by the prosecution if there is a claim of good character when the accused has, in fact, convictions of a similar nature. I saw that used only once but to electrifying effect. In this case, it was claimed that Baly and Kausen had not known that it was a policeman chasing them; they denied that they had said they were going to eat the eggs; they claimed no knowledge of German or Arab prices for birds and repeated that the eggs were for their own use. The defence agent then made a strategic error in suggesting that the possible fines were extreme. Sheriff Smith interrupted him to say that 'Parliament was of the view that this was a serious matter and that is why they set the fines so high.' The agent went on to claim that the men had learned about peregrines in this area from reading a book in Cologne library and that the vehicle was virtually worthless, as was their equipment.

In his summing up and sentencing, the sheriff made the very useful remark that 'this legislation creates a dilemma [in having no direct jail provision]: what do I do with people with no money?' He then proceeded to fine them £6,000 each with the alternative of imprisonment for non-payment, knowing that they had only £600 on them. He also said he didn't believe that they didn't know this was against the law and that 'this was a professionally-organised visit for profit'. In imposing a fine of a third of the possible maximum, he told them he was being lenient. He also forfeited their vehicle and all their equipment.

The Germans were taken to Barlinnie jail in Glasgow.

Barlinnie is not a nice place and it contains some unpleasant people. I know this officially, having received a written reply from the governor to my forwarded complaints from nearby householders who had seen prisoners fishing for 'seagulls' using bread on bits of string. They throttled the gulls, then threw out the bodies. The governor's letter was a masterpiece of tongue-in-cheek understatement: 'I will look into the matter but you must understand – we have some unpleasant people in here.' Fair enough. He now had two more. I genuinely hope he got the gull killing stopped.

This case still had one last twist: within a week, a German national flew into Glasgow Airport, carrying a bag containing £12,000 in Deutschmarks. He took a taxi to Barlinnie where he tried to pay the fine for Baly and Kausen. The prison authorities said they could only accept sterling. So the unknown German got a taxi back into the centre of Glasgow, changed the money and returned to Barlinnie. Stepping out of the taxi, he left the money bag on the back seat, only to see the driver pull away. I'm sure the warders and inmates heard some interesting new words at this point. It was then that the unbelievable happened: the taxi driver found the bag, saw what was in it and took it back to Barlinnie! The story made the national press.

Sometimes, I think God is looking the other way.

The following year, Baly and Kausen had their fines reduced by the Court of Appeal in Edinburgh to £5,000 each. Big deal. We still needed prison sentences under the 1981 Act.

What we had seen here, I believe, was a couple of greedy Germans trying to cut out the middle men – UK nest thieves, bogus breeding launderers of peregrines and German couriers or smugglers – but who had, in fact, miscalculated the laying dates of Scottish peregrines. They had arrived too early. Another week or ten days later and their haul would have been twice as big. They had also underestimated our defences, although I'd be the first to say that there was a fair degree of luck involved here. Once again, though, RSPB skills and connections were what counted in getting a successful outcome. These were still days of true 'partnership working' although we would have called it 'using common sense and working together'. We just got on with it.

Around this time, several groups of Germans were caught and a good deal of intelligence was gathered from within the falconry community suggesting that a high volume of live eggs and chicks were being stolen and smuggled by, or on behalf of, German nationals. In the early 1990s, though, this was largely unknown to the general public. One April morning, a worker at an active quarry beside the A9 in Inverness-shire arrived early and surprised two men in the quarry. They were carrying climbing ropes but what impressed him most was that they were speaking to each other in German. Being an active quarry, there were considerable quantities of explosives stored in a shed on site. The two Germans left, without properly explaining what they had been up to. The quarry worker came to the conclusion that they must have been international terrorists trying to steal the explosives and immediately contacted the police. He had managed to take the number of their car, a hired Mercedes saloon. This, of course, triggered a wave of intense police activity.

By the time the site manager arrived at the quarry, the police were there in force. Fortunately, he was well aware of the peregrines nesting in the quarry – local RSPB staff monitored the site every year – and came to the correct conclusion when he heard about the climbing equipment. The men had been peregrine thieves.

I was sitting in my office when the phone rang. Colin Crooke, my RSPB colleague in Inverness, had now got involved. He passed me on to the police officer in charge. 'We've traced the car to the Europcar office at the top of Leith Walk in Edinburgh. A DC Gosling at Gayfield Square nick is handling it. Could you go round and tell him everything you know about Germans and peregrine smuggling?'

The top of Leith Walk? Gayfield Square? That's about two minutes' walk from my office. I grabbed a couple of files and headed off at a run. As I was going into the police office, it struck me that I was a) about to downgrade the officer's inquiry to a 'bird matter' and b) that his name was Gosling.

He took it well. Particularly when I told him about the size of the fines being handed out and the type of people involved. A period of frantic activity ensued, with communication between the police, Customs and Excise and RSPB HQ. At some point it was decided – I suspect by Customs – that the Germans would be allowed to run until they were stopped at a UK Border. I also suspect that this was to allow for more serious consequences: the Endangered Species Act and smuggling legislation would come into play, with jail as the likely outcome. And so it came to pass. The two Germans were caught trying to go onto a ferry at Dover with an incubator hidden in their glove compartment area, containing several live peregrine eggs. They pled guilty and were given sentences of 18 months and six months in jail.

Working most of the time in Scotland, I was at the sharp end of the peregrine and golden eagle thefts. Year after year, I visited robbed nests and diligently reported and recorded the crimes. We knew who the thieves were and they knew who we were. Outside court, on the few occasions when they were caught, and during police searches of their homes in the Newcastle area, when we acted as expert witnesses, the thieves would talk to us on first-name terms. They knew that while the law stayed weak, they could carry on with relative impunity, facing not jail, but just a fine. They were very cocky. On one occasion, I was about to abseil into a nest in Moffatdale – an area notorious for the attentions of the 'Geordie gang' when I spotted a message scrawled on the rock face. 'Dave 88 3' which translates as, 'We took three chicks from here in 1988, Dave.'

A new and very powerful ally was about to appear, however: DNA fingerprinting. Already achieving a growing success using human DNA in the fight against crime, biologists were beginning to isolate DNA from wild and captive birds and animals. We immediately saw the potential: to be able to separate wild-taken birds from genuinely captive bred ones and to show that birds were unrelated to each other would be massively useful tools. We had long suspected (and been told, by the inevitable informants who infest any criminal enterprise) that the route taken by our stolen peregrine eggs and young chicks included 'laundering' within bogus captive breeding stations in the UK. Under ideal conditions, it is perfectly possible for captive peregrines to produce two full clutches, then broods of chicks in a single season. This takes time, expertise and a certain amount of luck. Some breeders' figures were just too good to be true.

As the 1990s wore on, a series of police and RSPB 'DNA raids' in England trapped several dealers in peregrines and goshawks. I was involved in one such raid in southeast England, where a man was found living in a modern ranch-style house with a dozen peregrine mews (breeding aviaries) in the back garden, next to a pond full of very expensive Koi carp, a new four-wheel drive vehicle and a speedboat. He gave his status as 'unemployed'! This man, and several others, ended up in jail, thanks not to the weak 1981 Act (with no jail provision in Scotland until 2003) but because they had sold on birds alleged to be captive bred, when they had in fact been taken from the wild. In English law, this is the crime known as 'deception' and comes under the Theft Act.

However, such was the lure of free peregrines and the profit to be made from an exciting trip up to Scotland that the thefts continued. Some years were worse than others, I presume because of variations in the market. Ironically, as the thefts diminished due to the effectiveness of the DNA cases, the police resource was growing, at least on paper.

WEDNESDAY, 28 MAY 1997

My day had not started well: a dental appointment at 9 a.m. had ruined a perfectly good field-work day in mid-season. To add to my annoyance, the sun was beating down. Still, I had spent the day before wandering round a beautiful part of Banffshire, with nesting buzzards and a large active badger sett, with no traps and no poison baits, against the expectations of my local guide. The phone rang as I sat in my Edinburgh office. A colleague from our North England office had received a tip-off that, as we spoke, peregrine thieves were heading for Moffatdale in a hired car. I thanked the caller and immediately phoned Sgt Graham Young, at that time the wildlife coordinator for Dumfries and Galloway Police. I gave him the information, along with an offer of help. 'Thanks,' he said, 'I'll get right onto it. No need for you to come down, we can handle this.' Slightly surprised, I put the phone down and started doing the paperwork necessary to record the two calls, but I couldn't get it out of mind. 'We can handle it'? How? You don't know the nest sites, you don't know the terrain, you don't know the thieves involved or their M.O... No, this is ridiculous, I shouldn't be sitting here, with my experience and knowledge, particularly of Moffatdale.

I grabbed my usual rucksack and filled it with maps, binoculars, scope and tripod, waterproof gear, first aid kit, water bottle, compass and camera equipment. With the usual 'I'm off!' to my secretary, I loaded up the office car and headed down the A701 towards Moffat. An hour and a half later, I parked in a lay-by at the end of a glaciated hanging valley.

I picked up my binoculars and scanned the crags at the far end, where a line of very familiar cliffs are located. Even at that distance, the two men creeping up towards one the several peregrine ledges were clearly visible. I switched over to my telescope and, as I focused, the equally familiar sandy-white hair of Leslie Mark Massey came into view. Massey was already well known to me, with a conviction regarding a peregrine nest in Dumbartonshire in 1993.

By 1997 I had had 13 seasons' experience of attempting to protect these birds. I had been involved in testing out alarm and radio equipment at various sites and knew that a deep valley like Moffatdale was a difficult proposition for communications. The mobile mast network was still fairly rudimentary in upland areas of Scotland at this time but by some miracle, I had parked at one of the only spots in the valley where I could get a signal for my mobile phone. I phoned Keith Morton, my assistant back in Edinburgh, and told him to phone the police urgently and tell them what was happening.

What to do now? I knew my own eyewitness evidence, at this distance, would be almost useless in court. The men were too far away to photograph. I needed another witness. Then came my next stroke of luck. Driving along the narrow Moffatdale road and about to pass me was the distinctively-marked National Trust for Scotland Seasonal Ranger's van from the Grey Mare's Tail (GMT). It was my practice to drop in on the GMT ranger at the start of the season – the beginning of April – and introduce myself. I had also in the past given pep talks regarding nest protection to the National Trust for Scotland rangers and their volunteers at the site. They had their own nesting peregrines, along with a long history of robberies.

I jumped out of my car and waved him down. Stuart McBurnie, the NTS Ranger, got into my vehicle. I handed him pen and paper and asked him to write down everything I said. At intervals I got him to look through the scope for himself, in order to fully corroborate what was taking place. My statement for the police related the unfolding tale of a nest robbery – I clearly saw Massey reach the top of the cliff and start to clap his hands (a widely-used technique to scare the peregrine off its nest and reveal its position); a peregrine could be seen repeatedly 'stooping' down past him and flying around, with agitated wingbeats. I then saw his companion tie a rope around his middle and start to lower him down the rock face. He arrived at the nest ledge and I clearly saw him picking up eggs and placing them inside his clothing (a technique used by egg thieves and smugglers alike is to sew pockets onto a shirt, in which eggs can be kept in relative safety and warmth). He then scrambled and was hauled back up to the top, where his companion untied him. They then packed the rope into a rucksack – the companion had carried both up the broken face of the crag – and started walking along the top of the crag.

At this point the police arrived – it was Graham Young, the WLO. I explained what had occurred and let him see the men through the scope. He told me a car containing two women and a child had been intercepted in the neighbouring valley and that we should go to the Grey Mare's Tail where we would be contacted later. He, meanwhile, was going to Moffat police office to direct operations.

I watched the men disappear over the horizon, heading in the direction of the next hanging valley. Stuart and I drove back to the Grey Mare's Tail where we were soon joined by Andy Dickson, the recently retired WLO, based in Moffat. Like myself, Andy was well acquainted with all the peregrines in the area – he had roped me into nests on many occasions and was a member of the local Mountain Rescue Team. While we were discussing what had occurred and what the next moves should be, two CID officers appeared, dressed in white shirts and shiny shoes. I again related my story. They said that they were trying to get a spotter plane up from Carlisle (the nearest available plane or helicopter; Dumfries and Galloway is a very small force and couldn't afford such expensive equipment). They advised us to stay where we were and await developments and drove off.

Andy and I both agreed that the most likely route the men would take would be via another vulnerable and often-robbed peregrine nest. We couldn't just sit there while that was happening! Off down Moffatdale we went again, parking my car and walking into the head of the second valley where we hid behind the stone wall of a circular sheep fank (a 'stell' or 'fank' in Scots is a sheepfold in English). We got out our bins and scopes in time to see our two thieves packing up their rucksacks in the distance, directly above the peregrine site. Two agitated peregrines could be seen above them. Andy knew that this site had contained already-hatched chicks. We made a mobile phone call to Graham Young, who told us the plane was on its way, and I reminded him to tell the pilot to stay high. If the thieves suspected they were being watched, they would dump their haul.

A few minutes later, Andy and I watched in disbelief as the two men stopped on the skyline on their way back to their car and could be seen staring up at a small plane flying in circles, only a couple of hundred feet above them. To quote a well-used George Carse phrase, we were 'dancing with rage'. All that hard work, from the initial handling of an informant, through to our stunning luck in witnessing two robberies, was being put at risk. The lives of a live clutch of peregrines and a brood of chicks were being thrown away. All because someone hadn't been given my message or had chosen to ignore it. As Andy later said: 'If we'd had had an anti-aircraft gun…'

The two men disappeared from sight over the high ridge leading to the valley where they expected to find their companions and car.

A short time later, we were joined by a young and fit police officer, who said he had been asked to go with me to the second peregrine site, check it out and follow in the footsteps of the thieves. At last, some action. We left Andy and walked into the hanging valley. Within an hour, we were standing at the top of the peregrine nest crag, looking at a freshly-dead chick. It had obviously been dumped by the thieves when they found that it had died, presumably while being handled and removed from the nest. I photographed the bird and the site. We climbed to the top of the ridge, from where we could see down towards the adjoining valley. By this time we had been told by radio that the two thieves had been apprehended approaching the road and taken to Moffat police station – there was no sign of eggs or chicks. We searched a long section of stone dyke, the only hiding place possible up there, but found nothing.

The following day I took the chick to the Central Veterinary Laboratories (CVL) near Penicuik. The resulting analysis showed that the bird had died from heart failure – of fright, basically – due to its rough handling by the thief.

One of my earliest challenges in the job was to find reliable professionals to carry out X-rays of both live and dead birds and animals. It was also important to find people who could be relied on to interpret those X-rays and to give statements with informed opinions on the cause of death or injury. My first such colleague was an old friend from my Arran days, by then a vet practicing in Edinburgh. 'Cammie' was a vet student, studying alongside Malcolm Wheeler (a childhood friend from Uplawmoor who has been for many years the main vet on Arran) when I first met him. He had approached an RSPB colleague after a film show and offered his services. When Cammie moved away, I was again lucky in obtaining the services of another Edinburgh vet practice. I was usually guaranteed a fairly rapid service when I arrived, as no one wanted too many questions from the assorted pet owners when this strange bearded man came in to the waiting room carrying ominous-looking black polythene bags (containing dead buzzards, kites or even eagles!) I then learned of, and made contact with, the government scientists of the CVL (Central Veterinary Laboratories) in particular the splendid Dr Ranald Munro, Scotland's first forensic veterinary pathologist. For several years I was cheered by the sight of Ranald's smiling face and his greeting of 'And what have you brought me today?' He was not only a hugely competent pathologist but also a doughty expert witness, a worthy match for the fairly vicious attacks by QCs in some of our court battles. I always learned something from our discussions, held over some poor unfortunate bird corpse laid out in his pristine laboratory. I hope my successors in wildlife investigations appreciate the groundwork we laid down.

Three days later, I returned to the area and met Bob Elliott, then the Head Ranger for NTS in Dumfries and Galloway and now my successor at the RSPB. It was a hot and sunny Saturday and we retraced my steps, climbing up past the second peregrine nest and out onto the 700+ metre ridgetop. We then slowly walked the seven kilometre descent to where the thieves were apprehended, searching stone dykes and dense conifer plantations for any sign of the missing eggs and chicks. We found nothing. It was a sad ending to what should have been a triumph.

MONDAY, 11 MAY 1998

I arrive at Dumfries Sheriff Court as a trial witness and get a cheery 'Hello!' from Massey on the way in. The Fiscal informs us that he has accepted a plea from the accused – to disturbance of peregrines at the two nest sites – which is rather unsettling as they have been charged with taking and possession of three eggs and three chicks of peregrines in addition to the disturbance charges. And what about the killing of the chick? In court, the Fiscal outlined the case, stating that the men had been seen at the nests, including during surveillance by a spotter plane. He mentioned German connections in relation to falcon theft and asked for forfeiture of all the climbing equipment.

The defence then claimed that it was just a family outing and that the defendants were keen birdwatchers. What I found most galling of all was the mention of a lack of evidence to uphold the charges of stealing or possession of peregrines. It was also claimed that the men had seen two groups of people near the nests. Strange, that. I must have missed them.

Fortunately, the sheriff didn't believe a word of it, pointing out their previous convictions regarding peregrines, and fined them a whacking £2,500 on each disturbance charge, making a total of £10,000.

It was a good result but the lack of a trial meant that the court, and therefore the public, never got to hear the full story of the destruction being brought about. This is an excerpt from my statement on this case:

The first record of a robbery at R**** C****, reported to the RSPB, was as far back as 1973, when a clutch of three eggs was stolen. At that time, the peregrine was a very rare bird indeed, with only six pairs breeding between Moffat and Edinburgh. Although this low number was mainly due to the effects of DDT and other environmental poisons, already banned by that date, the population recovery was held back by thefts at this time.

The site was again robbed in 1974, 1978, 1980, 1983, 1984, 1985, 1986, 1990 and 1991 - an appalling record, but by no means unique in southern Scotland. Robberies were mainly of eggs, but in two of these years, chicks were taken. To my knowledge, no person has ever been prosecuted for any of these thefts.

There then followed an unprecedented run of successful breeding over the last five years, only for the nest to be robbed again this year (1997).

THURSDAY, 12 FEBRUARY 1998

In Eindhoven, Holland, Wilhelmus Hubertus Josephus Enzlin posts a letter to a falconer in the north of Scotland. It is one of a series he has written, as he later admits, to falconers across the UK. In the letter, he asks if the falconer can supply him with 20 wild peregrine falcon chicks from their 'territories'. He tells the falconer to 'burn this letter' as 'it is always dangerous'. By offering to purchase wild peregrines, an Appendix 1 species, he has made a big mistake, committing an offence under section 8(1) of the Control of Trade in Endangered Species (Enforcement) Regulations 1997.

I have already mentioned that the relationships between falconers and the RSPB was not universally friendly at this time but I certainly did not share Enzlin's view that a random selection of British falconers could all be trusted to steal wild chicks on his behalf. Far from it. The falconer in this case was a good example – on receiving the letter he was appalled and immediately passed it to one of my colleagues in our Inverness office, who then passed it on to me.

It seemed almost too good to be true and I treated this windfall with some caution at first. Blunders by over-zealous government officials in the 1980s had led to a culture of claims of entrapment within the falconry world and I certainly didn't want to fall into a criminal's trap. The next move had to be a face-to-face meeting with the falconer.

And so it was that on my journey back from a visit to Wick, to identify eggs and photographs seized by the police from a persistent nest disturber up there, I dropped in on the recipient of Enzlin's letter. He told me that he had had a phone call from Enzlin a few days after the letter arrived. Apparently he could hear other people's voices in the room with Enzlin, as though he had co-conspirators. The falconer had stalled Enzlin, neither agreeing to nor rejecting his request. He gave me the letter and I told him we would deal with it and get back to him within a week. By now I was convinced that this was all very real.

A week later and I was discussing the letter with Sgt John Grierson, the Northern Constabulary WLO coordinator based in Aviemore. We were also discussing two poisonings and I was in my usual role of courier, taking yet another suspected poisoned buzzard, red kite and bait down to SASA in Edinburgh. I handed over Enzlin's letter and signed a production label – it was now officially evidence. This discussion led to the two of us sitting down with the Inverness Fiscal. He agreed that Enzlin had already committed an offence (so luring him across to Scotland could not be described as entrapment) and backed up our idea of writing to Enzlin, pretending to be a third-party peregrine thief. John came up with the idea of Alec Munro from Aviemore. We composed a letter which was duly posted to Enzlin and he took the bait.

It was at this time that I first used my connections with Holland, made through Hans Peters, an ex-policeman now working for *Vogelbescherming* [the Dutch equivalent of the RSPB], who was a good friend of the RSPB and a founder member of the Eurogroup against Bird Crime (EABC). He confirmed that Enzlin was known to own peregrines.

As the date for the supposed exchange of stolen peregrine chicks approached, at the end of May, a new name cropped up. Ivo van Lanen offered Alec Munro more money if he would deliver the birds to Enzlin at Calais rather than in Aviemore, as had been agreed. This was, of course, unacceptable to us: we had to catch Enzlin in the act on Scottish soil. Alec Munro, by now in touch by phone, said he was not prepared to take the risk of discovery during a long drive and a border crossing at Dover – a perfectly believable stance.

I worked out the most believable date for young chicks of a suitable size, which of course called for a knowledge of laying dates in north Scotland. The date for the exchange of 16 chicks for £4,000 was Sunday, 24 May. Shortly before this, John Grierson told me that he would be accompanied by a local gamekeeper, who was also a special constable, at the time of the arrest. I was very unhappy about it. Not only was I being squeezed out of what I saw as my case, but to use a gamekeeper was adding insult to injury. I had nothing against the man involved but I saw this for what it was – a political move to show police and gamekeepers working together. This was at a time when estate-based/gamekeeper criminal activity was continuing to run at a high level.

However, ever the professional and very curious to see what would be the outcome of months of careful planning, I agreed to take a backroom role as an expert witness. This was just the way things were going by then, with the police squeezing out their best allies for political reasons.

I arrived at Aviemore police office in the late morning of 24 May, in time to see two Dutch vehicles being driven through the gate. John was very pleased. They had arrested not only Enzlin, in possession of £4,000 in cash, at the car park rendezvous but had also caught van Lanen, the alleged paymaster, and his wife in a second car nearby. I helped with the car searches. In the van Lanens' car, we found paperwork mentioning peregrine chicks and their welfare.

Back in the police office, all three were interviewed through an interpreter. Off the record, Enzlin was very chatty and spoke to me about birds he had at home, which he was looking after for someone else. He struck me as rather a simple soul, utterly fascinated by peregrines. He immediately admitted his guilt. The van Lanens did not.

Once upstairs, I phoned Hans, who put me in touch with the Dutch Agricultural Ministry section, which dealt with the registration of peregrines. They were extremely interested and started making arrangements for official visits to Enzlin's aviaries. They later confirmed that he had six peregrines, all legally registered to another person. Sadly, their law at that time did not have any sanctions to prevent Enzlin keeping peregrines in future, no matter what law he had broken in Scotland. I told John that I had arranged for the suspects to be inspected in Holland, which seemed to appall his gamekeeper friend. 'You can't do that!' he said, to which I replied, 'I just did!' It was a fine example of the growing attempts on the part of the shooting community to undermine our work, which were to bear fruit over the next ten years and effectively slow up the real progress of the fight against wildlife crime. No matter how successful our work, it would be attacked by such people and their apologists, desperate to get rid of the threat we posed to estate-based crime, and always ready to believe any lie that was fed to them.

All three were held in custody until bail of £3,000 each was paid by van Lanen's father.

At a hearing in August, Enzlin pled guilty to a COTES charge (the Control of Trade in Endangered Species) of offering to buy wild peregrines. The van Lanens continued to plead 'not guilty'. The same date – Tuesday, 26 January 1999 – was set for their trial and for Enzlin's sentencing.

I can clearly recall my precognition (the term under Scots law for the statement, often just a sketchy account, which the defence can take from the Crown's named prosecution witnesses) by a solicitor working for the advocate who would be fighting the van Lanens' case. He asked me to expand on a point involving peregrine theft and smuggling – my main court role was to be an expert on such matters. I gave him the full half-hour lecture, after which he said he wished all witnesses would be so forthcoming. I told him that I was sick and tired of watching the blind leading the blind on matters of biology and wildlife crime in Scottish courts and that, in my eyes, justice would only be served by a court having real facts in front of it rather than ignorance and prejudice, as I had all too often seen on both sides. And I stick by every word.

The subsequent court case was as tedious as any I can remember (and some were excruciatingly dull). I had the misfortune to be the first witness and everything had to be translated into Dutch, a sentence at a time, for the defendants. I have lived in Holland and visited it many times and it's my experience that it is unusual to find a Dutch person who does not understand English, or speak it, very well indeed. In addition, the substitute sheriff seemed to be having trouble with his hearing and to top it all, we had a (false) fire alarm. Day One was adjourned after about an hour of this torture. Day Two started in the morning with continuation of my evidence (where would any of these cases have been without RSPB expert witnesses?) which lasted for over another hour. Then it was Willy Enzlin's turn. I will be polite and call his evidence evasive and contradictory. One question he could not avoid, though, was the Fiscal's first: 'You are Willy Enzlin and you earlier pled guilty to offering to buy peregrines?'

DAY THREE, 10 A.M.

I'm in the Fiscal's office, where she's telling me that, in her opinion, there is not enough evidence against the van Lanens to get a conviction. We still have Enzlin's sentencing, however. We went straight into court and the Fiscal deserted the van Lanens' case *pro loco et tempore*, for those of you who enjoy Latin. Such a phrase was just another example of how puzzling a court of Law can be to those it is meant to serve.

We went immediately on to Enzlin's sentencing. The Fiscal presented a short but complete account of Enzlin's crime and full confession of guilt, ending with a request for forfeiture of the Austin Metro he was driving and the £4,000 in his possession. The defence agent carried out a lengthy plea in mitigation, which was actually more of an attack on the van Lanens, basically describing Willy as a poor, unemployed, partially-disabled dupe, here described as an international criminal but actually doing it all for expenses. He wanted to get the best stock for van Lanen, the birds from an English source were too brown in colour, so he wanted real 'blue' Scottish peregrines. He claimed, on Enzlin's behalf, that van Lanen had no idea that these birds would be wild-taken. It was clearly being said that the £4,000 seized was the van Lanens' money. He also made great play of the £3,000 bail money for Willy, which was posted by van Lanen's father.

From his comments, it would seem that Sheriff Breslin was none too impressed by the plea in mitigation. He immediately outlined the high level of punishment possible – £5,000 and/or three months' imprisonment per offence – which was obviously reflecting the seriousness of the crime. He then went on to say that the whole affair had not been committed on the spur of the moment but perpetrated over a lengthy period of time, involving much correspondence and a trip to Scotland. He also pointed out the large number of birds potentially involved.

Taking into account Enzlin's two weeks custody, back in May, he had decided to fine Enzlin £2,000 (much less than the maximum) which was to come from his £3,000 bail. In addition – and this was the real stinger – he ordered forfeiture of the Austin Metro and the £4,000 cash. The van Lanens' QC, who had tried to save his clients' money by interrupting during the plea, only to be told by the sheriff that his points were 'not competent' and that it was 'not appropriate' for him to interfere, said to John Grierson outside the court that this was a fine for the van Lanens 'by the backdoor'.

I wasn't complaining. It was an unusually excellent result, with absolutely no harm done to Scotland's wildlife. There was an enormous press and media response. Justice was clearly seen to have been done and a message had gone out, again, that Scotland was no soft touch when it came to the theft of wild birds. I had a bizarre but friendly chat about birds with Enzlin himself outside the court. I was left with the impression of a bumbling, simple character being used by other, more sinister people. I may of course have been mistaken – by this time I had learned to avoid taking too much on trust.

Anyone reading this chapter may be under the mistaken impression that all our troubles with peregrine theft came from outside Scotland. This was not the case at all. Scotland could hold its head up high when it came to peregrine thieving, even if only because of just one man, Matthew 'Matty' Morrison, from Ayr. It always irritated me to see wildlife criminals described with nicknames such as 'the Moriarty of bird crime' (Colin Watson) or as daredevils, carrying out raids 'with military precision'. The fact is that most of these criminals were pretty ordinary petty thieves, who happened to be thieving something extraordinary – wild birds, animals or even plants. The reason we actually knew about them was that they got caught. One of the commonest reasons for getting caught was a lack of knowledge of the Scottish countryside and, in particular, how to move about in it without attracting attention.

Morrison was different. In addition to his peregrine stealing activities, he had also acquired a conviction for salmon poaching and I heard a persistent rumour that he had once been employed as an underkeeper on an Ayrshire shooting estate. He was also alleged to have been convicted for an undisclosed offence under the Protection of Birds Act 1954. Whatever his background, by the time I had to start dealing with his thefts, he had shown that he knew many nest sites, from inland mountain crags to the length of the Ayrshire coast and much of the Solway. He also knew how to get in and out of them. Add to that, his connections with pigeon fanciers and the 'travellers' who wandered these coasts and you have a one-man crimewave. I am under no illusion that the few times he was caught hardly even slowed him up and that he was responsible for hundreds of thefts.

By 1999 he had been convicted four times: for taking peregrine eggs (Wigtownshire), for possession of peregrine chicks (Ayr), for possession of peregrine trapping equipment (Ayr) and for taking live pigeons (Ayr). On sentencing him to a £200 fine in 1986, that sheriff was clearly frustrated at the lack of a jail sentence under the 1981 Act and told him if he saw him again he would 'Give him a huge fine with no time to pay and thus imprisonment'. This, however, was only the tip of the legendary iceberg. I had had several near misses, having watched him close to trapping sites. We had found trapping sites set up by him, we had found hidden nets and other trapping equipment, his son had even been filmed by a TV cameraman robbing a peregrine nest in Galloway while Matty (allegedly) drove the getaway car.

On one occasion, I was checking out one of his Ayrshire coastal trap sites that we had found. I was on my way to give a talk to SNH staff who were holding their annual conference on the Isle of Arran. This site, like all the others, was perfectly chosen, on a clifftop, within sight of a favoured peregrine area but just out of sight of any nosy passer-by. It had been recently used: the small freshly-cut grassy area was strewn with bits of nylon fishing line, used for nooses on the harness on the back of a live pigeon, and pigeon feathers from an unfortunate bait bird. In the centre of the level site was a piece of plyboard about 50 cm square. I lifted it up. Underneath was a small hollowed-out area containing a Fenn spring trap Mk IV, with a freshly-caught dead stoat in its jaws. He had obviously been getting problems with a stoat eating his tethered pigeons and had dealt with it. That's confidence for you, but it got worse. I left word with Willie Allan (WLO) about what I had found but had to go to my appointment on Arran. I came back the next afternoon, slightly weary from the excellent hospitality of the SNH – I had taken a guitar with me and stayed up late. At first I thought the site was unchanged. Then I lifted up the plyboard. Someone, presumably 'Matty', had taken the first stoat out of the trap, left it underneath as bait and caught a second one, which was lying dead in the trap. I wasn't happy. It was another opportunity missed.

When we received a tip-off in August 1999 from within the falconry world that he was active and trapping peregrines at the Heads of Ayr, it certainly came as no great surprise. Yet again, I set off for the Ayrshire coast, a journey that had reached the status of routine.

TUESDAY, 10 AUGUST 1999

At 7.30 p.m. I arrived at the Bracken Bay caravan site car park, about half a mile back from the magnificent headland known as the Heads of Ayr. In the car with me was Sgt Willie Hannah, the Strathclyde Police WLO for the area. The first thing I saw was Matthew Morrison's vehicle in the car park. An excellent start. Our expectations were high. Although I hadn't worked with Willie on a case before, we had met – his predecessor, Inspector Willie Allan, had spent many hours in the field with me on just such occasions but had now been promoted away – and Willie was aware of just what a big fish we were after here.

Discreetly, we parked the car nearby and walked down to the well-used beach path. As we approached the point below the area where I knew Morrison had previously set his nets, I was scanning the area with my binoculars. I then saw what I was hoping for – a small rectangle of freshly-cut grass, a good 150 feet up from the shore and about 50 metres down from the edge of the cliffs. I knew this place of old, having checked it out on several previous occasions. It could be accessed with care from above by someone with a good head for heights. We concealed ourselves behind a large rock and settled down to watch. It was time to get out the telescope. I then saw what appeared to be a feral pigeon in the centre of the trap area. The bird was very much alive but didn't move from one spot. I later found out it had been tethered between two set mist nets but that was as invisible to me as it would have been to any watching peregrine.

We sat for over two hours with no sign of Morrison and it was nearly dark. What should we do? Despite all the surveillance and chance encounters, I was still unsure of his actual methods when trapping. Would he come back in the dark? Surely not – clambering on that cliff was dangerous enough in daytime. I knew that peregrines, like many predators, will often feed early in the morning. Maybe he would come back then to see if he'd caught anything. Would he watch the nets which were presumably there? The biggest question, of course, was whether he had seen us and scarpered. We left the beach, got back to my car and drove down to Girvan, where Willie was based. Morrison's car had gone from the car park.

A few hours' sleep in Willie's spare room and we were back out again at 3.30 a.m., this time with the police at the Ayr office on full alert. Back to Bracken Bay we went in the dark. There was no car in the car park. This time we decided to get closer and ended up hiding behind a bush at the top of the cliffs (much to Willie's discomfort – he had no head for heights but got full marks for bravery). We had a view down and across to the trap site.

4.30 a.m. First light and the pigeon is still there. We are on tenterhooks and expecting Morrison to appear at any moment. The pigeon will have to look after itself as it's far too dangerous to risk an encounter with a thief on those cliffs.

6.05 a.m. We hear a peregrine calling. Suddenly, a juvenile peregrine flies down and attacks the pigeon, killing it immediately. I've started taking video film in the growing light. The young bird tries to take off but hits something (presumably a net) and takes a nosedive over the front of the trap area. A short while later, to my immense relief, it flies onto a nearby perch and starts pecking at one of its own feet. It is joined by an adult peregrine and they both fly off. I'm not happy about the pigeon. The excitement over, we sit behind our bush as the day moves on. By 8.30 we've relaxed and are quietly chatting, thinking we must have been spotted the night before, when out of the corner of my eye and within 30 feet of us, I see the man I know as Matthew Jack Welsh Morrison come up to the fenceline at the clifftop and look through binoculars at the trap site! We hold our breaths for what seems an age but can only be a couple of minutes – one glance to the side and he will spot us. He lowers his binoculars and heads away from us along the clifftop. I switch on my camcorder.

I filmed Morrison, carrying a small rucksack, cross the fence and walk to the gap in the clifftop, where I knew his path to lie, before reappearing on the trap site. He then looked carefully about him before retrieving equipment disturbed by the young peregrine. He didn't hang about. Within a few minutes, he again passed our observation point and again failed to see us. He then crossed the fence and headed over the fields towards the car park. We got up and followed him, with Willie talking to his colleagues on his radio.

Right up until the point when I saw the marked police car, with Morrison sitting in the back, I still thought we were going to lose him. I had had so many disappointments before but this time he was well and truly caught. Willie gave Morrison an official caution before he was removed (with his car) to Ayr police office to be searched.

We found a live pigeon in a soft keep bag and another, empty, bag in his rucksack. I advised the police to contact the Scottish SPCA and Inspector Hainey arrived soon after, taking the pigeon into care and saying he would get a statement from a vet with relation to its condition. I also contacted PC Ronnie Sewell, at that time the most experienced WLO in the Strathclyde Force, as I wanted a policeman of his calibre to help with the follow up.

The only sour note to the case came at this point, when we contacted the available depute Fiscal to ask for a search warrant for Morrison's house, a normal and vital follow-up to such a capture. I was able to advise on all the relevant sections of the 1981 Act (and indeed the Protection of Animals (Scotland) Act 1912 with reference to cruelty to the pigeon) but she seemed strangely reluctant to authorise a search. When his house was searched later on, it was done by police, without any wildlife expert present. We will never know what opportunities were missed.

Ronnie Sewell arrived and we headed off to search two other known Morrison trap sites on the same stretch of coast. It was of course perfectly possible that he had been running other sites with live pigeons at the same time. We drew a blank at those places and arranged to meet Willie Hannah back at the Heads of Ayr site. It had been a busy day and we still had a long way to go.

When we arrived at the site of the early morning activity, Ronnie and I scrambled down to where I had seen Morrison retrieving equipment and took photos of all that we found. A cord led from a wooden stake set in the ground to the remains of the pigeon. We also found several nets attached to short metal rods. These were all seized as evidence. While we were on site, we had two adult and one juvenile peregrine flying nearby.

Back to Ayr and a lengthy session of writing up notes, signing production labels and discussion of the case. After a meal with Ronnie, I went back to the police office and was handed a bag containing two dead owls, from a possible persecution case, to be taken for post mortem in Edinburgh. I got home about 11 p.m. It had been just another bizarre day in the job.

So far, so good. Next would come the usual long wait, the usual 'not guilty' pleas, the usual lengthy trial.

MONDAY, 14 FEBRUARY 2000

Ayr Sheriff Court. I was in the witness box for several hours giving evidence and being cross-examined by the defence. The trial lasted almost three whole days before the sheriff found Morrison guilty on all six charges, with sentence deferred for a month. Morrison's defence consisted of his saying that he had found an injured pigeon and was looking after it, that he had never been at the Heads of Ayr and that the net was for catching crabs!

TUESDAY, 14 MARCH

I'm back at Ayr Sheriff Court to see Morrison fined £2,000 for taking a peregrine, £500 for using a live pigeon to take a peregrine and £200 for causing unnecessary suffering to a pigeon. The sheriff admonished him (no penalty) on the other three charges (use of nets, attempting to take peregrines, possession of equipment) saying that they overlapped the other charges. It was not a bad fine for someone who gave his status as 'unemployed' but when you consider the words of the other Ayr sheriff, 13 years before, he got off lightly. There was still no jail provision under the 1981 Act but there was one within the Protection of Animals Act. £2,500 was the equivalent of five female peregrines if laundered into the UK system (legitimate birds were selling for £500) and from the Enzlin case the year before, we knew that some falconers were desperate for wild Scottish birds, so £2,500 wouldn't buy many peregrines, would it?

What I had not realized at the time was that the police had arrested and detained Morrison using the 1981 Act. This was serious procedural error, as there was no provision for arrest under that Act at that time. Over the years, I received several phone calls from delighted police officers in different parts of Scotland who told me that, 'We've just arrested **** after catching him stealing eggs/trapping finches/shooting a sparrowhawk!' My reply was always unequivocal. 'You'd better un-arrest him damn quick, there's nothing in the 1981 Act… unless he hasn't given you the right name and address!' It was an understandable mistake. While the press and media sensationalised all our cases, the legislation stayed stubbornly unchanged, so an inexperienced police officer would be surprised to find, that these criminals could not be arrested and would not face jail.

If only I had a pound for every time I gave that advice to a police officer – at first on a case-by-case basis but later when I had become heavily involved in training WLOs. This situation would not be rectified until the passing of the Criminal Justice (Scotland) Act 2003.

The case went to the Court of Appeal. On 1 March 2001, the two charges involving Morrison's possession of the live pigeon in his rucksack were quashed, as it had only been discovered by the police after he had been wrongfully detained at the police office. His fine was reduced to £1,500.

As we entered the new millennium, then, things were looking brighter for peregrines. DNA cases and testing significantly affected the black market and we saw nest robberies tail away. The RSPB in England were behind the first successful case in 1991 in which a commercial laboratory was used in a goshawk case – this was followed by at least 20 more cases, almost all involving my colleague Guy Shorrock. It was one of the more obvious links between a drop in crime levels and increased enforcement activity. Our years of racing around nests, trying to protect individual birds from thieves, were mainly useful as a training ground – for RSPB staff and some police alike – but the real job was done by targeting the market. It is an important lesson to those who have to use scarce resources. Without the experience of people like myself, though, a criminal can easily dupe the police and the courts when they do get caught.

And this crime has not gone away. As I write this (August 2010), a man called Jeffrey Lendrum has admitted taking 14 peregrine eggs from nests in Wales and trying to smuggle them, alive, to Dubai through Birmingham Airport. He was caught by an alert cleaner and by anti-terrorist officers. He got a 30-month jail sentence. It seems that there are still people out there willing to pay silly prices for wild-taken falcons.

I have focused entirely on peregrines in this chapter but there is also a story to be told about the theft of golden eagle chicks from Scotland, also for falconry, also for foreign and domestic markets. Fortunately, that threat seems to have been short- lived, due to excellent cooperation between European conservationists, the use of DNA testing and, of course, enforcement action. In England, goshawks (*Accipiter gentilis*) were also a common target of thieves – but those stories will have to wait for another time.

6

POISON

This is it, this is the one, the only wildlife crime in Scotland worth pouring investigative resources into, worthy of the full force of the legal system. If you actually believe in wildlife conservation, that is – which is, after all, the basis of the Wildlife and Countryside Act 1981, a law written to enshrine the idea of wildlife as important, as property. Property, of course, is the basis of most Scots law.

The damage which has been and is still being done to entire populations of birds in Scotland dwarfs any conservation damage caused by all the egg thieves and falcon thieves put together. I don't say that lightly and I certainly don't say it without the facts to back it up. Compare close to three decades of government annual reports, of analysed baits and poisoning victims with our knowledge of the pattern of distribution of raptors in Scotland and the match is absolute.

A glance at the geographic breadth and the stubborn persistence of these crimes gives the lie to claims that this is a rare and outdated practice. I was hearing that line in the mid-1980s. Gamekeepers would tell me that poisoning was the lazy man's method of vermin control. All I can say is that there must have been a hell of a lot of lazy gamekeepers out there since then.

Why do people use poison? Because it works. It does the job. It gets rid of whatever your hate is targeting. I use words like 'hate' in this context because the passionate hatred of 'vermin' is what makes the poisoner defy the law and lie to the police, the public and sometimes even to his employer. It's personal. The word vermin itself (think 'varmints' in the cowboy films) is a complete anachronism.

Our insistence on attributing human traits to animals has a very long history. Wolves are the classic species which has suffered from this 'give a dog a bad name' attitude, in their case literally, preached against from pulpits in mediaeval times. Foxes are 'cunning'. All birds of prey are 'fierce' and 'merciless'. This is a hangover from our very long history of sharing the world with animals. Except for those we could use for food, they were competitors, so we destroyed as many as we could. We were scared of some of them so we made up even scarier stories to tell our children as a warning. Then we told ourselves the same stories for pleasure. It's the basis of much of our literature, from Aesop's *Fables* to *Animal Farm*, but it is, of course, a lie.

Animals, including birds, occasionally show an ability to learn by experience in their – mostly short – lives. Normally, however, they are programmed by instinct. They have been hard-wired through thousands of years of selection to use their physical and mental attributes to take advantage of any food supply available. So if you put a thousand pheasant chicks into a cage in the middle of a wood, please don't be surprised when a fox or a buzzard decides to eat them, or indeed, in the case of the fox, tries to eat them all. They are not being vicious, they are not killing for fun. They are responding in a natural way to an unnatural food supply. The same, of course, applies to predators of red grouse, present in hugely and artificially high numbers on a totally artificial habitat, created by burning.

If spending their life killing vermin, most human beings would have to rationalize the destruction of so many live animals which are not being killed for food. The old stories of the cunning, fierce predator are dragged out and dusted off, particularly in the modern era, when the public began to ask awkward questions about what was going on behind the scenes

Unfortunately, these anthropomorphic ideas are not restricted to those people who want to kill animals they see as pests. Young birds and animals are 'cute', animals with teeth and claws are 'vicious'. Our society has reinforced a lot of these prejudices, which is fine, until you see the prejudices appear even amongst politicians in a Government Environment Committee, taking evidence from those who want to kill the aforementioned predators – sorry, 'vermin'!

And so to the poisoning of wildlife in Scotland, the area of wildlife crime which continues to flourish in this beautiful country. I dealt with so many cases of poisoning that it is difficult to choose which ones to relate. I have chosen cases which I hope will help the reader see the breadth of the problem and, more importantly, will show why it has been allowed to continue long after other hideous throwbacks to the Victorian era have long gone. As with many aspects of wildlife crime, historical context is essential if we are to understand the motivation and methods of the modern wildlife poisoner. I have no intention of writing yet another long discourse on the persecution of predators in Scotland, begun in earnest with the Clearances for sheep of the late 18th century and, in some cases, accelerated to the point of extinction by the invention of 'sporting estates' in the mid-19th century. It is, though, an important area of knowledge for any modern conservationist or, indeed, Scottish land manager, and I would strongly recommend Roger Lovegrove's masterly account of 'vermin' control in Britain through the ages, *Silent Fields*.

I have divided this chapter into poison types.

STRYCHNINE (BANNED FOR USE IN 2006; ILLEGAL TO POSSESS FROM 2005)

I will start with the wildlife poison probably best known by the public but the least recorded as a wildlife killer during the 1980s and up to the present day: strychnine. It's an ugly word for an ugly chemical. Strychnine (certainly up until it was first synthesized, as late as the 1950s) comes from the seeds of the strychnine tree which grows in the Philippines and China. Its use in tiny quantities, both as a poison and as a medicine, was first recorded in the UK in the 19th century. The chemical used in pest control in the modern era was actually strychnine hydrochloride, a water-soluble salt of strychnine.

Strychnine blocks certain activities of the brain and spinal cord causing characteristic severe convulsions (although it's by no means the only wildlife poison to do this). The bird, animal or human dies a terrible death, by breaking its own back, by asphyxiation or by exhaustion. It is to our shame that strychnine use for mole control – its last legitimate use as a wildlife poison – was only finally banned in 2006 and that ban came only after its inclusion in a European Directive gave our legislators no choice.

For many years it was only available under a permit system, run by the Agriculture or Rural Affairs departments of the UK governments. Tiny, one-gram bottles were the largest amount issued at any one time, through licensed pharmacists. Department officials had the right of unannounced inspections. I will again praise the Department officials I worked with here: they took this part of their work very seriously and record keeping and checks were exemplary, as I saw during many poison searches. There were also, though, several occasions when I saw bottles seized which had belonged to the old system: gamekeepers in possession of large quantities, in old bottles, with handwritten ink labels. A little of this stuff goes a long way. It had been killing for a long time, and I'm not talking about moles.

Whenever we seized a poisoner's kit, particularly in the successful searches of the early 1990s, we were almost guaranteed to find illegally-held strychnine. Judged by quantity of baits and victims found, however, it was a minor player during my time and becoming rarer. Only one incident comes to mind as being particularly noteworthy, showing not only the extent of wildlife poisoning but also the reasons for it and the attitudes involved.

In the late 1980s, after yet another poisoned golden eagle had been found and yet another press release from us, I found myself at what became a very familiar workplace, the self-op cupboard at the BBC's studio in Queen Street, five minutes walk from my office. It was a three-way interview between me, the BBC interviewer and the latest Convener of the Scottish Landowners' Federation (now the Scottish Rural Business Affairs Partnership, which has wisely removed the tarnished word 'landowner' from its name). The programme was chugging along in the usual way: I described the poisoning and gave an opinion as to the damage done to wildlife and the tourist economy. The new chap then made a tactical error, trying to elicit sympathy for the poisoner on the grounds of how horrible 'vermin' was. The exchange went as follows:

'Has Mr Dick ever seen a crow peck the eyes out of a live lamb?'

'Have you ever talked to a little girl whose dog took 16 hours to die from strychnine poisoning?' I was referring to a wildlife poisoning which 'went wrong' on Cawdor Estate.

That was pretty much the end of the interview.

The Scottish Government's WIIS scheme report in 2006 stated, 'Strychnine poisoning has been identified as the cause of death in 109 incidents submitted to the WIIS scheme in Scotland since 1972. Virtually all of these incidents were attributed to the illegal abuse of a pesticide to poison non-target animals. The most frequent victims were dogs, with the remainder comprising corvid species, cats and birds.'

I make no excuse for repeating the words of a Perthshire estate factor: 'Well, we didn't have any of these fancy chemicals in our day. We just used strychnine.'

MEVINPHOS/PHOSDRIN (BANNED FOR USE 28 FEBRUARY 1993, BANNED FOR POSSESSION 2005)

This is by far, for me, the worst poison to deal with. It's incredibly dangerous. One of Phosdrin's nicknames amongst the gamekeeping community was 'the Jolly Green Giant' due to its blue/

green colouring at full strength and its ability to knock down any bird or animal immediately. It was popular partly because of its toxicity at all temperatures, unlike the other poison of choice, alphachloralose, which was most effective in the winter months. It could therefore be used against a large target, such as a fox, at any time of year.

I only ever heard of one survivor of Phosdrin poisoning: Mrs McNab's cat on Edradynate Estate, Aberfeldy. Sadly, the same cat was killed by a vehicle soon after, no doubt having used up all its lives in one go.

MONDAY, 16 JANUARY 1984

I learned all about Phosdrin very early in my career. At the beginning of the third week of my month's induction, I travelled with Frank Hamilton, head of the RSPB in Scotland, to a Fatal Accident Inquiry (FAI) at Perth Sheriff Court. Such inquiries are very similar to a trial, with a sheriff presiding and witnesses giving sworn testimony.

This inquiry involved the death of a gamekeeper, Thomas Nicol, on a Perthshire shooting estate, Solsgirth, from, it was alleged, the accidental ingestion of Phosdrin.

The decision to attend was a good one on the part of my managers. On that day I saw the lid lifted, via sworn testimony, on the Scottish shooting estates' poisoning culture before it was firmly shut again. It would be 1989, five years later, before I would be able to get another such insight into poisoning reality.

The first witness was a Nicholas Alexander, the son of the estate's owner, who told the court that he had worked as an assistant gamekeeper there during his holidays. He said he had been asked to obtain Phosdrin from France in July 1981, as the keeper was about to run out of it but couldn't get hold of any.

A Dr Fiskin from Shell Chemicals, the manufacturer, gave a full description of the chemical and its legitimate use as a very dilute late infestation insecticide. He followed that up with the information that they knew it was being abused and that his company was trying to tackle this. One way was by the production of Phosdrin 24, 24% of full strength. They hadn't produced full strength Phosdrin (the subject of this FAI) for two years.

Under questioning, he gave the chilling fact that the lethal dose of full strength Phosdrin for an adult human was about six drops by ingestion (drinking) and only a little more by absorption through the skin. He described how it was abused by people using syringes and gloves. He said that he was aware that gamekeepers 'all over' were illegally abusing not only this chemical but alphachloralose and strychnine too.

The lawyers questioning him (acting for the man's family and his employer, the owners of Solsgirth Estate) made great play on the deficiency of the labelling on Phosdrin containers.

The court also heard that the estate factor had switched over to the purchase of alphachloralose in 1980 and had assumed that all the Phosdrin on the estate had been used up.

The dead man's wife gave the most harrowing account. Her evidence was that her husband had gone to a local pub and met the estate shepherd, who was complaining about losing lambs to foxes. He said he would deal with it. He had several pints of beer and whiskies, 'but wasn't drunk because he drove back home.' He then got hold of his Phosdrin and a rabbit carcass. He diluted the Phosdrin in a cup in his kitchen. He then poured the poison onto the rabbit carcass and walked out to the lambing park where he left it for the fox. He came back to the house and, being thirsty after drinking alcohol and walking up the hill, used the same cup to drink out of. The medical evidence was that he would have been dead before he hit the floor.

Now, all of that evidence was hearsay as she had not actually been present, but it had the ring of truth and she was not cross examined to any extent.

The sheriff eventually produced a written summary with recommendations on better labelling.

The whole affair had a surreal feeling to it. The witnesses were so matter of fact about their purchase and use of poison, as if it was the most ordinary thing in the world, like buying seed grain for the farm, or ammunition for a pheasant shoot. You would never have known that they were describing an activity made illegal more than 80 years before by the Protection of Animals (Scotland) Act of 1912.

It was, as I say, an eye opener. The following cases were often characterised by disbelief on the part of those caught using poison, as if we were the bad guys, as if no one had any right to criticise what they had been doing and getting away with, for generations, in their little kingdoms. Later on, of course, that changed, as the PR battle swung into action and denial became the order of the day. 'No one's done that for years… it's all hugely exaggerated… we are the real guardians of the countryside… there's only a few rogue keepers out there, a few rotten apples in the barrel.'

THURSDAY, 14 NOVEMBER 1985

Edinburgh Sheriff Court was always a busy court and I find myself standing in the witness box facing a very grumpy sheriff, who shows every sign of impatience. He has just interrupted my evidence to say, 'Mr Dick, I'm looking at the 1981 Wildlife and Countryside Act. Where does it say that the sparrowhawk is a wild bird?' I'm new at this game and, without thinking, say exactly what is on my mind. 'I'm sorry, your Lordship, but I find it odd to be standing here and asked about a point of law, I'm not a lawyer". His reply? 'Well, Mr Dick, I find it odd to be judging a case concerning sparrowhawks and pigeons.'

I didn't make that mistake again and started looking at all the detail in the Act, including the definition of a wild bird. I also started carrying a copy of the Act with me, not just to Court but everywhere I went. On several occasions, I actually passed this copy across courtrooms to sheriffs. I realised that the law would not automatically be brought fully into play at every hearing and that even a non-lawyer like myself could be helpful to police, Fiscals and sheriffs, who seldom saw conservation legislation, whereas I looked at it every day.

But back to the actual case. In early May 1985, a walker had come across a dead sparrowhawk in a birch wood close to Roslin Glen in Midlothian, a short drive, back then, from my office. The finder showed me the dead bird in situ and I then had a look around the rest of the wood. A short distance away I found a dead pigeon, opened up, with the tell-tale blue/green stain of Phosdrin on its flesh. Somehow or other I managed to get bait and bird analysed and persuaded the police to search the nearby gamekeeper's premises (the wood was part of his pheasant shoot).

We arrived at a group of ramshackle buildings surrounding a cottage on the edge of a strip of woodland. No-one was around. We found the usual detritus of the gamekeeping trade – deer skins, dead pheasants, a dead tailless fox hanging up by its snare, a gin trap with stake and new wire – and then we found two Phosdrin containers in two different locations. I carefully unscrewed the lids to find one empty but the other one full. I hastily screwed the tops back on, giving the police dire warnings about not touching the contents, no matter what happened.

Just a little later in my career, I would have known this case was a no-hoper, but the police and local Fiscal were somehow persuaded to proceed, prob-ably because they'd been told how lethal a poison Phosdrin can be. The fatal flaw, though, was that there was no provable connection between the ac-cused (a Mr S.) and the pigeon bait. Like so many after him, he would say that someone else 'put it there'. Although he had no legitimate use for Phosdrin, it was not then an offence to have the stuff (it would be many years before possession became an abso-lute offence – with the 2005 Possession of Pesticides (Scotland) Order, to be exact, 20 years later) – you had to be able to clearly show 'possession for use', a near impossible task. Many a poison case fell on that point. Quite rightly, Mr. S was acquitted through lack of evidence.

Over the years to come, I had to warn police officers many times about the danger posed by the chemicals found during searches. Possibly the worst situation I saw was at a farm steading near Dundee, when I physically pulled a young constable out of a ramshackle, roofless poison store, after watching him up-end a wooden box containing three rusting tins of CYMAG and watched water run out of the end of the box. I caught a distinctive whiff of the chemical as we exited: once smelt, never forgotten. CYMAG was used to gas rabbits and rats (legally) and foxes and badgers (illegally). It's a powder which gives off lethal cyanide gas fumes when in contact with moisture and, thankfully, is now banned.

Another 'fun' moment came as I walked into a CID room in a large police office, to see an officer throwing a large plastic container of aldicarb across a table to a colleague. I patiently explained that there was enough carbamate poison in the jar to kill most of the surrounding town. They had been given the jar to take fingerprints.

It was a lesson learned with another to follow. The next spring, I was out in the Uists and had been persuaded to give a talk to as many officers and Special Constables as could be rounded up by the local police sergeant, a Sgt McCorquodale, who was keen on catching the egg thieves and unlicensed photographers infesting his patch at that time. I was cautious about this, as I knew most of the specials would be crofters, and conservation was going through an unpopular patch in the Highlands at the time. The designation of Sites of Special Scientific Interest (SSSIs) and the 'goose wars' on Islay had met with strong protest.

I therefore made it plain at the start of my talk that I was only there to give them information about how to catch egg thieves and the like, not as an Aunt Sally for every gripe they may have with conservation. I was wasting my breath. With all the arrogance of my two years in the job, I warmed to my task and threw in an account of the Mr S. case, too, as an example of the evils of poisoning.

First question: 'What are the RSPB going to do about all the black-backs?' The great black-backed gulls (*Larus marinus*). Big sigh.

Next question? Well, more of a statement. I know S. – he's a nice bloke!'

In Scotland, you can travel great distances but should never assume gamekeepers and shooters haven't travelled too. There are only five million of us. I learned that lesson well and was very careful in talking about casework in public, unless I was very sure of my audience and subject. A lesson I repeatedly taught my English colleagues who lived and worked in a far more crowded and populated part of the UK but where, ironically, you could be far more anonymous.

Phosdrin seized from gamekeeper, Borders, 2003

ALPHACHLORALOSE (BANNED FOR POSSESSION, 2005)

I think I can do no better as an introduction than to quote from one of my background reports to a Procurator Fiscal, an addition at the end of my statement on the facts of a case. I was thanked for these many times by Fiscals, particularly early in my career. As I say, I hate watching the blind leading the blind in court. This report was written in 2003, but I originally compiled it in 1994. Since that time, alphachloralose had been replaced to a great extent by carbofuran as the poison of choice for wildlife criminals but we were still seeing it used, with 15 confirmed incidents in the UK in 2002.

This is a narcotic poison that kills birds by lowering their body temperature and causing death by hypothermia. In its pure form it is a fine white powder; some less pure formulas are produced containing a green dye (notably the Rentokil 16% formulation). Recent joint action by the Departments of Agriculture and Industry has led to approved formulations of this chemical being restricted to only two products at 100% and one at 16.6%. This change, and others listed below, have come about due to the acceptance by these agencies that this chemical has been widely abused. In 1985, alphachloralose was added to Schedule I of the Poisons Act (it had previously been a Schedule II poison) further restricting its sale. At the present time (2003) suppliers now insist on potential purchasers producing a current licence before releasing the high strength formulations for bird control.

LEGAL USE

It is used as a mouse poison at formulations of 4% and it is sold over the counter to the general public at that dilution (I believe it is an offence under the Food & Environment Protection Act 1985 to make up your own formulation) and it is illegal to use it against any other species including rats (on several occasions during recent court cases, it has been stated in mitigation that the possessor of alphachloralose was using it for that purpose). Its other legal use is as a bird poison using the high-strength formulations. This can only be done under licence with strict conditions attached. These licences are given out by SEERAD (Department of Agriculture).

The main users of this type of licence have in the past been pest control companies such as Rentokil, local authorities and, ironically, conservation bodies. Until the mid-

1980s the RSPB and the former Nature Conservancy Council both used alphachloralose to kill gulls on small islands to protect the nests of rare terns. This practice has now long been discontinued and was in no way comparable to the indiscriminate placing of baits on open land, even when targeted at pest species such as crows or gulls.

ILLEGAL USE

The RSPB, and indeed SEERAD, keep detailed statistics on the abuse of pesticides and the poisoning of wildlife. Over the ten years up to 1994, the most common poison identified in incidents of wildlife poisoning in Scotland, by a large margin, was alphachloralose.

Although statistics on an activity which has long been illegal (1912 Protection of Animals (Scotland) Act) are necessarily difficult to obtain, it was thought in the early 1990s that poisoning would decrease as pressure was applied to make its distribution more controlled. This does not appear to have happened, with poisoners turning to other chemicals, most notably carbofuran, as alphachloralose became more difficult to obtain.

ILLEGAL SALES

The wide availability of alphachloralose within the poisoning community appears to be due to a high level of illegal dealing during the 1980s. In 1989 a gamekeeper from north Scotland, after being heavily fined for poisoning and trapping, told the press that there were over 400 estates in Scotland using alphachloralose illegally. RSPB information suggests that this was an underestimate. The man who supplied this keeper with his alphachloralose was fined £5,000 in 1991 for supplying, storing and selling alphachloralose to Scottish estates. He was the proprietor of Moor End Game Farm, Whitby, Yorkshire.

Egg baits with alphachloralose, Leadhills, 1990

There have been continued reports and two confirmed seizures relating to the supply of alphachloralose from Eire into the UK. These reports have been linked to the game-shooting industry.

Although, proportionally, its use appears to have dwindled, I am sure it remains popular, particularly with older vermin controllers, who may have used it for many years.

POISON PRICES

During a 1993 search of an Edinburgh wholesalers, who were allegedly selling alphachloralose to shooting estates, it was discovered that they were buying in chloralose at £6 for 100 grams and selling it at £10. This would give a rough price of £60 per kilogram wholesale or £100 per kilogram retail. By contrast, Neosorexa, a well-known and effective proprietary brand of rat poison, retails at £10.50 for three kilograms.

The usual excuse for possession of alphachloralose – that it is used as a rat poison – is therefore shown to be ludicrous in financial terms. These proprietary brands are known to be effective and the addition or substitution of alphachloralose in rat control would not increase this effectiveness.

So alphachloralose – known variously in the gamekeeping community as alpha, sugar, salt and powder (and no doubt many other names I never got to hear) – has been a blight on raptor conservation in Scotland. Until the 1980s, I believe it to have been used very widely, illegally, in Scotland and by a broad spectrum within the rural community. Up to this point, I have been clearly and repeatedly naming gamekeepers as the main users of poisons: the evidence for that is massive and irrefutable. With alpha, only in this earlier period, it was also being used by some in the farming and crofting community, particularly in relation to the killing of corvids. The reasons for this are twofold. Firstly, it is not a particularly dangerous chemical to man (although a closely-related chemical, chloral hydrate, is the basis of the infamous Mickey Finn knockout drops, being far more toxic to birds than mammals. Secondly, it was being widely recommended as a crow killer by Agriculture Departments – its first recorded use as an avicide appears to have been in France during World War Two – albeit under licence. Unfortunately, there appear to have been very few studies into the real dangers of this chemical to protected wildlife, particularly through secondary poisoning, until 1974. At that time there were calls for the government in Scotland to remove restrictions on the supply and use of alphachloralose in order to kill crows which, as always, were being described as 'out of control'. The Department (DAFS at that time) carried out a controlled experiment on six farms – in Argyll and the Highlands – when over 1,000 hens' eggs were put out in the open. The result? Over 20 protected birds were killed, including six buzzards, some of them having fed directly on the poisoned eggs but the majority killed by secondary poisoning – feeding on the carcasses of poisoned crows or gulls.

Some of those involved thought that the risks to wildlife were acceptable but the RSPB and others strongly disagreed. The subject was still being brought up, sporadically, by farming and shooting interests until 1989. The public outcry after the poisoning by alpha of one of the first red kites reintroduced to the UK, one of only six released on the Black Isle, seems to have sounded the death knell for any legitimised use in Scotland.

Throughout my career I have heard people describing alpha as harmless. 'It only kills small birds – you can revive anything bigger and let it go.' That is wrong. Dangerously wrong.

WEDNESDAY, 12 MARCH 1986

For some weeks during early 1986, local residents had noticed dead herons turning up in the River Earn, near Kindrochet Fish Farm, a few miles to the west of Comrie in rural Perthshire. I visited the area and talked to one of the concerned neighbours. I looked at the fish farm from the nearby road. I was shown the body of a heron taken out of the river but which was only skin and bone, not enough for a post mortem analysis. I spoke to the local police, who had also been getting suspicious reports and, along with Iain Macleod, I travelled back to the fish farm with the police.

The initial intention was to have a talk with the manager and ask to look around. When we arrived, we immediately saw the remains of a large bonfire with bird feathers sticking out of it, which were unmistakably from a heron. We made a closer investigation and also in the fire I spotted a BTO ring (the British Trust for Ornithology, the organisation which administers the ringing scheme for wild birds in the UK). With the police in close attendance, I found seven large BTO rings and one large Danish ring amongst the ashes and lumps of melted plastic feed bag. In later years, I learned that every fish farm has a rubbish fire in which they burn old feed bags and other detritus. Melted in with the bags, I could see the bodies of several herons. We scooped up the contents of the fire after taking photographs, and placed them in black bin bags. No one from the fish farm appeared during all this activity. We spoke to a close neighbour and I recall them saying that they had lost their cat recently.

Probably my best tip for anyone working in wildlife crime investigation in Scotland would be to carry bin bags at all times. It will be when you least expect it that you find that dead eagle or smelly rabbit covered in granules. I used to describe myself, only slightly tongue-in-cheek, as the 'dustbin man' for the RSPB. I must have bagged a couple of hundred dead buzzards alone in my time, not to mention all the bits of hare and rabbit bait. If there's such a thing as post-traumatic stress disorder for a bird conservationist, I will have it. To be serious, though: always wear gloves, or at the very least use the bag pulled inside out to handle any suspect material, and remember that even a dead rabbit has dangerously sharp toes! Get that jab updated if you don't want tetanus.

After leaving the farm, we headed back to the police office. After promising to follow up the ring details with the BTO, to hand over the herons for analysis and to send a report with photos – and, of course, having completed the usual signing of production labels – we headed back to Edinburgh. At the East Craigs DAFS laboratory (later SASA), I warned Dr Ken Hunter that this would be a difficult one. We tipped out the hardened lumps of plastic full of bird remains in the car park. Although we had no direct evidence of poisoning, it was our only hope for any meaningful analysis – an X-ray of this mess would almost certainly be meaningless.

It was with some surprise, then, that I got a call from Ken a few days later, asking me to drop in next time I was passing as he had interesting news for me. At the lab I donned my white coat and gloves (provoking a real sense of *déjà vu*, taking me back to my days as a laboratory technician. I could almost hear Charlie, the Paisley Head Technician, bawling at me down a corridor!) Ken then showed me one of the most remarkable sights of many fascinating visits to his lab. They had managed to sift out six or seven animal stomachs from the mess I had given them. The first surprise was that six stomachs were from herons but one was from a cat! That neighbour's cat, most likely. Ken then produced his best sur-

The trio of pesticide analysts – Douglas Ruthven, Ken Hunter and Elizabeth Sharp – and their long suffering technicians should be seen as among the real heroes of this book, if any heroes there are. I would like to apologise now to Elizabeth for all the maggots I brought into her pristine lab. Hers was always a friendly face when I turned up with sacks full of dead wildlife from some dark corner of the country, sometimes just too unpleasant to be opened in an enclosed room. The DAFS/SASA car park saw some sterling post mortem preparation. Those early years, before political interference began to have its usual stultifying effect, we all worked as a team with mutual respect for each other. I was delighted to sing the praises of the East Craigs workers on several occasions to civil servants and politicians. In later years, though, as with the police, there always seemed to be someone trying to drive a wedge between us.

prise: inside each stomach was a perfectly preserved (and cooked!) trout fry, and inside each tiny trout fry was alphachloralose.

Twenty years later, at his retirement party in the shiny new purpose-built SASA building which he had helped design, on the edge of Edinburgh's Green Belt, I reminded him of what I saw as one of his best bits of casework. And it was all done in a couple of cramped rooms using techniques which were being invented as we all went along. Those were interesting times, indeed.

Ironically, the fish farm owner/manager, although fined £350 for his possession of dead herons, had his plea of 'not guilty' to the poisonings accepted. Once again, without any admission, it couldn't be shown who had used the fish fry to poison the birds. Wildlife offences are often like that, with no witnesses.

As part of my report to the Procurator Fiscal, I included a statement from the BTO which said that, according to their ringing statistics, in order to have found seven heron rings in that part of the UK, a total of at least 50 herons must have been killed.

Herons, by the way, are one of our largest birds. This poison in a minute quantity was enough to incapacitate them.

THURSDAY, 30 OCTOBER 1986

Another victim of alphachloralose has been found. This time it's a buzzard with what appears to be rabbit meat in its stomach, a standard poisoning. If there were a prize for retrieving the greatest number of poisoned common buzzards in Scotland, I would win, hands down. This bird had been found by a local walker and by some miracle had ended up reported to me and was therefore sent to DAFS East Craigs for analysis. I dread to think how many baits and victims were ignored or discarded by the public in those early days.

I had driven with Iain Macleod to the Haddo Estate (NB: not the Haddo House Estate, the adjacent NTS property and country park whose owner, Lady Aberdeen, was very helpful to the later, 1989 inquiry). This area lies about 25 miles north of Aberdeen, close to the River Ythan, and is a pleasing mix of rolling farmland and pinewoods. There are several major castles and big houses in this area, most of which had large-scale pheasant shoots at that time. I was involved in several poisoning and illegal trapping cases in that area.

We had a look round the given location and found a lot of set snares but no sign of poisoning. We started a wider

PC Mark Rafferty and Sgt Malcolm Henderson (WLOs) with seized poisons, Borders Estate, 2003

PC Mark Rafferty with poisoned buzzards, Barns Estate, 2003

search and soon found a freshly-dead crow and the remains of a rabbit, about one metre apart, at the edge of a stubble field close to a wood. We photographed these, then carefully bagged them up and took them for analysis. Close by, in the wood, we found a pheasant release pen with a 'feed ride', a linear opening in the trees with straw and grain laid out. Many of the tree stumps left by its creation had bits of very decomposed rabbit and pheasant draped over them, almost certainly poisoned baits but in 1986, the two poisons we knew about – alpha and Phosdrin – we considered too volatile, or soluble, to stay viable on an old bait. We left these in place.

We took the crow and rabbit back to Edinburgh and handed them over to the DAFS analysts. A few days later, we were told they both contained alphachloralose.

Time for another reality check: this was 1986 so no WLOs to handle any of this; the near certainty that the estate would hear about any official inquiry; the indisputable fact that a conviction under the 1981 Act was impossible, as no law against the possession of poisons existed, even if we could get enough evidence to identify and search a suspect. Those very, very few poison cases which had gone through under the previous 1912 Protection of Animals (Scotland) Act and the 1954 Protection of Birds Act had relied either on overwhelming eye witness evidence and/or a complete admission.

What should we do, then? My boss, Frank Hamilton – RSPB Scottish Director – wrote to the Factor, who was also the Lord Lieutenant of Aberdeenshire, to ask politely for an explanation for the poisoned birds and bait. His response? He said to Frank, on the phone, 'We get a lot of peo-

PC Rafferty photographs carbofuran in cupboard beside child's toys. Barns Estate, 2003

Above: The author with Angus Aird and Eddi Reader, Pigmeat, 1977

Below: Pete Ellis on Sanda Island ringing storm petrels, 1981

Above: Just fledged: golden eagle on ground, Lewis, 1983

Left: With Stirlingshire eagle chick, 1982

Last few metres of climb into eagle nest, 1983, Lewis

Right: Peter Cunningham with eagle chick, Lewis, 1983

Below: Birding gear, 1982, Rannoch

Above: Cain and Abel eagle chicks, Lewis, 1983

Below: Remote eagle country, Lewis, 1983

Above: Just-hatched golden eagle chick and egg

Left: Jayshree at eagle nest, Lewis, 1983

Above: Peregrine chick close to fledging

Below: Author with alphachloralose egg baits, 1988

*Above: Three peregrine chicks in nest,
c. two-and-a-half weeks old*

*Right: Iain Macleod and drowning set
gin trap, Atholl, 1986*

Author with poisoned golden eagle, Glenfeshie, 2006

Above: Sgt Malcolm Henderson with young peregrine chicks, Peebles-shire

Below: Buzzard on pheasant bait carbofuran near Loch Ken, 2000

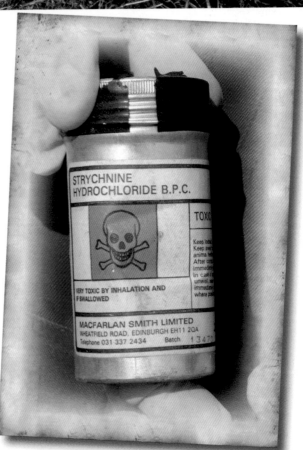

Above: Carbofuran-poisoned sea eagle on lamb bait, Turnalt, Argyll, 2002

Right: Strychnine canister seized from gamekeeper, Borders, 2003

Above: Dead eagle and buzzard
illustrating size difference

Right: The author and palm (aka
black) cockatoo, Chatuchak, 1991

Below: Carbofuran rabbit bait
showing dead insects

Above: Author releases peregrine bought in street market, Nanning South China

Left: Cockfight behind Chatuchak Market

Below: Author holding a Wryneck

Right: Author holding trapped long-billed vulture at Pinjaur Vulture Breeding Centre, 2006

Below: Skinning dead cow while dogs and vultures watch, Bikaner Dump

Above: Feral puppy on skinned cow carcass, Bikaner Dump, Rajasthan

Below: Vulture nest cliffs near Bayana, West Rajasthan

Above: Timon with local farmer and family, Bayana

Below: 'Poison in use' sign, Lothian

ple coming onto our land from the country park. It could have been a jogger who dumped the rabbit bait.'

The jogger theory was a standing joke in my department for some years. I believe the Lord Lieutenant's statement could best be described as an insult to Frank's intelligence. That 'planting of evidence' nonsense would become more popular as more gamekeepers were caught and prosecuted in the early 1990s, but that was yet to come.

So, in 1986, that was the end of it – a complete denial and no chance of further action. Another hard-won statistic and another sighting of the tip of the poisoning iceberg.

TUESDAY, 23 MAY 1989

Aberdeen Sheriff Court and George John Rodenhurst, head keeper of Haddo Estate, has just been fined a whacking £2,600 after pleading guilty to five charges involving the use of alphachloralose and gin traps and possession of an unlicensed pistol. His lawyer stands in front of a TV camera outside the court and reads a statement from him in which he claims that over 400 estates in Scotland have purchased alphachloralose and that four dealers are making a full-time living by supplying it. He is obviously not happy.

No joggers involved that time, then?

This was a landmark case for several reasons. Sheriff Alastair Stewart's comments were very pointed and very useful to me in later years. 'I find it rather ironic that Parliament permits the imprisonment of those who poach game but does not permit the imprisonment of those who set illegal traps or use illegal poisons to preserve it.' He also said that if, as had been said, alphachloralose was widely used on estates in Scotland, then that is a sorry indictment of the estates' 'wholesale flaunting of the legislation'.

Unlike all the other cases in this book, I had very little to do with the actual initial investigation. My contribution was restricted to giving the Fiscal a background report on the problem of wildlife poisoning in Scotland at the time and the details of the 1986 incident. With guilty pleas being accepted, I was not called as a witness. I did, however, help manage the absolute flood of press and media interest which followed this landmark case. I can recall covering the floor of my office with copies of newspaper reports on the case. The fact that Rodenhurst had been given the nickname 'Hitler' by locals helped the headlines, along with, of course, his claims of widespread poisoning on Scottish estates.

Without going into all the details, this case was investigated and put together by a recently-appointed Police Wildlife Officer, Jim Walker, aka Jim the Fish due to his knowledge of poaching legislation. Jim had used an informant to gain details of Rodenhurst's poisoning and trapping activities. The other investigator, however, made a more lasting mark on such cases. This was a local DAFS employee by the name of Alan Bone. Alan had a reputation for investigating potato fraud, crimes with serious financial and environmental implications involving the illegal sale and purchase of unlicensed seed potatoes from foreign parts. He was the man who spotted the wide implications of the Food and Environment Act 1985 (FEPA) for the investigation of wildlife poisoning involving pesticides. As pesticides almost always were – and are – involved, this was of great interest to me.

FEPA and the accompanying Control of Pesticides Regulations (COPR) (1986) were to become very familiar to me over the next two decades. It seems remarkable to me now that we hadn't spotted the potential for this legislation to fill the gap left by the rather feeble

1981 Act. Having said that, many Fiscals were very reluctant to use FEPA/COPR. I'm not sure why. I believe there may have been an element of unfamiliarity leading to worries about loopholes or, just as likely, a desire to simplify everything for the sheriff. The fact is that such laws which were directly aimed at stopping the abuse of pesticides had clearly been drawn up with poisoners in mind, in addition to being aimed at misuse by negligent agricultural and industrial workers.

The problem was that no-one had included those most directly involved in the detection, investigation and prosecution of wildlife poisoning in Scotland: the RSPB, DAFS, Police and the Crown Office. This might have been due to it being a piece of UK legislation, very much pre-devolution, with little or no scrutiny by Scottish MPs.

The first successful use of FEPA in relation to a wildlife poisoning case was at Perth Sheriff Court on 11 December 1990 when Gordon McGregor, head keeper on Glenfernate Estate near Pitlochry was fined £200, out of a total £1200 fine, for his possession of alphachloralose. McGregor was chairman of the local community council and a former Special Constable. The estate was owned by David Heathcoat-Amory, at the time a minister in the Environment Department of the Westminster Parliament. At the time of the conviction, he was a newly-appointed energy minister, which ensured a high level of publicity, including the fact that this was a first under FEPA.

WEDNESDAY, 7 FEBRUARY 1990

An Industrial Tribunal Hearing (now known as Employment Tribunals), Union Street, Aberdeen. Rodenhurst was not finished with his case – far from it. These tribunals operate under Scots Civil Law. One of the results of that is that evidence is very widely interpreted, leading in this case to a fascinating insight into the workings of gamekeepers, factors and landowners, the running of an estate and the purchase and use of illegal poisons and traps. For a few hours in a first-floor room of an Aberdeen Office, the entire poisoning iceberg was visible.

On Rodenhurst's side in this claim of unfair dismissal was Frank Lefevre, Aberdeen's best known QC; representing Haddo Estate was a Mr Macleod. Rodenhurst was attempting to show that not only were the estate fully aware of his illegal activities but that they had actively participated in buying his alphachloralose. The estate was just as keen to deny any knowledge and to justify the dismissal. Witnesses brought before the tribunal included Lefevre himself; the Chief Accountant of N.E Farmers, proprietary rat poison suppliers/agricultural merchants; Marcus Redway, the alpha supplier; Andrew Wood, an assistant factor at Haddo; the Earl of Haddo, the landowner; and Rodenhurst, the sacked headkeeper of Haddo.

Rodenhurst lost his claim but not before the public were treated to some very revealing evidence:

- Lefevre said that he believed R.'s claims of a local conspiracy against him. R. had 29 charges libelled against him, reduced to 12, then he finally pled to five. Legal fees were at first being paid by the shooting syndicate who later pulled out. R. pled guilty because of 'a lack of money and fear of a prison sentence'.
- Macleod made a strong attack on Lefevre, reading out all the charges to which R. had pled guilty. He claimed that R. had asked for a reference from the estate as he had decided to leave.

- N.E. Farmers produced invoices showing that the estate had been buying large quantities of proprietary brands of rat poison during the time of the offences.

- Marcus Redway (M.R.), Moorend Game Farm, admitted selling alphachloralose to R. in 1986 1987 and 1988, listed as 'rat poison' on invoices, when veterinary medicines supplied at the same time were named. Claimed it was an effective rat poison. Said R. had asked for it 'for rats'. Named Martin Edgar as one of his commission agents, who 'may have supplied the estate' with alphachloralose. Put up defence for its use against rats 'and our local council uses it against seagulls… it's not dangerous like Phosdrin'. R. had it weighed out and put in plastic containers marked 'rat poison'.

- Tribunal member put it to Redway that he was disguising an illegal product by calling it 'rat poison'. M.R. also told tribunal he would supply any keeper who phoned and asked for alpha as a rat poison.

- Andrew Wood, assistant estate factor, said that he hadn't known alpha was illegal but that he wasn't involved with the ordering of it anyway. He also said that the head factor Farquharson would have seen all invoices.

- In 1987, all employees were sent a letter instructing them not to use 'illegal activities'.

- Lefevre said that such a letter, saying you should obey the law, was merely to 'keep the estate's hands clean'.

- The Earl of Haddo, the landowner, said that his relationship with R. was not good. He said he was aware that R. had a previous conviction for assault but was unaware that he also had one for pole-trapping.

- Rodenhurst had been a keeper for 21 years plus three years working with his father as a boy. When he started at Haddo, previous staff had been resentful and the shoot was poorly run. When asked if the previous keeper used poison, he said, 'I don't know… he was a good keeper and therefore difficult to catch.' He took 60 gin traps off the under-keeper when he started. Said the warning letter from the estate was 'to keep the estate right'.

There followed a long diatribe against the police, accusing witnesses of partiality and accusing the estate of reneging on him.

He then gave a fascinating insight into his in-depth knowledge of alphachloralose, including the fact that you should only use it at temperatures below 55° F. He also gave the usual rant about councils and the RSPCA using it to kill gulls and that it was only the pure form that made it impossible to revive protected species; with the 25% strength, he said, there was the possibility of an 8 – 10 hour revival period. This is, of course, dangerous wishful thinking. Although some large birds and animals will recover, it can and does kill eagles and even some foxes stone dead, as I have seen for myself.

He followed this by a strong attack on Redway, saying that he was a highly experienced agrochemist with a vast experience of alpha and who wrote 'rat poison' instead of alphachloralose 'to keep his feet clean'.

Fascinatingly, he also went on to say that alpha is the last thing he would use for killing rats, as where rats are warfarin-resistant they are also alpha-resistant. 25% strength alpha in particular would be ineffective.

He claimed that Captain Farquharson (the estate factor) knew all about the purchase and use of alpha. He quoted Captain F. as saying, on several occasions, 'Your only crime is being caught' and that he has 'paid his fine'!

It's impossible to know how much of that can be taken as the absolute truth. One thing, though, is for sure: they can't all be telling the truth. What can definitely be gleaned from the tribunal is that alphachloralose was being supplied to estates, probably routinely and in large quantities, under the guise of rat poison.

Certainly since FEPA/COPR in 1986 and possibly since 1912, the use of alphachloralose as a rat poison has been illegal. The main reason for this is the danger of secondary poisoning – stupefied rats wandering into the open would be eaten by, and therefore kill, predatory birds. No professional rodent controller would use alpha against rats: only people caught using it illegally would claim that.

The final chapter on the Haddo Estate saga was written on Friday, 12 July 1991when Marcus Redway of Moorend Game Farm, Whitby was fined a total of £4,900 with £2,000 costs at Whitby Strand Magistrates Court. He pled guilty to 14 charges of offences against FEPA/COPR. He admitted illegally supplying, storing and selling alphachloralose. No doubt his legacy lives on in many estate cupboards all over Scotland. As part of the investigation, the Ministry of Agriculture Food and Fisheries (MAFF) investigators found invoices showing he had been selling alpha (listed as 'rat poison') at prices of £45 to £50 a half kilogram.

Of course this didn't stop poisoning. I doubt it even slowed things up, but at least it would mean that no one could deny what was going on. Or so I thought.

Jim Walker, the police officer who had worked hard to produce such a good result in the initial court case, resigned his position as Police Wildlife Liaison Officer in November 1989. On 20 February 1990, an article appeared in a national newspaper, alleging that he quit 'because he believed the police were reluctant to treat countryside poisoning as serious crime. He left the post as Grampian Police launched an inquiry into an alleged poisoning at Fyvie Estate, next door to Haddo. Mr Walker's help was not requested during the Fyvie investigation, which was handled by police at Turriff.'

Now that's pretty strong stuff regarding a serving police officer: even implied criticism of your force is seriously frowned upon by senior officers. The fact is that that I saw several such WLOs either quit or get moved on after apparently becoming too successful in their field of work.

Monday, 2 April 1990

I was in my seventh field season as an Investigations Officer, my tenth in the Scottish uplands. Things were still pretty hit and miss, as the following fiasco of a case will show. Some of it was down to plain bad luck but mostly it was down to apathy on the part of the police (with the exception of the poor put-upon local constable on the day) and the usual lack of cooperation from estate staff.

I had received a report of a suspicious dead buzzard, lying close to the remains of a rabbit, which had been found by a walker over the weekend. (I later found out that the walker had been given permission by someone on the estate, someone who obviously forgot to tell the gamekeeper; I can recall three such blunders in my time, including the Atholl poisoned eggs). This was on a grouse-shooting estate near Abington, in South Lanarkshire, later variously named by the newspapers as Leadhills Estate, Abington Farms or Hopetoun Estate.

I drove to Abington from Edinburgh with my colleague, Oonagh McGarry, a birdwatcher/ contract worker from the RSPB office. This estate was known to be hostile to walkers and conservationists in particular – my predecessor Pete, had had rather brusque correspondence with the owner regarding a poisoned peregrine and local raptor workers were not welcome there either. In such circumstances I occasionally took a female companion with me, on the basis that we would appear more like normal walkers. There was, of course, no legal hindrance to our walking on such open land in Scotland.

Oonagh was pleased to be out of the office but became witness to a frustrating and disheartening series of events. We walked up a hill to a position overlooking the estate – a stone dyke was the sharp dividing line between the green heavily-grazed sheepwalk of the neighbouring farm and the regular brown strips of the managed grouse moor. Unfortunately for them, generations of buzzards were attracted to this ridge, where they could hang in the up-draughts spying out the M74 on one side – with its plentiful supply of roadkill – and also the grouse moor, no doubt full of rabbits and voles due to the regular killing of any predators. (To quote a Borders gamekeeper, when asked by George Carse if he ever saw hen harriers on his grouse moor, 'Aye, we see them whiles but they dinnae bide lang!').

As we arrived at the wall, we saw a man wearing a deerstalker hat, accompanied by a boy, get out of a red pick-up and walk over and enter a crow cage trap. I was able to read the number of the vehicle as it drove away below us a short time later.

We walked across to the area where the dead buzzard had been reported and found a dead rabbit but no bird. It had presumably been picked up by the keeper but could just as likely have been carried off by a passing fox, which would die anonymously elsewhere. I put on my gloves (by then a standard piece of kit in my rucksack) and bagged the rabbit. We walked towards the crow cage but then spotted a fenced-off area containing two dead sheep. I could also see a couple of set snares inside this stink pit or midden, to use the working terms. It was a standard system for catching foxes in Scotland. I was unaware of legislation such as the Dogs Acts (1906 – 1928) which makes it an offence to leave sheep unburied in a position where dogs can get access to them and spread disease, or the Animal By-Products Order 1999, with similar restrictions. It was another example of the *laissez faire* attitude towards legislation that I saw on a routine basis on shooting estates, from unattended and unlocked firearms and ammunition to the illegal use of traps and poison. Strange, though, how they suddenly became very concerned about the niceties of legislation when it's being used to prosecute them.

What wasn't so standard was the presence inside the stink pit of a little nest of four brown hen's eggs, all with the top of the shell knocked off. They were bait, laced with poison which on later analysis proved to be alphachloralose. This was a belts and braces man, then, setting snares for the foxes and poisoned eggs for the winged predators. We had plenty of circumstantial evidence of poisoning when added to the reported buzzard next to the rabbit. It was time to get police help, including a search warrant.

At this time (1990), such a scenario was taken as sufficient evidence to allow for a search of land by the authorities, whether police or Agriculture Department staff or both, either under a J.P. warrant or under the provisions of FEPA/COPR. This was often used to great effect, as it was essential to move fast after the discovery of baits and victims – word gets round shooting estates very fast indeed. With the arrival of so-called partnership working, protocols and intelligence-led working, a lack of urgency, common to those not directly involved in nature conservation, kicked in with a vengeance. It was my job to protect nature and I always imagined some other creature being killed while we waited days or even weeks for a follow-up. This did not make me a pleasant person to be around at such times.

As late as 2001, it was still being argued in court (Perth Sheriff Court, in this instance) whether or not the police and Agriculture Department had the legitimate right to follow up circumstantial evidence with a search of land and premises. The case in question involved carcasses with blue granules on them and several dead buzzards. It was a very hard-fought case – a CID officer involved said that his cross-examination had been worse than being in a murder trial, but I routinely had to put up with that – and resulted in a fine of £2,400 against a gamekeeper, Malcolm Kempson. The appeal failed, giving by Stated Case the green light on such searches. We had been carrying them out since the early 1990s anyway, depending on the enthusiasm of those involved.

We walked out and drove to the nearby Abington police station, a lovely old sandstone building nestling amongst tall deciduous trees and within sight of the estate's moor. There we met a young constable who was about to have a very bad day at work. I explained who I was and what we had been up to before we arrived at his office. To give him his due, he didn't try to bluff and immediately said that this was his first day in this country office, having been transferred from the city. (Abington is within the Strathclyde Police Force area, which also includes the entire Greater Glasgow conurbation and stretches out as far as the island of Tiree in the Inner Hebrides: in terms of staff it is the second largest force in the UK, after the Met.) He knew nothing about wildlife or wildlife law but said he would phone his sergeant, down the road in Biggar. This he did and his sergeant agreed to drive across immediately. So far, so good. Ten minutes later, while we were sharing cups of tea, his radio roared into life. There had been a fatal accident on the M74 so there'd be no sergeant to help today…

Right, what next? I showed the constable my copy of the 1981 Act and explained that as there was no such thing as a wildlife search warrant (some forces eventually had those drawn up but it wasn't until the email era that the Crown office standardised such matters) we would have to convert a standard theft warrant. I had seen this done many times with the words 'stolen items' crossed out and replaced by 'live birds', 'dead birds', 'birds' eggs', 'traps' or 'poison' with the relevant sections of the 1981 Act added in. My input to this process was essential, not least because warrants could only be issued for certain offences and/or involving certain species. A flaw in a warrant and a case would get thrown out of court. I saw one of my cases fall because the wrong date had been written on a warrant by a police officer – a genuine but damaging mistake.

OK, let's get the warrant typed up, then: first find the typewriter and type (no electronic keyboards here), slowly and carefully, with two fingers. We pass on the vehicle number from the keeper's pick-up. Get on the phone to the computer at Swansea. It checks out to Leadhills

Estate; a police colleague tells the constable which keeper has that vehicle, we get an address, a cottage close to Leadhills village.

Now, a J.P. to sign the warrant. Searching for a list in the office drawers, here we are, the nearest is Kenny Wilson. His occupation? Head keeper of Leadhills Estate. Perhaps not, Constable, there might be a bit of a conflict of interest there, don't you think? He eventually settles on a farmer J.P. who lives a few miles to the south. We drive along bumpy single-track roads and arrive at the farm house – we're in luck, the farmer's there. 'What's this about then… let's have a look at the warrant… Oh, him, he's a good bloke, he comes and does my foxes for me!' Great. Today is just getting better and better.

At last we drive up to the suspect's cottage and there's the vehicle parked outside – maybe our luck has turned at last? The constable knocks on the door, just as I notice that the vehicle number is one digit different from the one I noted earlier. 'Stop! It's a different motor, the estate must have a fleet of them.' 'Never mind,' says the constable, 'let's search him anyway.' 'No, we bloody won't,' I say, 'I'm not getting involved in an illegal search!' At that moment, the keeper comes to the door, the constable has seen reason and says, 'Sorry, wrong house.' 'Oh dear,' says the keeper, a big smile on his face. We drive off.

We drive half a mile to the tiny police office in Leadhills village and meet the local (off-duty) cop, who tells us that the man we are after lives a few doors up. We eventually arrive at Tommy Murray's door. We explain why we are there, the constable introduces me and we start a search of vehicle and garage. Tommy is friendly and relaxed, no doubt having received a helpful phone call to say we were on our way. We find nothing of interest except a dummy peregrine egg. He denies any knowledge of poison on his beat. The constable asks him to accompany us to the location of the poisoned eggs. 'You'll have to check with my boss, Kenny Wilson,' is his reply. This is nonsense: there was no requirement for that, either legally or morally. Against my advice, the constable goes to Wilson's house close by and when he comes out is an angry man. 'Wilson says he doesn't have to come with us.' He's obviously had a flea in his ear from the head keeper/J.P.

We drove down the glen and parked the car at the closest farmhouse, walked in and retrieved the baited eggs. I photographed the eggs and locus and then we walked over the surrounding area in case their might be more offences taking place. We found nothing and headed back to the police office.

I signed labels for the rabbit and the eggs and Oonagh and I headed back to Edinburgh. I got home at around 10 p.m., having started work in my office at 9 a.m. – just another routine 13-hour day.

When analysed, the rabbit and all the eggs were found to contain alphachloralose. No one was ever charged.

I would be back on that estate several times, when it was under different management, right up to my retirement in 2006.

THURSDAY, 20 SEPTEMBER 1990

At this time the corvid cage trap known as a Larsen trap was a relative newcomer to the gamekeeper's arsenal. To a veteran of illegal traps like myself it looked suspiciously like a hawk trap, a multi-section portable cage with a decoy/bait compartment and one or more trapping compartments. The trap is usually sprung by a bird landing on or touching a split perch, which is holding the trap door in place against the action of a strong spring. We were aware that these traps could catch raptors: they had done so during their licensed experimental use by the Game Conservancy and, as I say, are quite similar in design to hawk traps which have been used through the ages.

Newly-licensed by government Open General Licence from 1988 – anyone with authorisation from the landowner could use one, with no requirement for inspection or individual licensing – the traps were designed to be used with live crows or magpies as bait. Such birds would attract territorial birds of their own kind. We had received anecdotal evidence that they were being successful in catching unwanted corvids and some optimists were even saying that it would remove the need for illegal poisoning but – you've guessed it – we also began to receive reports of people placing live pigeons in Larsen traps in order to trap birds of prey. Hawk trappers traditionally use a live pigeon as bait.

When I got a call from Malcolm Henderson, the Borders WLO, saying that a Larsen containing a live pigeon had been found next to a pheasant release pen on a shooting estate, I knew what was going on. We had been working on cases for over three years and had got used to each other's methods. Malcolm had one of the longest careers as a WLO in Scotland, being one of the first to be designated in 1987.

I drove down to Jedburgh police office and met Malcolm. This was an office I got to know extremely well: it saw some of my highs and lows in the struggle against wildlife crime and I owe thanks both to the friendly civilian staff and the police officers who often met me in the canteen, dishevelled and thirsty after a hard day's 'hill-walking'. He had identified the gamekeeper for the area we were about to visit. We drove to the hills above Bonchester Bridge, parked up and started to walk up the steep grass hillside, Malcolm in his uniform and me in my waterproof clothing, carrying my ubiquitous rucksack.

In front of us – and between us and the reported site of the trap – lay a narrow strip of medium-height pine trees, which we started to walk through. To our astonishment we found ourselves looking at a set pole trap, a spring trap set on top of and attached to a seven-and-a-half-foot post beside a pheasant pen. This was one of the rarest offences I came across, as by this time such blatant practices were fast disappearing. Illegal since 1904, the pole trap is one of the most horrible methods of 'vermin' control: birds get caught by the leg or legs when they land on the trap and are left hanging upside down to flap their lives away, through loss of blood, exhaustion or shock.

I took photos for evidence (no cameras were issued to 'ordinary' police officers back then) and Malcolm sprang the trap. Half an hour later, we were standing looking down at a Larsen trap containing a live pigeon in the decoy section and two set trap sections. I took more photos. The Larsen was inside a recently-occupied pheasant pen.

While here, I noticed a dead pheasant poult which appeared to be have been plucked of its feathers – possibly an indication of predation by a bird of prey – but with a white substance on its breast. We both looked at this for some time, wondering whether it could be a fungal growth. Fortunately we decided to take it for analysis – it was later found to be alphachloralose. After checking out another two nearby pens we returned to the car.

Malcolm then drove to the keeper's house, which was about half a mile away. We met the keeper's wife, who showed us some stuffed birds of prey in the house. We looked around the back garden and steading buildings. We found an identical Larsen trap in the back garden, set and baited with a live collared dove. In the garage, we found a plastic container labelled 99% alphachloralose and containing white powder. On the same shelf we found a syringe, a plastic container with grain in it and a plastic box containing wooden sticks with white gunge adhering to the ends. We also found a labelled strychnine jar, three-quarters full, in a wooden box with an unlocked padlock attached. The garage itself was unlocked. Malcolm seized all the items as evidence but we left the Larsen trap, being unsure of the status of collared dove in this context.

We then left the cottage and headed back up the hill to look for the keeper, Jimmy Haining. We met him sitting in his Land Rover, close to the Larsen trap pen. Malcolm told him who we were and that we had found illegal things on his land. To my surprise he then admitted using the Larsen trap to catch birds of prey and followed that with an admission that he was using alpha-chloralose too (but he took protected birds home and warmed them up!). He then backtracked and said, 'You know goshawks don't come back to a kill.' We hadn't mentioned goshawks.

He then started to give the usual 'I'm really a conservationist' line. 'I told that Dave Dick about an eagle,' he said, to Malcolm. I waited till he had finished before saying, 'I am Dave Dick,' bringing that particular conversation to an end. (A couple of years before he had phoned me to pass on information about a failed, one-off breeding attempt by golden eagles in Dumfries-shire).

In case anyone reading is this is still under the illusion that we were dealing with 'a few rotten apples in the barrel', 'unprofessional part-timers' or any of the other terms used by gamekeepers' representatives to deflect attention from a blatant and large-scale problem, I should point out that Jimmy Haining was a well-respected, long-service professional keeper who also lectured in the legitimate use of strychnine for mole control at the Borders College.

Two days later Malcolm returned and charged Haining with the offences we had discovered. Haining made admissions to all the charges. You may think that that would be that, cut and dried. You'd be wrong.

THURSDAY, 20 JUNE 1991

Jedburgh Sheriff Court and Jimmy has got himself a QC – or more correctly, Jimmy's boss, a wealthy Austrian banker, has got Jimmy a QC. Kevin Drummond, QC, who walks in to the Fiscal's office just before the trial is due to start, where I am having a last-minute conference as was the normal, efficient practice by 1991. Kevin announces that he is going to win this case because section 19 of the 1981 Act does not permit a constable to enter land and search for evidence. The Fiscal may have been used to this robust, even arrogant approach but I wasn't and in my naivety, combined with experience of section 19 in court, I blurted out, 'Do you really think that's what Parliament thought, when they drew this up?' The resulting angry out-burst ('You may be very good at what you do out there, Mr Dick, but in here, I'm in charge!') was my first sight of an apparent lack of control which I have since witnessed many times.

He was as good as his word. Drummond put forward the defence that 'a constable has no power to enter land to search for evidence without a warrant' and Sheriff Paterson agreed. Not guilty on all charges. Not easy to take when you've actually seen the man admit crimes to your face. That's the way court cases go, though, and I'd learned a long time before to take the rough with the smooth. The next day I was on a plane heading for Indonesia to investigate the large-scale smuggling of endangered parrots. I always had plenty of work on the go, with little time to brood on the failures.

TUESDAY, 21 JANUARY 1992

The Fiscal in the Haining case, Mr Whitelaw, was not impressed by the sheriff's decision and passed the case on to the Crown Office, with the suggestion that it should be sent to the High Court of Justiciary in Edinburgh for a Crown Appeal. I attended the Appeal Court, a very solemn affair where three judges, in full ermined regalia, produced a 'stated case'. Their conclusion was 'that the only question which we have to determine is whether the construction which the sheriff placed upon Section 19(1)(d) was the correct one. We are satisfied that the construction of the sheriff is an erroneous one... we are satisfied that he arrived at the wrong decision in this case... and remit the case to the sheriff to proceed as accords.'

THURSDAY, 23 APRIL 1992

Jedburgh Sheriff Court. Sheriff Paterson finds Haining guilty and fines him £100 each on the two remaining charges, of setting a pole trap and laying poisonous substances.

Was it a victory for conservation? Even in 1992, that was not a very impressive punishment. I, along with the police and the Fiscal had spent days preparing a case in which the accused had admitted everything to the police at the time of the alleged offences. What was most important, though, was the Stated Case. It blocked one attempt at inventing a legal loophole. It was in no way, though, the end of attempts to prevent wildlife investigations by spurious questioning over investigation 'without landowner permission'. That was still a hot topic when I left the RSPB 15 years later.

Alpha is still turning up in wildlife poisonings – unsurprisingly, given the levels allegedly being sold and smuggled into the country. We received several pieces of information about smuggling routes but usually with no hard evidence. One case, though, showed just how simple it could be for a keeper to get hold of the stuff.

SPRING 1995

A young RSPB scientist/fieldworker is on his first week of his first contract, studying upland waders and their habitat. He is walking along a high grass ridge above the heather moor of Farleyer Estate near Aberfeldy. It's over 500 metres above sea level: eagle country, raven country. Then he sees the hen's egg. That's not right – it looks like one of the photos that Dave Dick showed us on our training and induction day. I'd better phone him up.

Well done, that man! I used to issue dire warnings about what I would do to any staff member who didn't report suspicious activity. I knew what could happen to wildlife if bait was neglected – I spent a large chunk of my life bagging up the casualties. I also knew how frustrating it could be if evidence was removed.

I realised the importance of this find immediately. This would not be my first visit to this estate. In 1989, I followed up a report of uncovered set spring traps; in 1990 a shot-out hen harrier nest and in April 1993, I had retrieved a dead buzzard and rabbit baits from Farleyer, which had led to my making an unsuccessful search of keepers' premises with two SOAFD (Scottish Office Agriculture and Fisheries Department) officials. Donald Ross and John Hunter from the Perth Office were a formidable double act with whom I had several successful cases in those early days. They didn't worry about politics, just went straight in and searched all estates, farmers and keepers in the area without discrimination. That's still my favourite approach: no one can complain of bias. That day, unusually, we were unsuccessful. We had failed to get access to one locked shed and someone had got to another just before us, leaving tyre tracks in the snow. To complete the set, I also helped the police later on, in 1996, when a buzzard was found, still alive, in a gin trap a few hundred metres from the keeper's house.

Back to 1995 and by this time, Alan Stewart was on the scene as the Tayside Police Wildlife Liaison Co-ordinator. Alan returned with me and the contract fieldworker to the mountainside and retrieved two hen's eggs, full of alphachloralose.

This time a search went ahead without RSPB involvement but with police and SOAFD – Alan Bone , the man from the Haddo case, had been included. The most worrying find was a Lea and Perrins sauce bottle containing Mevinphos, unlabelled, in his unlocked Land Rover. Most interesting though, was a jar of alphachloralose with a Tipperary address on it. The keeper, James Lambie (an underkeeper at the time of the 1993 search), admitted putting out six baited hen's eggs on the hill 'to kill crows'.

Lambie was in trouble and then did something for which I had no precedent – he shopped his boss.

Lambie said that he had been given the alphachloralose by his previous employer, a neighbouring estate owner, who had brought it back from Ireland. This was brought to the attention of the Perth Fiscal. On 31 October 1995, Lambie was fined a total of £2,500, for offences under the 1981 Act and FEPA, including his possession and use of the alphachloralose.

A separate 'pleading diet' was set for the landowner for a week later. At the last minute the case was abandoned when it was noticed that the charge had gone out of time. A case had to be first heard (accused served notice), within six months of it coming to the attention of the Fiscal. This was – I hoped - sheer incompetence. I wrote to the Fiscal pointing out the importance of the case and how we were unlikely to get another chance like this and got an apology, for what that was worth. I saw several cases go out of time during my career but none were as damaging as this one. The signal to those who could substantially cut back on poisoning overnight would have been clear. It was very, very frustrating. As with 'cause and permit', we never saw this chance repeated.

The Wildlife and Countryside (Amendment) Act 1991 had made it an offence to 'knowingly cause or permit' any person to kill or take wild birds (section 5) or wild animals (section 11) by the already-listed prohibited methods. This was the result of the growing alarm at the amount of estate-based crime being revealed by our work. The theory was that the poor downtrodden keepers were being forced to illegally trap and poison by their managers (head keepers/factors/landowners) and that this amendment would protect them. They could point out to their oppressors that they, too, risked prosecution if an individual keeper got caught.

Not a bad theory, but it fails to take into account the nature of this type of employment – who would employ a whistleblower in this industry? Everything rests on getting a good reference. So, 19 years after this amendment, I remain unaware of its ever having been used successfully in Scotland. That fact should speak volumes about the true source of these crimes.

CARBOFURAN: BANNED FOR USE IN UK IN 2003; BANNED FOR POSSESSION IN SCOTLAND 2005

MONDAY, 18 JULY 1988

I had spent a very pleasant afternoon watching a male marsh harrier flying over a reed bed. A local farmer had called me after seeing a food pass between a male and female bird – a good indication that the birds were nesting there. This was confirmed by the local Raptor Study Group and today this pair has been joined by several other regular breeding pairs of what is a very rare breeding bird in Scotland. This might strike an unusually optimistic note in this narrative, I know, but it is a reminder that some things were improving.

I phoned in to the office as I would try to do once a day from a phone box, in these pre-mobile phone years, to be told that there had been a tip-off about someone pole-trapping goshawks in the east neuk of Fife. Unusually, the location given was very specific.

Although it was now going-home time for most folk with a normal job, I knew I was only half an hour's drive from the locus, so I set out for the Boarhills area. It was a pleasant summer's evening as I walked along the edge of a field of barley, heading for the small wood mentioned by the caller. At the edge of the field and close to the wood I found a dead wood pigeon with a plucked breast. So far, so normal – birds of prey will often pluck their prey, beginning with the breast area, before starting to feed. A closer look, however and I saw a cut into the meat on each side of the exposed keelbone. In each cut were a number of small blue/black granules. The granules meant little to me at the time but the method was clear – this was a bait. I photographed and carefully bagged the pigeon. Then I crossed over into the wood. A thorough search revealed no sign of any traps but I did find a locked shed and many used shotgun cartridges – it was obviously a well shot area.

Carbofuran in coffee jar labelled 'turnips', Barns Estate, 2003

The next morning, I took the pigeon in to East Craigs for analysis. A few days later I got a phone call. 'Those granules were carbofuran.' It was the first time I'd heard the word spoken. I was full of questions and, as usual, the DAFS staff had the answers. Yes, they had come across it before in an abuse/misuse context: several blackbirds and a cat had been analysed from one incident in 1987. Where was the incident? Cupar, Fife. Well, there's a coincidence!

July 1988 was well before we all got our act together regarding coordinated RSPB/police/DAFS searches. No serious follow-up ensued, although it was of course reported to the police at St Andrews.

Over the following three years, a trickle of records of carbofuran abuse were picked up. always in Fife. It seemed

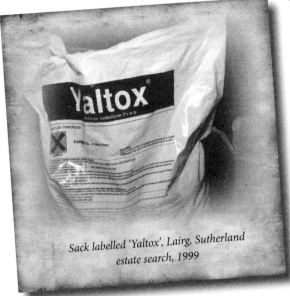

Sack labelled 'Yaltox', Lairg, Sutherland estate search, 1999

to be a local problem. Carbofuran, sold as Yaltox, was a legitimate agricultural chemical, albeit one which was so dangerous that it could only be legally used by trained operators using deep drilling machinery. The other poisoners were carrying on as usual on Scottish estates with their winter/summer combination of alpha/Phosdrin.

THURSDAY, 10 JANUARY 1991

I got a tip-off in late 1990, from a very reliable source, that a company calling itself Fife Pheasants, based in Largo, were supplying Phosdrin to their customers. This was the opportunity my boss, Andy Jones (Head of Investigations section at HQ) had been looking for. In 1991, three separate sting operations were carried out on poison suppliers, one each in Scotland ,England and Wales. These were all televised. Despite the continual denials, back then and still today, we had shown that poison was being widely supplied to the shooting industry throughout the UK.

One of the reasons I look back on the early 1990s as a sort of Golden Age for wildlife crime investigation is that there was a proliferation of good investigative journalists, both in the press and media. One such person was Callum Macrae, in January 1991 working with a TV production company called Hand Pict, based in Edinburgh, and now an award- winning TV journalist specialising in the more dangerous parts of Africa and the Middle East. They were making a short programme about wildlife crime and when we told them about the Fife opportunity, they jumped at it.

So, on a cold January day in Fife, I watched in a lay-by as Andy got wired up by the technician before heading off in a car into the Fife Pheasants premises. It was basically a one-man show. A man called John Hutchison, who described himself as a local gamekeeper, met Andy, whom he thought was managing a shoot in Ayrshire, and discussed an order for pheasant poults for later in the year. Andy brought up the subject of predators and John was off and running. 'Buzzards are 70 % of your problem. Try some of this, that'll sort it.' He handed Andy a bag of Yaltox and wouldn't take any money for it. He also talked about using pole-traps on site round his pheasant rearing area. And all of it was taped.

Andy came back in a high state of excitement. 'What's Yaltox?' 'Carbofuran. There's enough there to poison a whole town, never mind some buzzards.'

We knew that Hutchison was due to go home from his work shortly, so the team waited till he got back to his cottage and then Callum doorstepped him with the full TV camera. Of course he denied everything and shut the door in Callum's face. Job done.

I later took all my information – my statement, a copy of the tape and film – to the local Procurator Fiscal who sat down and discussed the case with me at length. His opinion? Regrettably, there wasn't enough to be certain of a conviction. I believe it boiled down to Scots Law not allowing for a conviction on a person's admissions alone. I was disappointed at the time.)

So, with carbofuran in the early 1990s, the genie was soon well and truly out of the bottle. It started appearing on shooting estates in the Highlands, then in Perthshire, then the Borders, then everywhere. It was always referred to as Yaltox by informants and by the few who were caught using it. This was revealing in itself. There are several trade names/products with carbofuran as the main constituent, yet at first we were always seeing Yaltox. I became very interested in this new chemical and learned as much as I could about it.

It is made in both granular and liquid format. The granular form was already banned in the US following large-scale bird kills. Like alpha, birds are particularly susceptible but unlike alpha, it is very toxic to humans – in its pure form, more toxic than strychnine, as Ken Hunter told me. Unlike alpha, it was effective at any temperature, at any time of year. It rapidly began to replace both Phosdrin and alpha. While it was still a legitimate agricultural chemical – mainly used as a soil pesticide for turnips and other root crops – I was told several times that it was easy for a keeper to get it from agricultural staff on the same estate. This also came out in at least one court case.

TUESDAY, 7 DECEMBER 1999

A small shooting estate in the far north, near Lairg, Sutherland. I always welcomed a trip up there – it held fond memories of chasing eggers in the 'simmer dim', hearing wailing divers on peaty lochs and – last but not least – the hospitality of Stuart Benn, my ex-assistant, at Inverness on the way up.

We made a bleary-eyed pair out on the hill. As was already becoming an annoying trend, the police had decided the RSPB should stay away from the keeper's premises during searches. It was a small estate but a big enough hill which we were scouring for poison baits and victims, with a constable in full uniform. When we got called back, we were shown the haul: a plastic alpha container of laboratory-grade chloralose and sacks of carbofuran in a locked estate shed. The most interesting item, though, was a multivitamin bottle containing a small quantity of carbofuran. This had been found in the head keeper's gun cabinet, which was often where the more dangerous poisons on estates would be found.

When asked about the large amount of carbofuran in his store, the landowner told the police he had bought it to put on carrots in the walled garden. We calculated there was enough Yaltox there to supply a small farm for several years – no one even mentioned the fact that you couldn't use a legitimate drill for the granules in a walled garden, as you need heavy equipment. The clincher for me was when the Agricultural Department official attending (this was a FEPA pesticide follow-up) said he had never seen Yaltox before, so it wasn't exactly commonplace for use in the Highlands.

The case had really started in 1997 when the very decomposed remains of a red kite were found on the estate – to the finder's surprise, SASA analysts managed to trace carbofuran from the dessicated corpse. It was calculated that the bird had lain dead for at least six months. A short time before the search, a carbofuran poisoned raven had been found in the same area.

In my early days I had become aware that the deadly poison Phosdrin would kill any fly landing on it – a bait with dead flies or beetles was an almost certain bet. When Yaltox –

like Phosdrin, an insecticide – started to be commonplace, we noticed that baits were often covered in dead insects, most noticeably the almost indestructible sexton beetles but on occasion baits were turned black with the bodies of hundreds of small flies. A secondary effect here was that the normal process of a corpse's biodegradation was being halted, at least in those areas where carbofuran was present. On many occasions, therefore, the evidence of poisoning was being preserved by the poison itself. Baits would degenerate to a skeleton with scraps of carbofuran-laced sinew; victims' mouths, gullets and stomachs would be preserved while the rest of the body decomposed.

Alphachloralose had no such effect and would eventually break down, leaving a bait or victim impossible to analyse. Phosdrin, whilst a deadly nerve toxin, breaks down very quickly in the open air. I believe this effect is common to all carbamates, the chemical group to which carbofuran belongs. Other types have recently appeared as part of the poisoner's kit.

Despite all of the above and a letter from me to the Fiscal, pointing out the now widespread abuse of carbofuran and alpha, he marked the case 'No Proceedings', describing the keeper's possession of a vial of carbofuran as a 'small technical offence'. The carbofuran and alphachloralose were in labelled containers in a locked shed. We would have to wait for the Possession of Pesticides (Scotland) Order 2005 before such blatant anomalies could be addressed by the law.

Monday, 22 March 2004

'Over here! I've got another one!' The man in the flat cap, blue jeans and buckled wellies was calling to PC Mark Rafferty. There were six of us in the line, carefully picking our way through the young conifer plantation with its thick carpet of pine needles and long lines of brash, cut branches from some recent thinning job. We all walked across to where gamekeeper Stephen Muir was poking at a pile of brash with his stick. The distinctive mottled brown-and-grey, black-and-white corpse of a buzzard had been revealed from its hiding place. This was buzzard number six or seven. I had already lost count since Muir showed us the first three where he had buried them under rocks and a tree root at the edge of the plantation. This one, like the others, was carefully photographed and catalogued by the joint police/SEERAD/RSPB team. It was a well-practised series of moves, from identification, to photographing in situ, to bagging and labelling. An onlooker would have immediately recognised that these people knew each other and had worked together many times before. The only odd man out and onlooker was Stephen Muir.

Four hours earlier, at 8 a.m., a marked police Land Rover and an unmarked estate car arrive at a group of houses and garages grouped around a central square about a quarter of a mile into a sporting estate in the Borders. As we pull in, I see the nearby 'big house', a baronial mansion at the end of an avenue of daffodils and screened by tall deciduous trees.

Uniformed policeman are knocking on the door but no-one is home. Discreet inquiries are made next door and, eventually, a Japanese-made covered pickup drives in behind us through the arched entrance to the square. The gamekeeper has arrived. 'Mr Muir?' 'Yes?' 'I'm PC Rafferty and these gentlemen…' Introductions are made all round. We all move into the keeper's house. It is explained to Muir that poison has been found on the estate and that an official search is going to take place. We are all now in the living room of the house when a man appears at the door. 'What's going on?' Polite but inquiring. I can immediately tell by the clothing and accent that this is either the estate factor or the landowner. It turns out to be the landowner's husband. PC Rafferty explains the situation. The newcomer looks serious and asks if he can have a word with Stephen, now, as he has to leave on urgent business? 'Certainly, but I will have to stay in the room with you.' This from PC Rafferty. We all stay.

'Stephen, have you done anything wrong?'

'No, sir, I have not.'

'That's good enough for me, officer. Now, I really must get on…'

I realise that there are six of us in a small house and suggest to PC Rafferty that a couple of us wait outside while he conducts his search. If he finds anything needing my skills, he can call me back in.

I'm standing outside in the square with Angus Macaskill of SEERAD (Scottish Executive Environment and Rural Affairs Division) when a middle aged, elegantly-dressed woman appears through the entrance archway. She walks straight over to us. 'What's going on? I am the owner.' Angus explains that poisoned birds have been found on the estate and a search of the gamekeeper's house is in progress. Our conversation then continued.

'This is the midnight knock on the door!'

'It's actually 8.30 in the morning.'

'Who are you?'

'I'm Dave Dick of the RSPB.'

'It's a police state.'

Angus: 'I'm Angus Macaskill from the Scottish Executive. We have the authority to search any land and buildings when banned pesticides have been found.'

'Everyone knows the Executive are against shooting – all my friends have been raided.'

Angus: 'Actually, I'm a shooter myself.'

'Well, there's too many of these harriers about anyway. And what does it matter if a few kestrels get killed?'

She then left.

Kestrels? Birds famous for their mouse-eating habits – what possible harm would they cause to a shooting estate? This lady was either very ignorant about wildlife or had become confused by anger.

The action soon moved to an open-sided garage area taking up one side of the square, one corner filled with children's bikes and plastic cars. A free-standing wooden cupboard, within three feet of the nearest bike, is opened up. On a shelf stands a grey music cassette holder which PC Rafferty opens up, to find several cassettes wedged against a Nescafé jar, complete with label but stuffed full of blue- black granules. A second Nescafé jar, also full of blue granules, is then found in a paint tin inside an old wooden cupboard, also feet away from the kids' bikes.

This juxtaposition of everyday objects and deadly chemicals, traps and weapons is something I've seen on many occasions on gamekeeper searches. I've heard investigators say that there is no point in searching dwelling houses, as no one would be so stupid or irresponsible, as to keep such things near them or their family. They're absolutely wrong. I've seen alphachloralose next to the cornflakes, a tin of CYMAG in a bedroom cupboard with damp on the walls and many instances of live ammunition in ashtrays and in vases in living rooms.

This jar has a handwritten label stuck on one side: 'Turnips.' That's interesting. A clear case of getting your defence in first. The legitimate use for carbofuran, the poison which had killed a buzzard and a goshawk on the estate and the reason we were there, is to kill soil insect pests of crops like turnips, but only when drilled professionally into the soil using agricultural equipment by a trained operator. We all (SEERAD, RSPB and police) recognised the granules as identical to carbofuran seized on other searches. Later analysis confirmed this. It is a deadly poison and it's illegal to decant it into an unlabelled container. More importantly, it was the same chemical identified in the two birds of prey already found on the estate and analysed.

Stephen was asked about the poison. He denied any knowledge of the jars. By this time the estate factor had appeared and told the keeper that it would be best to admit any knowledge of poison, or poisoning, to the police. The denials continue. It was decided to carry out a search of the estate, starting with the location where a member of the public had found the two dead birds of prey. We all moved to a hilltop immediately above the steadings. We soon found a line of dead rabbits and pheasants, cut open and with blue granules liberally sprinkled all over them. This is when Muir finally decides to confess to the police that the poison in the garage is his and that he has placed these baits.

It is decided that we form a line and carry out a systematic search of the area. Muir joins the line and in a bizarre parody of a pheasant drive, we begin to walk through a conifer plantation and an area of open mixed woodland surrounded by ploughed fields. We find dead buzzards everywhere – under piles of brash but also literally hanging from trees where they have died in flight or have fallen off a perch. One bird has made it a few hundred metres from the baits to die in the centre of a ploughed field. None got further than a quarter of a mile. We retrieve over twenty dead buzzards in this one small area. It was a shocking sight, even to a hardened investigator like myself, but the most unusual sight by far was that of the keeper helping us, with apparent enthusiasm, to find the birds he had killed.

FIVE MONTHS LATER: WEDNESDAY, 25 AUGUST 2004, SELKIRK SHERIFF COURT.

After the usual attempts at plea bargaining by the defence agent, this time resisted by a Depute Fiscal with a very strong case, guilty pleas are entered and a sentencing hearing is held. This begins, as always, with the Crown (Depute Fiscal) describing the case to the sheriff. Always crucial to the outcome, this consists of a concise but hopefully inclusive précis of events from the police report and any other sources available to, or asked for, by the Crown. It should also give some opinion on the severity of the charges and any background regarding the damage, real or potential, of such crimes. On this occasion, the Procurator Fiscal presents her case excellently. The sheriff casts an eye around the unusually busy court and fixes on the packed press benches opposite. 'There are some people who may think they know what is in the public interest here... and others who do not.' It was a strangely cryptic remark. 'Is there anyone here who can tell me why there should be such strong public interest over the killing of 20 buzzards?' The Depute Fiscal then pointed me out as a representative of the RSPB. I was called to the front of the Court. This happened to me three times in my career and I would not recommend it to anyone of a nervous disposition. Sheriff Farrell asked me about the importance of buzzards in the countryside and what effect they might be having on the 'balance of nature', a revealing question, as the shooting industry use the same term when trying to justify killing predators. I gave a robust defence of buzzards and their place in nature and also pointed out that the putting out of thousands of reared pheasants on the estate was what really upset any balance. Predators would quite naturally respond to that, although buzzards are not noted pheasant killers. I also pointed out the fact that the Borders relied heavily on tourism, which was damaged by the activities of this poisoner. I was then thanked and sent back to the body of the Court.

Defence mitigation consisted of stating that pheasant rearing and shooting was a non-profit making part of the Estate, that the owners were totally unaware of the poisoning and that the keeper, who was 38 years old, had worked there for 17 years. It was also added that pheasant shooting had now been suspended and that Muir had been kept on in other employment. There was then the utterly unfounded suggestion (and of course with no evidence put forward and no chance for the Crown to respond in kind) that the first poison findings were the work of a trouble-making 'conservationist' who was a mile away from the nearest right of way. It was a clear attempt to muddy the waters and appeal to that sheriff's known decision on a previous 'no landowner permission for access' decision on a wildlife case (McLeod, Peebles Sheriff Court).

My notes of that day show what happened next. (See across).

After the sentencing I left the building pursued by the media – two TV companies and at least ten paper or radio journalists – and spent the next two hours giving interviews. Halfway through, a spokesman for Wemyss and March Estate appeared, refusing to give his name to the media but reading a

... Sheriff himself suggested Muir would not be losing his job (!?) ... then gave £500 fine for culpable and reckless conduct and £5000 for baiting and killing birds while admonishing him on his possession of carbofuran for the purpose of killing – no reason given for that admonishment. No threat of imprisonment except for a casual 'I see I could give out a fine of £80,000 or six months prison,' in a tone which suggested that would be ludicrous.

prepared statement which said that Muir would remain suspended while 'an internal investigation' was completed. He also said that all shooting was suspended that year on Barns.

In my interviews I said that this was a significant, large fine but that I was disappointed that Muir had not at least been threatened with prison. Many articles later appeared to suggest that I had wanted him jailed. My strongest comments were kept for the estate, saying I was astonished that he had not immediately lost his job.

Despite a conviction for one of the worst poisonings I have heard of in the UK over the past 25 years, a few months after the Scottish Parliament voted overwhelmingly to change the law to allow for imprisonment for such offences due to their seriousness, and despite his having lied to his employer in front of the police and several civilian witnesses, Muir is still employed on that estate.

I have seen well over 50 gamekeepers in Scotland convicted of wildlife offences since 1984. Very, very few have ever been sacked.

That was in 2004, two years before I resigned, and not a lot had changed since Rodenhurst in 1990, the first serious poison conviction. We'd had dozens of court cases; hundreds of poisoning incidents, including sea eagles, golden eagles, red kites, hen harriers, peregrine falcons, goshawks, buzzards, various wild animals, working dogs and pets; huge amounts of publicity; and condemnation of poisoners from all sides, including landowners' and gamekeepers' associations.

Last year, 2009, was reported to be the worst year on record for wildlife poisoning in Scotland.

7

ON BECOMING AN EXPERT

The RSPB's clearly-stated policy has always been that it is the police who should be enforcing wildlife crime legislation. For most of the 1980s and early 1990s, I was cautiously optimistic that that goal was moving closer in Scotland. From being an impossible dream, it looked like becoming an achievable reality, thanks to an increasing amount of real casework: not just recording crimes but actually being involved in court cases. This meant a growing network of experienced police officers with actual casework experience. They were, for the most part, your ordinary cop, front line constables with all that that entails. They were responsible for many different duties and always subject to pressure from a sergeant or inspector. Wildlife crime never was, and still is not, a high priority within general policing, no matter what senior officers might say in public. I'm pleased to say that my work in a couple of cases changed that locally, but the statement stands for most of Scotland.

The Wildlife Liaison Officer network started in England, when a very senior officer from a force in the south, who happened to be a birdwatcher, helped as a volunteer in the annual 'catch the egg thief' operation run by the RSPB and Kite Committee in the Welsh Borders. While he was there, he saw not only the dedication of the team but also what they were up against. When my southern colleagues also gave him the real facts about the breadth of wildlife crime – including within his own force area - he decided to do something about it.

And so the first Wildlife Liaison Officers (WLOs) were designated. Scotland wasn't far behind – I made sure of that. Through a combination of direct approaches to Chief Constables (or at as high a level as we could get access to, usually a Superintendent) and use of the media, we were gradually able to convince senior police officers that having a Wildlife Officer in their force would be good for PR without causing a drain on resources. The network grew in an almost random fashion, certainly without any coordination between forces, although I occasionally heard, off the record, of Chief Constables putting gentle personal pressure on each other. Nothing succeeds like success, though, and I knew the enormous benefit of pushing forward the casework of these early WLOs in the press and media. If I hadn't done this, no one would have. Not only were there no dedicated press officers in most police forces at that time, there were none in the RSPB in Scotland either!

The earliest Wildlife Officers were called Wildlife Liaison Officers for a reason. Their job was to act as a coordinating point between a case officer (usually the unfortunate constable who received the initial report of an alleged crime) and those with specialist knowledge of wildlife and the countryside, members of Raptor Study Groups and badger groups and so on, people like me who might be called experts. It was not envisaged that they would act as case officers directly handling casework.

That, of course, was pie in the sky. For a start, the actual cases were always untypical of other police work and therefore needed a lot of work. No Procurator Fiscal would want or agree to handle a wildlife case without a decent background report attached to the police report. Understandably, in the early days at least, the Fiscal had to be convinced of that unchanging dictat, 'Is this in the public interest?' by a presentation of facts such as the conservation status of the bird or animal involved. That, of course, was not exactly a normal constable's area of expertise. An experienced WLO would eventually learn such facts, or at the very least know where to access them, and that meant coming to – guess who? Some of the early WLOs, mostly volunteers with a personal interest, would bring some wildlife knowledge with them, but a little knowledge could be a dangerous thing.

In the Borders (Lothian and Borders Police) the first WLO was a constable, Donald Ritchie, with a hobby interest in game shooting. He was a pleasant enough man but I don't recall any serious casework coming through him during his short tenure. When he left in 1987, I received a phone call which should be a lesson to those foolish enough to believe the 'lore of the countryman' rubbish. 'Hello Mr Dick, my name is Sgt Malcolm Henderson. I'm phoning from Jedburgh police office. I've been told you are the man to talk to. My Chief Constable has appointed me as the new Wildlife Officer for the force. Now, I admit right away that that's because I'm a shooter – I don't know anything about birds!' So both good news and bad. He wasn't a volunteer but was honest enough to admit that he was no wildlife expert. That was far, far better than some blow-hard who thought he knew all about wildlife and wildlife crime because he shot a few pheasants on a local estate or had once locked up a deer poacher. I was to meet a few of those in years to come. I mean this as no slur on Malcolm, of course, who went on to be one the longest-lasting and most dedicated WLOs and with whom I worked on many successful cases. He resigned from his post as a Wildlife Crime and Environment Officer in 2004. Now in retirement, he is a highly competent birdwatcher specialising in goshawks.

In Dumfries and Galloway, the first wildlife cop was a Sergeant Ken Bruce. He had a lifelong interest in birds, in particular the common buzzard, and was one of a tiny band of policeman who had dealt with wildlife casework before the development of WLOs. This smallest force in the UK in terms of staffing, although certainly not in terms of area or wildlife interest, had two WLOs by the early 1990s, splitting the area into west and east. In 1988 I first met Andy Dickson, a constable based at Moffat and, importantly, a member of the local Mountain Rescue Team. I helped Andy become a lifelong peregrine watcher and over the next few years he helped rope me in to what you might call some of the more interesting cliff nests around Moffat. This was, of course, one of the most heavily- targeted areas for egg and chick theft in Scotland and I owe a lot to him. Together, we also put in a lot of time giving training talks and back-up to the volunteers at the National Trust's Grey Mare's Tail site. It became a testing ground for some of the ingenious alarm systems made by an Edinburgh-based birdwatcher, Jim Steele, who also happened to be an electronics boffin working for Hewlett Packard. Our best capture at that site was a gang of Geordie housebreakers who wandered into our field of interest to the obvious pleasure of the local police.

In Strathclyde, we had Willie Alan based around Ayr, who was so keen to become a WLO that in 1991 he actually made the trek through to my office in Edinburgh to get advice after seeing some TV publicity about our work. We had several years working together, mainly investigating the activities of Mr Morrison, his notorious local falcon thief. Ronnie Sewell, a constable based at Helensburgh, was another lifelong companion I met through wildlife work. Perhaps his most impressive case was a successful admission and conviction of a fish farm worker who poisoned hundreds of gulls using the deadly chemical NUVAN. I spent a gruelling day, helping him interview over 50 staff members at this large site until the final breakthrough. The most high-profile WLO from that force however, has to be Finlay Christine, the Mull WLO, who appeared on the scene in 1996. Strathclyde, the second largest force in the UK, with an enormous personnel resource and a wildlife environment which stretched from Glasgow tenements to the machair of Tiree, was a disappointment to me throughout my career. We received remarkably few reports of wildlife crime. Remember the words of the governor of Barlinnie? 'We have some unpleasant people in here.' Well, the same could be said of many towns and the city of Glasgow and, coming as I do from generations of Glaswegians, I can say that with confidence and without prejudice. For the majority of my time, and certainly during the 1980s and 1990s, this force merely paid lip service to the WLO network, designating Superintendents of each Division as WLOs and then putting no resources into either casework or crime prevention. Those few officers who did take this type of crime seriously were all too often doing so in their own unpaid time with little thanks for their efforts.

Central Scotland, which had at least one area with a serious egg theft problem, eventually designated Inspector Ian Cameron in 1994, although individual officers at Lochearnhead and Callendar, in particular, worked closely with us as we tried to stop golden eagle egg thefts.

Fife, a known problem area for estate-based poisoning in the East Neuk and finch trapping in the West, eventually came on board around 1997 with the appearance of Constable Ronnie Morris. Ronnie 'retired hurt' after several years of unsuccessfully attempting to get resources for wildlife crime work. He had even put together his own WLO network of interested officers across the force area, before his frustration caused him to drop his wildlife role.

Grampian was a bit of an exception to this litany of senior police apathy, again, at first, due mainly to a series of very dedicated individual officers who always had to work above and beyond the call of duty to get any success. Jim Walker, John Sellar and Roddy McInnes fall into this category. Jim Walker soon resigned in disgust, John Sellar moved on to a fascinating career working in Switzerland for CITES and Roddy McInnes moved on to other police work.

In Northern Constabulary, containing perhaps Scotland's most valuable wildlife resource, I built up my own network of excellent police contacts by finding keen individual officers who happened to have become involved in wildlife casework. That involvement was completely arbitrary and mainly came about as a result of geographical accident, through having been posted to an area with a high incidence of egg theft or simply by having been the man on shift when an incident occurred. I watched some of these guys move up through the force to Inspector level or higher, or into CID, throughout the 1980s and 1990s. As with the other forces, much of that experience and contact was lost when the three Ps of Partnership, Protocols and Politics made their appearance, demanding that we deal with one Coordinator or risk the wrath of the force. What a waste that was. Jim Neil (Tongue), Paul Eddington (Bettyhill and Ullapool), Michael Macdonald (Rhiconich and Bonar Bridge), Colin Soutar (Morvern) and many others, from Kingussie up to Orkney: all these officers worked hard and successfully on individual cases.

Lastly, we had Tayside and again a number of good keen officers who just happened to be around at the right time. John Watson in Aberfeldy, for instance, already mentioned in the 1987 Glen Lyon egging case. The ace in the hole there, however, turned out to be Bob Macmillan, already a Superintendent in the late 1980s. Bob had been a keen merlin and eagle fieldworker in the 1970s and had dealt with at least one golden eagle poisoning before my time but which I had heard of. Perthshire was a hotbed of estate-based crime and I spent many hours on those moors, following up poisoning, trapping and shooting reports with varying success. Wildlife crime had also come to much wider public attention through the thefts of osprey and golden eagle eggs and, I'm pleased to say, some successful court cases. As the Scottish WLO network grew, it was obvious that this force was crying out for more resources. In 1993, Alan Stewart, a serving Inspector at that time, was appointed as the Force WLO coordinator with

PC IAN HUTCHINSON

One of Tayside's earliest WLOs was PC Ian Hutchison, whose friendly face belied his fierce love of nature and his previous employment as a Military Policeman. Ian and I worked on several cases together, including one major gamekeeper case involving finch trapping, the use of gin traps, stuffed animals and allegations of poisoning. Despite our hard work and the fact that we found a mass of evidence, the case fell for the simple reason that Tayside Police failed to give him any back-up officers on the search, leaving us both in a very exposed position. This culminated in a thoroughly undeserved dressing down from the local Procurator Fiscal after a 'lost' trial, the inevitable result of too little manpower leading to poor recording and poor coordination by the Prosecutor. Ian should be remembered far more positively, as the instigator of Operation Easter, the highly-successful joint RSPB and police operation targeting egg thieves. An early computer buff, he spent a week on secondment with me (Tayside led the way on this when partnership really meant what it said) and saw the potential of the mass of data already held by my section on our secure database. 'Why don't the police have this stuff?' came his astonished cry. 'Because they've shown absolutely no interest in keeping it and wouldn't know what to do with it if they had it!' I replied, speaking from experience. 'We'll see about that!' said Ian. This led to an initial meeting in Northumbria between RSPB Investigation staff and representatives of several forces on both sides of the Border, including Ian and those English forces with known thieves or egging problems. It was agreed that Tayside would be the coordinating force for the UK and that the idea was to target the main offenders, both on the road and in their home areas. Ian retired on health grounds soon after this and is now the sole paid employee of Scottish Badgers, carrying on excellent wildlife work. Alan Stewart took over the huge role as coordinator, and there followed years of chivvying forces all over the UK to keep their information updated and of leading what to date has easily been the most successful wildlife crime initiative ever attempted in the UK. There's been a massive measurable drop in egg thefts following many successful cases, including in recent years the jailing of a few persistent offenders.

three officers under his supervision. Like every other Scottish WLO, these were part-timers, meaning that they had somehow to fit in wildlife investigation work with their other duties.

In 1997, Alan was appointed as the first full time WLO in Scotland, albeit as a civilian, having retired from the police on the same day. I believe this was mainly due to Bob Macmillan, at that time an Assistant Chief Constable and nearing retirement. He had a network of WLOs split between the East and West Sections of Tayside, several of whom I had worked with on cases in the past but to all of whom I was to give training on wildlife investigation work. Things were looking good.

Monday, 7 May 1990

We are leaning against the side of a marked police car parked at the end of a rutted track in Highland Perthshire. We are in a grassy field and the bright white, newly-washed, saloon car looks out of place amongst the mole hills and broken-down dykes that lead up over the skyline. The officers are in uniform and trying to look nonchalant in front of this civilian, despite their Inspector's words of advice at Pitlochry – 'This is Mr Dick, he knows all about this type of thing, he's been at it for years so he'll keep you right' –while actually fascinated by the group of figures who have appeared on the hillside. Four very tall men and one short, obviously being escorted. The short man is wearing hill walker's clothing but the four tall men are in uniformly-dark clothing – and carrying rifles. They are Royal Marine Commandos from HMS *Condor*, Arbroath, who hand the short man over to the police and, after exchanging a few words with me, walk away silently back up the hill and out of sight.

Back at Pitlochry police station I stand beside the 'hillwalker'. Although young, he's already a notorious egg thief. He looks utterly exhausted as the duty sergeant lists in slow and exact detail all the items which have been seized from him. He then charges him with all the items as 'possessions for use in an attempt to take osprey eggs.' In a moment of false bravado, the young man says, in an East Midlands accent, 'I was going to make a run for it, you know!' The sergeant and I both burst out laughing

On Tuesday, 7 August 1990, at Perth Sheriff Court, Wayne Short from Coventry was fined £2,500 and had his car forfeited.

This was one of the most successful uses of the military in bird protection. In the late 1980s and early 1990s, several different regiments were used to protect individual osprey, red kite and golden eagle nests in Scotland, England and Wales. It was a mutually beneficial series of operations – those in charge of training soldiers were delighted to have an opportunity to test their best men against 'live targets'. From my point of view, I have always preferred the physical presence of watchers at nest sites to the continually irritating electronic surveillance and alarm systems, which have an uncanny knack of breaking down at vital moments.

But there were fraught moments, even when working with elite troops. I will always remember the conversation I had in a hole in the ground with a Glaswegian Special Forces soldier, about to begin his several-day stint. His troop had just been briefed by me (don't go too near the birds, here's what egg thieves look and act like, here's what to do with any eggs they may have stolen), a police inspector (here's what to do and not to do with your suspects) and a Forestry Commision Ranger whose patch we were on. 'Mr Dick, Mr Dick….' I was last out and walking along a narrow muddy path when the man in black caught up with me. 'Is it alright if we take out the odd deer?' 'No, it isn't ****** alright! The Ranger would have a ****** fit!' 'Aw, go on, there wullnae be any loud bangs…' The deer wouldn't have known what had hit them and neither would any egger. Perhaps it was fortunate that no-one turned up that time and the birds got their young away safely.

One of the most annoying situations I had to face in the fight against egg thieves, but one in which I did not hesitate for a second in making my decision, involved another group from Arbroath. On Saturday, 6 May 2000, a group of Royal Marines caught two notorious egg thieves red-handed, taking osprey eggs from a tree nest near Aviemore. This watch had been organised by Roy Dennis, ex-RSPB manager and now a wildlife consultant. Only three days before, Roy and I together had briefed the Marines and the police. We were all delighted with this outcome: a clear message was being sent out to the egg thieves. Unfortunately, the legal system took a very long time to run its course and by the time a trial was finally arranged (yes, these two men were actually pleading 'not guilty') it was well into the winter of 2001, more than a year after the capture and also some months

The author in evidence suit at osprey nest

after the terrible events of 9/11. I received a phone call from the Inverness Procurator Fiscal (I was, as always, an expert witness in the case and had been discussing its development with the Fiscal from the start). He sounded rather embarrassed. 'Mr Dick, I am perfectly willing to call these Marines as witnesses but am told that the Regiment will be leaving for Afghanistan at any moment and they will therefore lose their chance to go there. Without them, the case will collapse. What do you think?' No matter how galling it was to see these two thieves get away with their crime, I could not stand in the way of young men who had spent their whole lives waiting to go on active service. It wasn't the kind of decision I'd expected to be making when I started in the job.

Another example, of successful close working with police started as yet another bird poisoning case but turned into something altogether different. With a lifelong interest in natural history, I was of course well aware and concerned that a variety of non-bird taxa were being targeted or harassed by wildlife criminals. Often these animals had little or no legal protection from cruel treatment or even removal from the wild. The animal in this case is an exception.

As a force, Strathclyde Police do not have a good record in resourcing the fight against wildlife crime. When the first Wildlife Police (then called Wildlife Liaison Officers) began to be appointed by a few far-sighted forces around the UK in the mid- to late 1980s, the response from Scottish forces was muted. Strathclyde took the easy route of appointing Divisional Superintendents as WLOs, meaning that any real wildlife cases were dealt with in the usual *ad hoc* manner by the lower ranks. The force, though, could say that it had around 20 WLOs.

It was, though, my experience with this force, as with many others, that despite a lack of encouragement from above, there were always officers who had an interest in investigating wildlife crime. This interest usually took the form of a love of nature, allied to a strong dislike of criminals thumbing their noses at the law – the ideal profile for a wildlife officer, in fact. One such officer was Inspector Willie Allan, based at Ayr, a sergeant when we first met and last spotted as a chief inspector.

Willie and I worked on many cases and reports of falcon theft and finch trapping in Ayrshire but also the perennial and widespread crime of bird of prey persecution. I was disappointed, then, when he told me that he would not be able to lead a search of a suspected buzzard poisoner's premises near Sorn. He reassured me that he had found an able substitute in PC William 'X.' based at Mauchline police office. 'He knows nothing about wildlife law, but he's keen.'

TUESDAY, 5 OCTOBER 1993

I arrived at Mauchline police office at 6.15 p.m. The only person there was a uniformed police officer, sitting at his desk smoking a cigar and reading a copy of the Wildlife and Countryside Act. 'You'll be Mr Dick of the RSPB?' 'Aye.' 'Here, this is a great read, some of the names of these things are hilarious...' He then read from some of the little-used lists of flowers and insects. My heart sank. It was just my luck. Not only did he have no experience of wildlife investigation but he thought he was a comedian, too. By the end of the night, though, my respect for Willie had grown by leaps and bounds. He was a quick learner.

Three buzzards had been found poisoned by alphachloralose, a narcotic rodenticide still at that time the most commonly-used by wildlife poisoners, although already being restricted to those die-hard poisoners linked to game shooting. The area where the birds had been found was well within the boundaries of a pheasant shooting estate, where the 'vermin control' was carried out by a single gamekeeper. Further local intelligence

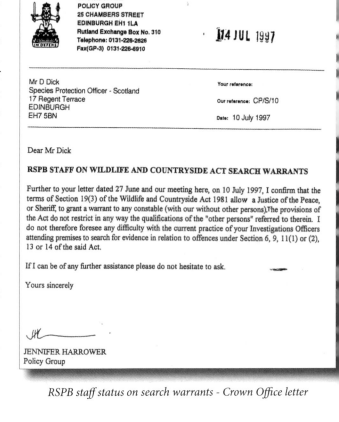

RSPB staff status on search warrants - Crown Office letter

pointed the finger at this same man. Willie Allan had arranged for a search warrant to be available if necessary but in fact, when we arrived at the keeper's house, he made no objection to our looking around. (As the fight against persecution became increasingly bitter, and resistance to the law better organised and more entrenched, such a 'friendly' search without a warrant became a thing of the past).

Willie, the keeper and I began looking round a small hut adjacent to his house, set in rural surroundings. The first thing I noticed was a chest freezer, always interesting in such a search. I have on many occasions found that poisoners and other persecutors of wildlife keep their dead victims frozen, presumably for sale to taxidermists at a later date. Aware, as always, that the police were in charge of any search, I asked Willie if I could look in the freezer. 'Go ahead.' The following conversation still ranks as one of the best examples I could give of explaining a keen police officer's way of thinking, as well as being a fine example of the black humour that got me through my long days. The keeper was standing beside us throughout.

'Willie, there's a sack in the freezer. Can I open it?'

'Go ahead!'

'Look, Willie!'

'What is it?'

'It's a badger, Willie…'

And now the killer line: 'Is that good?'

'That's very good. You know that Wildlife and Countryside Act?'

'Aye.'

'Well, there's a Badgers Act…'

'A Badgers Act!?'

'Aye, and I think you can get the jail for it…'

'So we take the badger?'

'Aye, we take the badger.'

The keeper chipped in. 'I found it dead on the road, I was keeping it to have it stuffed.'

During the hour or so that followed, with nothing else of interest found or seized, the keeper said, 'See that badger – I snared it!' and, ten minutes later, 'See that badger? I shot it, to finish it off…'

A post mortem showed that the badger had indeed been shot and that its stomach was full of grain, presumably from a pheasant feeder. On 12 June 1994, at Ayr Sheriff Court, after a lengthy court proceeding, the keeper was found guilty under the Protection of Badgers Act 1992 of killing and possession of the badger and was fined a total of £500.

For the rest of his career in Strathclyde, Willie was known as Billy the Badger.

Mull is really worth a chapter on its own. During my first peregrine contract in 1981, I had often gazed across from the mid-Argyll coast at its imposing cliffs. My first visits were in the company of other RSPB staff when we visited the site of the first breeding attempts and then to the site of the first successful breeding, in 1985, of the reintroduced white-tailed sea eagles. Due to the very real threat from egg thieves, the site had been protected throughout the season by Keith Morton and Dave Sexton, both now senior staff members. The eggs of some of the first-known osprey breeding attempts, in the mid-1950s, had been stolen and if eggers had known the whereabouts of the first returning sea eagles, there would have been a queue of them eager to repeat those 'feats' and make their name.

For several years after this, things were relatively quiet on the island. The presence of several pairs of successfully-breeding birds was known to a few local farmers and landowners and a small but growing number of birdwatchers. The first rumblings of discontent were coming from a couple of sheep farmers, though. Mull already had a reputation as a place where golden eagles were not always welcome – the previous NCC manager told me in 1981 that he would be chivvied about eagles whenever he visited the island. We now had a presence on Mull in Richard Evans, who became an expert not only on the eagles but also on the island politics during this fraught period. He was a good friend and companion to me and an even better one to Mull's wildlife.

Inevitably we began to hear rumours from within the notoriously gossipy and leaky world of egg thieves that nest sites were known and were being passed around. The greatest damage is done at the very dangerous interface between boastful twitchers and real thieves. By March 1996, all my instincts were shrieking 'Mull' at me and we got a last-minute anonymous tip-off. As bad luck would have it, I also got a new manager right at that time. I informed him, out of courtesy, that I would be off to Mull at the end of the month for at least a week. He disagreed. So I took a week out of my precious leave – in fact, in those years, I seldom used all my leave and the concept of time off in lieu would have meant my spending a large chunk of the winter on holiday – and headed for Mull.

I drove up the 'eggers' trail' which I had followed at this time for so many years – the Trossachs, Glen Lyon, Orchy, Glencoe, Morvern and back to Appin, noting every parked car and every passing car in the Glens, waiting for the 'click', dropping in on a gamekeeper here and a stalker there, all friends and acquaintances from earlier hunts. The snow-tipped mountains and their black-and-brown birch-clad slopes always look superb in late March, when the weather can be stunningly bright and clear and then change to a full-blown blizzard in the twinkling of an eye. All was quiet. At last I arrived at Oban and took the ferry across to Mull.

Thursday, 28 March 1995

It's early evening when Richard and I walk across the road from the small whitewashed police office and into the public bar of the Craignure Inn. It's my first time in there. Everyone stops talking, like a scene from a film ('Don't go out on the moor tonight, boys!'), a gigantic figure behind the bar (Billy McGregor, the legendary landlord, an ex-Royal Marine out of Glasgow's wild East End) looks at Richard and says one word. 'Well?' 'We got them!' The bar rang with loud cheers. I didn't put my hand in my pocket all night. It was the start of a wonderfully unhealthy relationship with that bar and the Mull locals. Don't tell me that the man in the street doesn't care about wildlife.

Almost as soon as I had arrived on the island, two days before, Richard had been told by a local van driver that he had seen a carload of young men acting suspiciously near a golden eagle's nest. We passed this on to the police, along with the car number. Thanks to the RSPB database, as always, the car was traced back to a notorious young egg thief, and a frantic search ensued. The police had almost given up – 'Maybe they've already left?' – when PC Finlay Christine spotted the car parked outside a B & B, almost within sight of the main police office in Tobermory. Discreet inquiries were made. The men were due to be leaving on the Oban ferry the next day.

Thursday morning, 5.15

Richard and I are up and moving, getting into position on hillsides overlooking a sea eagle nest. Never take your eye off the ball – we may have isolated one group of eggers but that was no guarantee that there wouldn't be more out there. My experiences on the north coast and elsewhere had taught me that. Fortunately, all was well at the nest we were watching and by 10.55 we arrived at the ferry terminal in Craignure in time to see the police searching a car which had been pulled out of the ferry queue.

One of the aces we held in the long game of cat and mouse with egg thieves was that they regularly underestimated the professionalism of Scottish police officers. I was surprised and rather appalled to find, after some years of having to stand and watch, that there was almost no training in the interviewing of suspects during the average constable's career. However, Finlay Christine was no 'average constable'. He had moved to Mull looking for a quiet life after years spent policing in Glasgow, including working in frontline firearms squads.

We had kept a discreet distance, mainly because I might have been known to them by sight, the downside of a long career and the use of the media. I was smuggled into the tiny police office and updated on the case so far. All three suspects were known to me, all three had previous, egging-related convictions. This was a serious crew and a seriously good capture. They had cameras and used film, abseil rope, climbing spikes, a small net, head torches, a catapult and weighted line, rucksacks, binoculars, a sheath knife, night vision equipment and marked OS maps. In fact, all the equipment your top-line egg thief would need. The next few hours were a pantomime of the eggers being brought one at a time out of the small cells and questioned about their equipment, their whereabouts and what they had been up to while on Mull . I would then be brought out of the toilet, discuss progress with the police and then return to my place before the next suspect was brought out. As expected, they treated the police like idiots and made significant admissions. After the films were processed and Richard and I were able to study the photos and their marked maps (which included sites for osprey, golden eagle and dotterel nests across Scotland), it became clear that they had robbed at least two golden eagle eyries where they had photographed the eggs in their nest. Unfortunately, without the actual eggs as evidence, they could only be charged with disturbance to the adult birds.

I reminded the police that to be an egg thief clearly means you have an egg collection and that this was a golden opportunity to gather more evidence by having their home addresses searched. That may seem obvious to people like my colleagues and me, who had been through this many times, but most police have not dealt with egg thieves before. There then followed the usual desperate attempts to get English forces to carry out searches. One of the eggers was from the Liverpool area – I recall the Mull police being given chapter and verse on how busy the duty Inspector was and that he couldn't spare resources to look for bird's eggs. We kept at him until he finally relented. The clock is always ticking in this kind of case: one phone call and your evidence can be spirited away. The case resulting from such a house search was quite often far more important than the original capture in the field.

So that's what I did on my holidays in 1996. On Monday, 3 February 1997 two of the men were fined £2,000 each, the sheriff saying that 'The penalties are ludicrous. It is ridiculous that

I am unable to impose a prison sentence.' He then went on to do just that for the driver of the eggers' car, who was driving while disqualified. The sheriff's point was repeated many times in the mass of publicity which followed this case. It was another step in the long, long wait for a change in the law.

The best result here, however, was that Strathclyde Police and the people of Mull woke up to what was happening to their wildlife. This lead to the Mull police (Finlay Christine and Sgt Erskine) being given time and personnel each spring to set up an operation to protect the eagles of Mull, under the generic title of Operation Easter. At least two more egging cases came out of Mull in the following years. Many islanders joined a new Birdwatchers' Club which provided volunteer watchers for many years. Eventually, Mull was branded 'Eagle Island' by the tourist board, leading to a huge boost to the local economy. Any egg thief now would have to run the gauntlet of involved locals, visiting and local birdwatchers, RSPB staff and well-informed police officers.

On a personal note, it also led to me playing many gigs at the Craignure Inn, but that's another story.

The cases I've described above are only a sample of what was an increasingly large, complex workload. I'm not saying that all of my managers were ignorant or uncaring – I always received glowing annual appraisals, including suggestions from my manager to 'take it easy.' He recognised that I worked very hard and they always included comments from me about wanting more staff and resources, but they never materialised. There was always some excuse. 'Wait until we've finished Regionalisation, we need to set up education, planning, fundraising…' Meanwhile, with more and more well-publicised incidents and court cases, the membership and the public in general wanted more to be done, creating a spiralling workload.

In addition to the casework, all of which had to be catalogued and recorded for inclusion in the increasingly-sophisticated computer database – card index files were a thing of the past – I became increasingly embroiled in the Raptor Study Groups, eventually organising the first Scottish Conferences. These were joyful affairs, for although we were all aware of the huge battles we had on our hands, we were all enthusiasts, sometimes meeting for the first time, and a huge amount of valuable information began to be exchanged. The beginnings were laid of the very sophisticated science-driven network and initiatives that exist today. The success of our Scottish Raptor Groups had been noted by our neighbours and my colleagues across the UK and beyond. I was in demand and attended inaugural meetings of Raptor Groups in Cumbria, Wales, Northern Ireland and Eire and gave advice to several more, from northeast England down to the New Forest. All of that had to be fitted in with my Investigations work, but I was still young and keen. We eventually set up committees and systems, including an overall Scottish Raptor Study Group (SRSG) with Patrick Stirling-Aird as secretary. Thank God for him – I was never one for paperwork when I could avoid it. Patrick, an already seasoned peregrine fieldworker with a passion for the species, was also a lawyer and part of a landowning family – unusual credentials for a RSG member. He was quite rightly made an MBE in later years for his raptor work, including much hard work on government inquiries.

The WLO network also needed regular servicing. It should never be forgotten that the RSPB ran the first 11 UK WLO Conferences, which at the time seemed no only normal but quite right and proper. Any note of defensiveness here springs from the fact that I inevitably have to refer to the modern decline in the relationship between the RSPB and the WLO network, with certain elements within the justice system behaving today as if the RSPB wants to usurp and potentially disrupt the enforcement of wildlife law. How did it ever get that bad?

In those days the UK Conference moved to a different force area each year, lately with different Investigations staff in charge. My own turn came in autumn 1994, when I was given the task of organising the Belfast Conference. I thought at first that it was a poisoned chalice, but it turned out to be one of the best conferences ever, helped massively by the IRA declaring a ceasefire during the run-up to it. My organisational work there was mainly cosmetic, the real work being done by my secretary, Catherine Douglas, and the outstanding RUC Inspector and WLO, Mark Mason.

1994 was also the year of the first Scottish WLO Conference, which I organised jointly in Glasgow with John Ralston of SNH. Scottish Natural Heritage, which rose in 1991 from the ashes of the Nature Conservancy Council, would never take a frontline role in the fight against wildlife crime. The origins of this organisation – the result of a fairly blatant political hatchet job from Westminster – meant that the new régime was visibly nervous of anything resembling controversy. Crime investigation, and particularly court work, which must by its very nature be played out in the public eye, was becoming very controversial due to the increased lobbying by shooting interests. The funding of conferences, administration and publicity was seen as reasonably safe ground. The name of SNH is not steeped in glory when it comes to casework – most of the good information I received from SNH employees was on the understanding that they remained anonymous. All rather ludicrous, really.

In between all this organisational and political faffing about, of course, the criminals were still hard at it. Our experience of cases on both sides of the Border was building up nicely. I regularly supplied police officers, and even Fiscals, with the wording of successfully-used charges from previous cases. We helped draw up templates for wildlife search warrants and were generally referred to as experts in the field of wildlife crime investigation, from the handling of evidence at the scenes of crime using film, digital photography and video cameras, right through to being a safe pair of hands as crown expert witnesses in wildlife court cases. Our expertise was well known within the Crown Office. Keith Morton and I spent many hours with Robert Shiels, a Crown Office official and now an Honorary Fellow at the School of Law at the University of Edinburgh, compiling the first two editions of *Reports to the Procurator Fiscal: A Guide for Non-Police Reporting Agencies* – the rules of engagement between bodies such as the RSPB and the Scottish justice system.

By the early 1990s, at first at the insistence of individual Fiscals but later on as a matter of course, we were attaching background reports on the conservation status of any wild birds involved in a case, on our knowledge of the extent of the alleged crime and on the use of the legislation so far in previous cases, and were often listing previous convictions by the alleged offender. All this was taken from our legally-held and legally-run database, often the only source of Summary case information, particularly regarding English cases, which we advertised widely and publicly to Fiscals and WLOs alike. The only limitation on this perfect partnership was staff time to input the daily flow of information.

On two occasions I was asked by a sheriff, puzzling over an appropriate sentence, to provide a report directly to him on the conservation implications of a crime. I have already mentioned that I was occasionally unexpectedly called on to stand up in court, after being pointed out by a Fiscal, to give a totally unprepared explanation of some point of bird conservation. That was perhaps the most gratifying acknowledgement of my academic and practical knowledge and a clear recognition that the 1981 Act was a piece of conservation legislation based on science, not just on common knowledge.

It would be a mistake to think, however, that everything was running smoothly in the rarified atmosphere of Sheriff Courts. Human error and personal prejudice were evident at times, making a mockery of even the most perfectly prepared case. Two cases prove the point, both dealt with by what was perhaps Scotland's most eccentric sheriff at the time, Sheriff Ewan Stewart. In 1992, Sheriff Stewart, now long deceased, had the distinction of being the only sheriff to be dismissed from office in the latter half of the 20th century.

On Tuesday, 8 August 1989, at Lochmaddy Sheriff Court, the Fiscal, Mr McClory, outlined the Crown case against Alastair Hugh Scott, gamekeeper on South Uist Estate. He had been seen on 4 May 1989 by Stuart Benn, my assistant at the time, checking rabbit baits he had earlier put out, laced with alphachloralose. He was found in possession of three poisoned hooded crows. The Fiscal highlighted the fact that the baited area was frequented by golden eagles and buzzards which had been put at risk. Scott was pleading guilty. Sheriff Stewart, himself a sheep farmer, commented on the threat posed by crows and admonished him, a peculiarly Scottish judgment by which no penalty is imposed. He added that he wanted Scott to pay £300 to the RSPB 'for their trouble'.

Stuart Benn inspects a legally-set Fenn trap, c. 1990

This, of course, did not make me happy. I was quoted in the next day's *Glasgow Herald*, saying that I would use the money to go back and catch Scott again. This article caught the eye of a Sheriff David Noble. On Thursday, 10 August 1989 at Campbelltown Sheriff Court, as he gave a £500 fine to an Islay gamekeeper, Gillian Diviani, who had pled guilty to putting alpha eggs into a crow's nest, Sheriff Noble said, 'I take a different view from Sheriff Stewart who earlier this week admonished a gamekeeper.' That came after I was called out of the body of the Court and asked to make a ten-minute defence of the place of crows in nature.

It's 1991 and a sunny afternoon in Dornoch Sheriff Court where the trial of two alleged egg thieves from Liverpool has been dragging on. Charged with attempting to take two diver eggs and being in possession of an egg collector's kit, one of the men has already pled guilty to possession of oystercatcher (*Haematopus ostralegus*) eggs. I'm in the witness box giving expert evidence about egg collecting and the equipment they had. I've been there for hours. The defence lawyer, a Mr Harkiss, is getting visibly agitated. He's getting nowhere with his cross examination. Very unusually, it's starting to get personal and I don't think he liked me. Even more unusually, the sheriff has done nothing to stop our 'conversation', which has contained such gems as 'You think you are the man in the white hat, don't you, Mr Dick?' 'I don't wear white hats.' In a verbal flourish, the lawyer makes what he thinks is a telling point, turns to the sheriff – and stops mid-sentence as he realises, to his dismay, that Sheriff Ewan Stewart appears to be asleep. His head is down on his hands, his eyes are shut, his wig is slightly askew.

A dreadful silence follows. In despair, the lawyer looks across at the Fiscal, Henry Westwater, who is leaning back in his chair, smoking. Eventually Henry, with a look of resignation, makes a dumb play of lifting something heavy with both hands, then pulling them wide apart, as if dropping something. Harkiss catches on and lifts a heavy legal book off the table in front of him and drops it with a crash. The sheriff's head comes up and I am being questioned once again, as though nothing has happened. We continue for the rest of the afternoon until the trial is adjourned, part-heard, and a new date is set for continuation. It never resumes as Sheriff Stewart has been removed from office. The egg thief, who had already pled guilty, is fined £50 but the other man on trial has his case abandoned.

Not all sheriffs were like that, of course, but I was often exasperated by their apparent lack of understanding of the gravity of many of these cases, particularly wildlife poisonings where deadly chemicals were involved, despite the combined efforts of RSPB, police and Fiscals working together. All too often we were made to feel like the joke at the end of the news, despite obvious growing public anger at the wildlife crimes being unearthed.

I think of David Minns as a conservationist of the old school. He will consider those before him – men like George Waterson and Seton Gordon – in the same light, as the torch has been passed on. David's generation were the first and unlikely full-time conservationists and were no doubt delighted to be so. Without exception, they had come into the conservation world from another profession or livelihood. In David's case, it was school teaching, but I know of former flower shop managers, accountants, lawyers, laboratory technicians, crofters, scientists and farmers who made that jump in the 1960s, 1970s and early 1980s. It was the mid- to late-1980s before conservation-based college or university courses began to churn out the next generation of conservation professionals.

In the 1960s this really was a jump into the unknown. There were no careers for such people. They had a passion for birds, plants, mammals or simply nature as whole and they followed their hearts. These people are unsung heroes, building up entire organisations such as the RSPB using their wits and, above all, mucking in with every job that came up. In David's case he founded, and continued to run, RSPB members' groups and film shows all over Scotland while simultaneously fighting the big guns of oil companies around the North Sea and learning from scratch how to lobby local and national politicians. This culminated in the stupendous international battles of the Flow Country forestry, Duich Moss peat extraction and the Cairngorms skiing developments. He was an eloquent and tireless campaigner for a better deal for Scottish wildlife.

Larsen trap illegally baited with live pigeon, Selkirk, 1994

By the time of the case outlined below, he was as seasoned a campaigner as the UK's now large and experienced conservation lobby could muster, but even he was shocked by what went on in this Scottish Sheriff Court. At the time he was in charge of the Public Affairs section of RSPB Scotland, with an interest in any activity that impinged on the public face of the organisation. Like those other stalwarts of the early Scottish RSPB, John Hunt and Frank Hamilton, he had served his time in the bad old days carrying out 24-hour nest watches for egg collectors and falcon thieves and was well aware of my work in Investigations, but had never attended a court hearing where a gamekeeper was on trial. He wanted to see for himself what I was up against.

In late August 1993, a birdwatcher out walking had come across a set Larsen trap, a legal portable crow and magpie trap, containing a live pigeon as bait. Not surprisingly, given the location and the bait, the trap had caught a goshawk. Goshawks are the pheasant keeper's public enemy number one and so the bird, along with any local buzzards or sparrowhawks, was undoubtedly the target. The trap was set in the middle of a pheasant shooting estate. The birdwatcher was horrified and released the goshawk, apparently unharmed, but could not release the live pigeon as it was padlocked into its trap compartment. The trapper was so confident of not being reported that he had locked the compartment to prevent 'do-gooders' from releasing his bait, a repeated and annoying problem for legitimate crow trappers in some areas, as not everyone thinks that using live crows or magpies as bait is acceptable. By locking the compartment, though, he had sealed in the evidence against himself.

The birdwatcher reported his find to the police. A friendly and knowledgeable policeman contacted me and we went to the site and concealed ourselves in nearby trees. A few hours later, a quad bike appeared with two young men on board, who went to the trap and re-set it (we had sprung it to protect other birds) and drove off. The two on the bike were identified by the police as an under-keeper and the landowner's son. The estate keepers were interviewed by the police and the head keeper admitted originally setting the trap in order to catch a goshawk. This admission was unusual, to say the least. In my already considerable experience, keepers at the time never admitted anything or pled guilty in court. Local talk was that he was carrying the can for the landowner's son, as there could be no question of the boy having to appear in court.

All this, then, led up to the head keeper appearing before the local sheriff.

Monday, 27 June 1994, the day of the court hearing, arrived, a full ten months after the trap was found. This was in fact a fairly short timescale, with most of these cases being dragged out by the Defence for well over a year. As David and I sat in the crowded court, we heard the accused head gamekeeper plead guilty to setting the trap to catch a goshawk. We then watched the Fiscal stand up and begin to outline the prosecution case and charges. The sheriff quickly interrupted him. 'What? You mean I can't kill these birds if they are taking my pheasants?' This local sheriff was involved in pheasant shooting. David and even I were flabbergasted. I had seen sheriffs apparently ignorant or contemptuous of basic wildlife law before, but this was perhaps the worst example so far.

It didn't make a good start for the Fiscal, who carried on with his job but must have known that he was getting nowhere. The defence QC, Kevin Drummond, now the sheriff at this same court, then waded in with mitigation, mainly revolving around the claim that the keeper was merely trapping the goshawk to move it elsewhere. This claim was unproven and came with not a scrap of evidence

The sheriff then merely admonished the head keeper – giving him a warning but no financial or other penalty – and we left the court, stunned and angry.

A man had admitted intentionally catching a goshawk, a Schedule 1 rarity and could have faced a fine of up to £5,000. A law whose very existence was the result of perhaps a century of struggle by conservationists had just been trampled on. If I felt bad, I could only imagine the shock and disillusionment felt by David Minns.

8

INTERNATIONAL INVESTIGATIONS

One area in which the RSPB were well ahead of the game was in international connections regarding wildlife law enforcement. In the early 1990s, when Andy Jones was head of my section, the first meetings of the Eurogroup against Bird Crime were hosted at our UK headquarters in Bedfordshire. They were a fascinating eye-opener for all of us. RSPB staff heard about all the fabulous 'exotic' species which our mainland European counterparts were trying to protect, while the foreign delegates got a chance to see what was, to their eyes, the stunningly large RSPB operation. I will always treasure the comment from Terje Axelson, the Norwegian delegate, on seeing the 9 a.m. rush of suited administrators heading into The Lodge: 'But why do you dress up for each other?' It brought to mind a similar comment by Iain Macleod, my first (and, at around 6' 4", by far my tallest) assistant in the mid-1980s, who was growing frustrated with some real or imagined obstacle put in our way by one such HQ 'base rat': 'The difference between you guys down here and us up there is that you carry briefcases and we carry rucksacks.' That was an insult back then. How times have changed!

The membership of the EABC was at first entirely composed of northern European countries and I recall meeting delegates from Dutch, German, Norwegian and Danish conservation NGOs. Our biggest shared problem was the activity of travelling German falcon thieves. Crimes committed in Scotland were being duplicated from Greenland to Turkey; with the opening up of Eastern Europe and the dismantling of the USSR after 1989, these thieves were also moving into central Asia. Particularly fruitful was the cooperation with German conservationists, who appeared to have very good working relationships with the German authorities. They were most unhappy about the depredations to their own peregrines and eagles by those same German thieves who had spread out into the world. Some excellent cases across Europe were successfully completed thanks to exchanges of intelligence on these people.

As the 1990s progressed, membership grew to include southern and eastern European NGOs from Malta to Romania. It was a genuine delight to see the enthusiasm with which these NGOs were working, often with the most meagre resources. Some of the work they were doing could quite rightly be described as courageous, such as facing down armed illegal hunters in Italy and Malta where the local population was, at best, apathetic. I'm sure the organisation will have become far more complex politically and perhaps less friendly – such

152

is the apparently inevitable course of any association – but I genuinely hope that the solidarity and determination I saw then have survived.

Most of these NGOs were still in their early phase of development and, like the early RSPB, the emphasis was on species protection, the direct effort to stop the killing or theft of rare birds. This, of course, made them very sympathetic to the work of my department. They were also very aware of the long history of both wildlife legislation and the RSPB within the UK and I was saddened to have to enlighten some people on the massive problems we were continuing to face. There were some surprises on our side of the fence too. We discovered that some of these countries had far stronger legislation, and certainly stronger enforcement by the police and courts, than we did. I recall how pleased we were to see two notorious English eggshell thieves, caught in Finland, receive a massive fine, a jail sentence and a ban from travel to any Scandinavian country for five years. In Scotland, at that time, they couldn't even have been arrested for the same crime. One of my English colleagues, Joan Childs, later carried out an extremely interesting piece of work collating all the wild bird protection legislation extant in the EABC member countries.

While all this networking was going on through my department at RSPB HQ, we were rather left out up in Scotland. I saw my colleagues getting regular trips – hardworking ones, I'm sure! – to mainland European countries while I plodded on with our own poisoners and other ne'er-do-wells.

But be careful what you wish for. By the beginning of 1991, I was aware that the RSPB had formed an unusual alliance with the Royal Society for the Prevention of Cruelty to Animals (RSPCA) and the Environmental Investigations Agency (EIA) to coordinate a campaign called 'Ban the Wild Bird Trade'. I have no idea what the genesis of the campaign was but its strongest argument, as far as I was concerned, was the fact that it was, with very few exceptions, illegal to trap wild birds in the UK but that we were importing thousands of live birds each year, trapped in the wild, from other parts of the world. We were being hypocrites. Campaigning by the RSPB in the early part of the 20th century against the widely-practiced trapping of finches for the pet trade had led to UK legislation as early as 1933.

I got a phone call from Andy Jones at HQ. 'You've got a sabbatical coming up, haven't you?' 'Yeeees…' 'How do you fancy going to Thailand?' 'I'd love to, but what's the catch?' 'We need someone to kick off the Ban the Wild Bird Trade campaign.' Ah, right.

One of the better ideas that RSPB management came up with over the years was the sabbatical programme. After being employed for seven years (very biblical!), all employees were entitled to a month working and/or travelling on a sabbatical project. A generous sum of money was provided to allow this. The project had to be connected to conservation and be run past the sabbatical committee to be assessed for suitability. People usually chose to travel abroad and to work with one of the many emerging conservation NGOs in a similar capacity to their work at home. The smarter staff members, or the more impoverished ones, used most of the money to pay for a long-haul flight to a destination where the cost of living was low and where there were new exotic birds to tick. Most of us were birders back in the 1980s, don't forget.

Not only did this excellent system quite literally expand the horizons of staff, it also gave a boost, through the import of expertise, to many struggling bird societies across the world.

153

I was the only one in Investigations at that time with real experience of the East. I had travelled with my Gujerati wife, Jayshree, to her sister's traditional wedding in North India in 1981 before we took a fascinating wander round Gujerat, Rajasthan, Delhi and Mumbai. Sadly, I had also returned in 1986 to scatter her ashes at a meeting of rivers in rural Gujerat.

The campaign team's research had identified Thailand as a centre for trade in birds, both legal and illegal. The UK was importing thousands of birds, mainly parrots and finches, but the trade involved millions of birds when the three big markets – Japan, USA and Europe as a whole – were taken into account. Using the brotherhood of birdwatchers, that wonderful, unofficial, international network, in addition to more official bodies such as WWF, Andy had homed in on Thailand as a country where the illegal trade in endangered species appeared to be rife and where, clearly, international dealers were operating. He also had a good friend in Bangkok, Derek Thomas, who was willing to help. All he needed now was an investigator with some experience of travel in the East and who would not be too put out by working undercover in a totally alien environment. Guess who sprang to mind?

The campaign was based on the idea of showing the public and decision makers in government that international (CITES) and national laws, supposedly protecting wild birds, were being widely flouted and to show the massive scale of trade. The RSPCA were focussing on the welfare side of things, from cruel trapping methods to the appalling conditions of transport. We already knew that there were high rates of mortality during the long journeys the birds had to make from remote jungle, bush or savannah to the cage in the local pet shop. We needed to show this in as graphic a manner as possible.

A frantic period of study ensued, mainly regarding parrots and their trade. I visited Edinburgh pet shops, not expecting to see much, and was astonished to find an Appendix 1 (of the Convention in Trade in Endangered Species – the CITES list) parrot from the Caribbean on display in a shop round the corner from my office. In what could almost be a motto for my whole tenure as an Investigations Officer, you don't know until you look for yourself.

Scotland as a whole, however, was not a big importer of live cage birds by 1991. We had a larger trade going in illegally-trapped native finches. The real action was talking place in the south of England, closer to the main trading ports and the wealthy buyers of the London area. What I did soon discover, though, was the scale of the sums, many thousands of pounds, being paid by collectors for rare and endangered parrots. As I had seen with birds of prey, a lucrative market will soon attract criminals. Two days before leaving for Thailand, I paid a very useful visit to the premises of a major bird importer in Essex. I was able to see some of the rare cockatoos and commoner finches and mynah birds from the Far East, which I expected to encounter closer to their native habitat.

As the time for my departure got closer, I started to feel more trepidation about the trip but was also greatly looking forward to solo travel in a new country. The old wanderlust I had felt in my long-haired guitar-toting days was coming back.

THURSDAY, 7 FEBRUARY 1991

After an extremely long series of flights I eventually arrived in Bangkok. I had never changed from my frugal student/itinerant musician/contract worker days and had booked myself on Biman (Bangladeshi) Air, the cheapest ticket I could find. I had left Heathrow at 3 p.m. and arrived in Bangkok at 10.30 p.m. local time the following day, after 24 hours of travelling, including a nine-hour wait in Dhaka airport. At least I got a couple of bird 'ticks' while gazing out of the terminal window.

I was met by Derek Thomas, my local contact, a Welsh birdwatcher on an exchange package with a local university where he lectured in mathematics. He had married a local university administrator, the very charming Lek, whose knowledge of local matters and, of course, ability to translate for me were invaluable. I regret never having seen them again since that time but I've never really had the funds or the time to travel for pleasure.

They took me in a taxi, through the noisy madness that is the Bangkok traffic, to my hotel in the centre of town. We then ate off a tin table, sitting on folding chairs, on a nearby pavement. The wonderful street food appeared, as if by magic, out of a narrow doorway and I had my first introduction to those dangerous little green cartwheels always supplied with food in Thailand – cross-cut slices of small, very hot chillies. I can't stress how indebted I was to Derek and Lek – my solo travels through Thailand would have been a lot more arduous had it not been for their good, practical advice. However, I was there to work and had meetings scheduled for the next morning.

In a hotel well used to foreigners ('farang' was one of the Thai words I quickly came to recognize), my breakfast the next morning resembled that of any UK B & B, except that my boiled egg came in a glass. Eaten in a courtyard bathed in the wonderful cool morning light that makes the East so beautiful – and comfortable – before the roaring heat of the middle of the day.

Off I went to the offices of the Wildlife Fund for Thailand (WFT), affiliated to the World Wildlife Fund (WWF), as it was then known. The WFT has the great advantage of having the King of Thailand as its patron, as in a country where the royal family is universally revered, that carries a lot of weight. I was introduced to the splendidly named Khun Pisit na Patalung, a charming and urbane Thai and the Director General of the WFT.

We got down to business right away. He gave me the names and addresses of four major traders and showed me press cuttings about the wild bird trade in Thailand. He told me that Thailand was a major staging post between the supplying neighbouring countries, such as Vietnam, Laos (both non-CITES signatories) and Kampuchea and also Indonesia, far to the south and east and western Europe, often via eastern Europe, with zoos being involved in laundering protected species, which were later sold on.

He told me that although, on paper, Thailand had wildlife protection laws, corruption was rife within the government departments supposedly enforcing them. As an example, he mentioned Bangkok's famous Chatuchak weekend market. Forest department officials, he said, could be seen confiscating protected species from traders on a Saturday (and indeed I later witnessed one such raid) but the same animals and birds will be back on sale on a Sunday after money has changed hands. WFT had been fighting this for years but it could take that long to remove just one corrupt official.

He told me where the main country trading centres were inside Thailand, a catalogue of wonderful names: Lampong (north Thailand), Surat Thani (Myanmar border), Nakhon Sawan (central Thailand), Nong Khai (Laos border) and Aranyaprathet (Kampuchea border).

My next meeting was with Phillip D. Round, one of those talented, energetic ex-pats whom I met in several places round the world, who give you the impression that they would have done well wherever they had ended up. He was an academic ornithologist and a leading light in the Bangkok Bird Club, with an encyclopaedic knowledge of wild birds in Thailand. He had, quite literally, written the book – *A Guide to the Birds of Thailand* – and had also, famously in the birding world, rediscovered Gurney's pitta, a beautiful thrush-like bird, in a fragment of lowland jungle in southern Thailand in 1986. The bird had been thought extinct for decades. Phil was delighted to see someone from the RSPB, telling me that 'we need all the help we can get'. I had had a similar reaction from the WFT. No pressure, then!

The next day, Saturday, I had my first, fascinating trip to Chatuchak market. We travelled by tuk-tuk through the dead flat, traffic-choked streets of Bangkok to what has to be my favourite market in the world. Pass the large declamatory sign at the entrance and you enter another world: streets of tightly-packed stalls selling everything from 'real silk clothes as worn by the Laotian Royal Family' to giant water scorpions, laid out beside the vegetables in the food section.

TUK-TUKS

A common sight in many Asian cities, the tuk-tuk is a sort of box with padded seats and open sides, balanced on the back of a three-wheeled scooter with the driver perched at the front. My first experience of these terrifying machines was in the city of Ahmedebad. I can still recall driving at break-neck speed, weaving in and out between sacred cows, donkeys, camels, pedestrians, buses and lorries and veering away at the last minute from oncoming traffic, the driver playing his large bulbed horn all the while and driving with one hand. I, meanwhile, sat attempting to make polite conversation, squashed in with my beautiful, brightly-saried sisters-in-law, while inwardly praying for deliverance.

The Bangkok variety were a bit less dilapidated and better decorated but the driving style was universal: go as fast as possible and hang the consequences. I could never imagine telling a tuk-tuk driver that I was in a hurry. My best advice to a tourist new to Bangkok is to take a tuk-tuk ride, an unforgettable experience, but have a good belt of Mekong whisky, the local rotgut spirits, before you get in and hang on tight.

Furniture, pottery, wall hangings and a large open stall from which Thai pop music blared out on huge speakers and dancers, male and female, leaped around displaying the multi-coloured scarves on sale.

Lek went shopping while Derek took me into the animal area. Amongst the stalls selling dogs and puppies, pigeons, pheasants, peacocks and fighting cocks, colour-dyed chicks and ducklings were around 50 stalls selling wild birds. At first I thought these were all finches, my first sight of the standard wild bird market with hundreds of little birds crammed into wooden slatted cages, with shafts of light through the dusty air picking out the constantly twittering and fluttering captives. As we moved deeper through the shade, though, I began to take note of more exotic species – kingfishers, hanging parrots and even a toucan, a South American bird.

Even more unsettling – with my Scottish Investigations Officer's hat on – were the large numbers of ingenious and very cheap bird traps on sale.

I then saw a more open stall with a number of live parrots chained to rough wooden perches. Two things immediately caught my attention. I passed my camera to Derek and asked him to take a 'tourist photo' which just happened to have the bird stall in the background.

I was standing beside a palm cockatoo, a native of New Guinea (Irian Jaya/ Papua New Guinea) and northern Australia, an CITES Appendix 1 listed species, banned from trade across the world, certainly including Thailand, Australia and Indonesia, long before 1991. The second thing that caught my eye were the credit card stickers, pasted on the crudely-drawn and rather ironic forest mural with its mix of trees and sawn-off stumps. Trying to appear casual, I caught the stallholder's eye and asked, 'How much for the palm cockatoo?' '25,000 baht' – or £500.

I could have gone home then, job done. It was a blatant breach of international conservation law: a stall selling endangered parrots, obviously aimed at international dealers, as shown by the credit card stickers and the dealer's practiced English.

We continued looking at this stall: several more cockatoos, including another Appendix 1 species (Moluccan or salmon-crested cockatoo) and sulphur-crested cockatoos. Eclectus parrots. Macaws. native to south and central America. All captive bred? Not at those prices.

Things became even more surreal when we moved to the adjoining area, where we found a rhea and two wallabies. Yes, you could buy anything in Chatuchak!

Both Pisit and Phil Round had mentioned the problem of wildlife restaurants, where the expensive meals on offer included wild bird and animal meat. I was already aware of the Chinese medicine trade in animal products, including endangered species, but until now had been unaware that restaurants were also a threat. Lek had got hold of an address for such a place, on the edge of Bangkok, from one of the Chatuchak stallholders, so we decided to go and take a look but to eat only vegetarian food if possible!

We got a taxi to the Rangsit marshes for a little light birdwatching and then, through clouds of orange dust in the tropical sunset, took a very hairy ride on the back of three motorbikes to our destination, the Restaurant Cobra. It lived up to its name. As we arrived, we saw a cobra being killed and prepared for eating. We also saw cages outside the restaurant containing a large monkey, a Brahminy kite, two koels, a hornbill and some fruit bats. Whether these were a sideshow zoo for the patrons or destined to be eaten, we never found out – I can only hope it was the former.

Inside, the restaurant was much like any other. We were seated at a table and handed menus. I am pleased to say that the entire menu was written in Thai script, utterly incomprehensible to foreigners, showing that at least this wildlife food was aimed at the locals only. Lek started to translate. 'Cobra, cobra and chips, cobra and spaghetti, bat, bat with chips…' and so on. It was like a bizarre, tasteless Monty Python sketch. There was a section listed as 'ordinary food' from which we made our choice and had an acceptable Thai meal. I then got Lek to ask if we could take the menu as a souvenir? The waiter looked puzzled and went off to ask the manager, who returned quickly and started a rapid fire conversation with Lek, in Thai.

'Right, we're leaving,' said Lek. 'He won't let us have it.' The manager was looking cross. We quickly paid up and left. I was worried. 'What's wrong, did he suss out that we were conservationists?' 'No,' said Lek, laughing, 'he thought I wanted to start up a rival restaurant for English people and was going to steal his ideas!'

It was one of the many misunderstandings that have made my foreign trips amusing. Never make assumptions when you don't speak the language.

Here is a traveller's tale I often tell, to illustrate the folly of making assumptions about people in a place like India. It's a hot December afternoon, in a bus station in Agra, and we've been waiting for an hour in crushing heat. I'm the only white face on a packed local bus, due to leave for the town of Bharatpur, close to one of the world's great nature reserves at Keoladeo National Park. A long-haired man in tatty clothes, wearing a satchel, gets on the bus. He glares at the passengers and then pulls a book out of the satchel and begins to read from it, talking loudly and then waving the book around. Everyone ignores him – old men, children, wives with saris pulled over their heads, my wife Jay – and they all stare out of the windows at the dusty yard. The man becomes agitated and starts to shout and then stuffs the book back in his bag and stalks off the bus.

I turn to Jay and say 'What was all that about? Was he some sort of religious fanatic?'

'No, no, he was trying to sell a joke book.'

'A joke book? What were the jokes about?'

'They were Mr Singh jokes. People make jokes here about Sikhs being stupid, like you make Irish jokes at home, but we've all heard them before...'

Not in a thousand years would I have guessed the truth behind what I saw. Another lesson learned from that great teacher, travel.

It was time to start travelling to try to find signs of illegal trade around the country. I knew that I couldn't go to all of the places mentioned by WFT. I decided to go to the borders with Myanmar (formerly Burma) and Kampuchea (formerly Cambodia) and visit Chiang Mai in the north. Sadly, I had no time to look at the Laotian border. I travelled by plane, rail and local bus and walked miles through dusty little towns, looking at pet shops and asking about dealers. Every day was an adventure.

THURSDAY, 14 FEBRUARY

I left Chiang Mai airport in a small prop plane. Even that had been dramatic: I had been shown onto the wrong plane and, only realising the mistake at the last minute, got the right plane to lower its steps after waving at the pilot from the runway as he started moving off. We flew west towards the border with Myanmar over the brown dusty landscape far below. I had chosen the town of Mae Sot because of its location on the border and its write-up in the *Lonely Planet Guide*: 'It's a type of Burmese-Chinese-Karen-Thai trading outpost, which is slowly becoming a tourist destination.'

After a taxi ride into town, shared with two adventurous elderly American ladies, from the very small and very hot airport, I booked into the Siam Hotel, then took a *songthaew* (shared taxi) to the market. Disappointingly, there was no wildlife for sale. Another *songthaew* to the border, where only a trickle of water runs in the Moei river and I can see people walking about in the village on the other side. Oh well, at least I've seen Burma.

The *Lonely Planet* again: 'Waley... 26 km from Mae Sot... an important smuggling point' sounded good to me, so the next morning, I get yet another *songthaew* to Waley. I would highly recommend this means of transport if you want to understand rural life in Thailand. Whole families travel in them with all manner of livestock. My attempts at conversation, using my 20 or so Thai words, were always acknowledged and people were universally helpful to this odd-looking *farang* asking about birds. A *songthaew* is also incredibly cheap.

Following a glowing reference in a guide book, I am dropped off in Waley and start to head for the border, a few kilometres walk away. The walk has been described as a pleasant stroll through thick woodland to the small border post. I get to the edge of town, but see no forest. I can see the border flag in the distance and I start to walk towards it. It's starting to get hot but I'm enjoying some unusual birding – two male Chinese goshawks are lazily circling above me, a group of noisy jays are calling, crow-billed drongos are sitting near a tawny eagle, and a roller and a sunbird dazzle in beautiful blues and purples.

My reverie is broken by a car pulling up beside me and a uniformed man shouting in Thai. He waves me across. I notice that there are three other men in the car, all wearing some sort of uniform. They open a back door and I get in. No one says a word as we speed down the track, leaving a plume of dust, to a small brick building with a Thai flag flying next to the Moei River. The entire landscape shows signs of recent logging: some log piles are scattered about the hummocky ground which slopes down to the fringe of trees at the water's edge.

I am ushered into the building and pointed into a chair next to a hatchway in the wall. The men disappear into a side room and shut the door. I'm getting worried. I've obviously stumbled into a restricted area.

A young woman appears with a glass of water, which is very welcome. Eventually one of the uniformed men returns. I ask him if he speaks English. 'Yes, a little.' 'What am I doing here?' 'This is a cottage hospital. We saw you at the side of the track. It's too hot for you, you will get heatstroke. We are doctors!'

As I say, make no assumptions when you don't speak the language. They gave me a lift back to Waley and I asked them about the area. They strongly advised me against going near the border and said I should certainly not to try to cross it. The area was still full of anti-government (Myanmar junta government) Karen people who often had Western mercenaries fighting alongside them. If a government patrol were to see me, they said, they would think I was a mercenary and shoot me.

I returned to Mae Sot in the evening where the comedy of errors continued. I showed a group of men in a café pictures in my *Birds of Thailand*. One of them pointed at a picture of a hornbill and said in broken English, 'My friend has one, I can take you there!' We all jump in a car and drive several miles up a dusty track to a farmhouse in the middle of nowhere. They talk to the friend who takes me into the house and shows me a magnificent three-foot high carving of a hornbill. I take several photos of it and smile and drink tea before being driven back to my hotel. Lovely people and very helpful!

My attempts on the other side of the country were no more successful. I had been told by WFT of a market at Aranyaprathet, on the border with Kampuchea, the site of the huge refugee camp shown at the end of the terrifying film *The Killing Fields*. 'They sell everything: gold, guns, parrots.' It was just on the Cambodian side and I thought it would be worth a visit. I hired a taxi-motorbike to Poipet where the border was easy to spot. The Thai side was brown, parched grass and withered crops, while Kampuchea was a line of thick jungle, presumably because the Khmer groups were preventing logging. It was under a violently repressive régime which was accidentally preserving one of the world's richest habitats. To cut a long story short, we were turned back at gunpoint (so that's what an AK47 looks like, close up!) by a group of soldiers wearing headscarves, manning a makeshift barrier about 300 yards into the forest. 'No *farang*! No *farang*!' I wasn't about to argue.

I returned to Aranyaprathet, rather dejected. Although my travels through the country had shown interesting domestic trade in a variety of bird species, mainly in pet shops, this was not what I was looking for. I came across a cafe, called Kim Kim, which to my surprise had a menu written in English in the window. In 1991 this was most definitely not a tourist town. When I went inside, I found that it was full of UN refugee workers and this was obviously their R & R HQ. I sat down next to a group of young Americans and, for the first and only time, broke my strict rule – I told them what I was doing. It was a good decision. They were able to tell me the market I had tried to go to had been shut down four months ago and that they only ever let Thai traders through anyway. Then one of them said a remarkable thing. 'Are you aware that Pol Pot sent a message to the international community last week, saying that he and his followers will respect wildlife conservation? I can get you a meeting with the Khmer, they could be very useful to you.' A meeting with Pol Pot's Khmer Rouge, which had killed millions of people and forced city dwellers out into the countryside to labour in fields and whose leader was obviously using conservation to try to whitewash his crimes against humanity. I didn't think so.

It was one of my finest hours. I turned to the young man and, summoning up all the bullshit management-speak I had recently had to endure back home, I said, 'Thanks very much but this sounds like a major policy decision on the part of my organisation. I will have to run this past my line manager for a full corporate decision. I'll get back to you.' I left shortly after and headed back to Bangkok.

On my next visit to the WFT offices, the charming DG listened to my traveller's tales. Regarding the cleared forest at Waley, he said, 'Ah yes, it is illegal to cut down virgin forest and sell wood such as teak from Thailand, so they cut it down anyway, ship it across the border and re-import it as Burmese teak. The local police chief will be involved. It would be dangerous to appear too interested.' Great. Then I told him about not getting to the jungle market at Poipet. 'Oh well, the last time I was there, a gunfight started and we all had to lie on the ground.' Thanks for forgetting to tell me that the last time I was here.

I made one last visit to Chatuchak and yes, the usual illegal 'offers for sale' were continuing. It was a hot afternoon and I wandered out of the animal stalls looking for a cool drink. I find a pleasant-looking bamboo-lined bar with a beautiful Thai girl serving. I order a Coke. As I gaze around, stupefied by the heat, I notice a guitar amplifier with a guitar case leaning against it. Two young men walk in. Another guitar appears, then a set of bongo drums. This looks good: maybe I'm going to hear some real Thai music. They launch into their first number, 'Hoochie-Coochie Man' by Muddy Waters. I walk up to the bar and order a beer this time.

The next morning I'm packing, slightly hungover, thinking back to a great night of conversation and guitar jams with Ju and Krai, my new Thai friends. I empty the pocket of yesterday's shirt and find a business card – in Thailand, everyone has a business card. – and wonder what Ju does for a living? 'Ju ***, Cargo Handler, Thai International Airways.' You jammy b*****! Another link in the trade chain and a big opening for information.

I realise I may be giving the impression that this was not a successful trip. Far from it: my attempts to contact dealers in Bangkok had paid off and it was time to call in the rest of the team.

I flew back to England overnight on 26/27 February and faced a bit of culture shock after three weeks' travelling round Thailand. There was no time to rest, though. Two days later, I was heading back to Bangkok with my colleagues, Andy Jones and Karen Bradbury, on a very different mission. This time we met a locally- hired film crew and started to put together the campaign launch, an exposé of illegal trade. Surreptitiously we filmed the bird dealers in Chatuchak, pretending to be dealers ourselves. Amongst the interesting characters we met was an Israeli man, who was buying live giant scorpions. When we asked him how he got them home, he said he simply crammed them into a suitcase for the flight. If customs ever opened his baggage, they shut it again very quickly and waved him through. So much for wildlife controls.

We then started visiting the wildlife dealers' premises which I had identified on my first visit. Our first attempt struck gold. We arrived in a taxi at the dealer's compound on the edge of Bangkok to face large, locked gates. We rang the bell. A thirty-something American woman, with a distracted air and sporting some home-made tattoos on her arm, invited us in, saying that her husband, the Thai owner of the business, was away but that she could show us round.

'I've just this morning got your fax,' (sent from a fake address with a fake company's headed paper, asking for their price list). 'Here's our price list, we only give this to serious customers.' She handed Andy a sheet of paper. He looked at it and handed it over to me and Karen without comment. We looked at a long list of birds and animals with prices. At the head of the page we read 'Tiger: $*,000, elephant: $*,000' and in the bird section, 'Gurney's pitta: $150.' Keeping my face straight, I handed it over to Karen.

So, wild tiger and elephant and one of the world's rarest birds, all openly and completely illegally offered for sale.

'We were wondering if we could look at your stock? Do you mind if we video this for our business partners at home?' 'No problem,' said the woman, who by this time had told us she had worked as a croupier in a casino in Las Vegas before marrying her Thai animal dealer.

We then spent a surreal hour or so filming a large variety of parrots, eagles, reptiles and mammals, with a running commentary from our American guide. One comedy moment came when I almost sat on a latticed box full of cobras.

Our taxi returned and we drove off after thanking our new friend profusely and promising non-existent bird orders in the future. Fantastic! We had high quality close-up video of protected species, with the dealer's wife giving us chapter and verse about where they came from and how much they sold for. We even asked about the elephants. 'Oh, we have

The author and seized tiger cub, WFT office, Bangkok, 1991

to put an order out, it might take a couple of weeks to get them for you...' and the same went for the Gurney's pitta.

The rest of that week was taken up with filming more background material. This involved a visit to the WFT offices, where by a great stroke of luck we saw two tiger cubs, newly confiscated by customs. They had been found 'hidden on the person' of two Thai prostitutes as they walked onto a Taiwanese freighter in the docks. At least I got 'tiger in the hand', to use a bird ringer's phrase.

We also had a trip to Chiang Mai zoo to get more captive bird and animal footage. It was interesting to see hill tribes people (Hmong, Karen), in traditional dress, staring at cages of their native wildlife.

Until we were actually in flight over Bangkok, we were all worried about being stopped and having our film taken off us: with corruption rife, you just never knew. Much relieved, we finally got home and a short time later our film was shown on TV as a main item on the national *Nine o'clock News*. The campaign had been launched and my first sabbatical was seen as a resounding success.

This was a happy time at the RSPB. Each member of the Investigations section had been given a world region to research in terms of the bird trade. Similar expeditions to mine to Thailand were later carried out to the Caribbean, the US and West and East Africa. I myself was back in Indonesia (Java) two months later, photographing Moluccan cockatoos openly on sale in street markets in Jakarta. All of us came back with similar tales of open illegal trapping, dealing and international trade, all professionally filmed and catalogued. We had a series of successes in tightening up conditions of transport and some airlines stopped carrying live birds entirely.

In December 1992, I travelled with a team of RSPB Investigators and Hans Peters of the Dutch Bird Protection society, *Vogelbescherming*, to Hong Kong and mainland China, showing that even Hong Kong, still a UK outpost at that time, was not able to fulfil its CITES obligations. Mainland China was an eye opener, with live birds of prey openly on sale for food in street markets in contravention of their own domestic laws.

It wasn't until July 2007 that the EU put in place a permanent ban on imports of wild birds. This was certainly precipitated by the 2005 bird flu restrictions but the Ban the Wild Bird Trade campaign, started by RSPB/RSPCA and EIA in 1991, was surely the start of the process. It is a largely forgotten conservation success.

I was still at the wrong end of the UK for regular international work but opportunities came unexpectedly. A three-day trip to the south of France in October 1992 (with a French civil servant and a member of FACE, the European Hunters' Union) came as part of a fact-finding mission on licensed thrush trapping for food; I gave a talk on golden eagles at the AGM of LIPU (the Italian equivalent of the RSPB) in the Alpine resort of Cortina d'Ampezzo; I carried out research in Saxony, Germany, for a Cook Report investigation into the theft and illegal trade of peregrines; a visit to Brandenburg, Berlin, was made to help local police deal with a huge haul of eggs, seized from several German collectors; and my second sabbatical took me to the Matobo Hills in Zimbabwe to help with research on black eagles. All of these trips were squeezed in, somehow, between the growing number of Scottish cases and court appearances and the madness of each year's bird breeding/egg stealing/chick thieving/raptor killing season which were all my responsibility with one assistant and, at first, one secretary/administrator.

One unexpected trip started with a call from HQ. 'BirdLife Malta has asked us if we could provide training in wildlife law enforcement for their local police, customs and military personnel. It means a week in Malta. How do fancy doing that?'

I had been to Malta once before, back in the mid-1970s, on a holiday with my first wife Marlene and two university friends. I remembered a very hot, barren-looking group of islands, full of tourist hotels and crowded beaches. I was also aware that it had a shocking reputation for the shooting of migrant birds and that it lay in the direct path between Eurasia and Africa, a major bird migration route.

What was the catch? There's always at least one. Firstly, it had to be in June and Malta lies off the coast of North Africa, where it's known to get quite warm in mid-summer! Secondly, they wanted me to take a wildlife policeman with me to talk directly to their counterparts. By 2001, a lot of the goodwill built up between myself and the police had been systematically destroyed by the shooting lobby. Some of the best WLOs had resigned because of a lack of resourcing and undue pressure from their own senior officers.

Alan Stewart lecturing Malta police, June, 2001

I was determined to take a Scottish policeman: I would, after all, be describing the Scottish justice system. He or she would have to be experienced both in wildlife crime and in training. There was only one serious candidate: Alan Stewart. We had had our problems after a promising start working very closely on setting up Operation Easter, for instance. That was a case of egg theft, though, and we disagreed strongly – and do to this day – on how to stop estate-based crime. Alan's links with gamekeepers, and his habit of trying to squeeze the RSPB and Scottish SPCA out of inquiries which had themselves been initiated by the work of those organisations, had by this time led to a lack of trust.

Alan was no doubt surprised to get my call but he rose with enthusiasm to the task, as I knew he would. Within a couple of weeks, we were flying into a very hot Malta. We dumped our clothes in the borrowed apartment in Sliema and were then given a crash course on Malta (almost literally, given the enthusiastic driving of Justin Vassallo, a young BirdLife Malta volunteer) with visits to Buskett Woods and the Dingli Cliffs, two shooting hotspots.

TUESDAY, 19 JUNE 2001

In designing the course, I had been very aware of the differences between Scotland and Malta

Author lecturing at BirdLife, Malta office

BirdLife Malta President, Joseph Mangion, ringing

Maltese wildlife police with Ray Galea and the author

and keenly conscious of my lack of knowledge of their 'on the ground' problems of enforcement. I also knew from the teaching and training I had already carried out that it is a very useful technique, for both teacher and student to get the student to share their experiences. It also breaks the monotony of lecturing. Day one, therefore, was an introductory indoor session, describing our work and the history of our organisations (RSPB and WLO network/Tayside Police). Despite the pleasant lecture room with fans blowing and an attentive audience, I was looking forward to the planned outdoor trip on day two.

The majority of delegates were ALE police officers (Administrative Law Enforcement) and were made up of one Inspector and ten lower ranks. We also had three customs officials, two government inspectors and three members of the Armed Forces of Malta, along with the very helpful presence of Ray Galea, a BirdLife Malta stalwart.

Ray and Inspector Miruzzi had decided on an itinerary which was to include both shooting and bird-trapping areas. In addition to the biannual barrage of shotgun pellets aimed at migrant birds, from tiny swallows to herons and eagles, bird trapping was also very popular.

In Malta, unlike in other southern European countries, these trapped small birds are for the cage bird trade rather than for the table.

We all jumped into a minibus and headed for the stunning Dingli Cliffs on the southwest of the main island. The entire island of Malta is a series of bare limestone escarpments and terraces. It is a particularly arid, unvegetated place, especially in high summer, with the exception of the protected Buskett Woods and the odd patch of bright green cultivated ground. Trees are scarce, although the ubiquitous Australian eucalyptus has caught on. We were again told about the dreadful, indiscriminate blasting of any migrant bird coming within range of the crude stone hides built into hillside ridges. Space on this small island is at a premium and that applies to shooting hides, too, with people having their own traditional shooting spots. Shooting may claim such 'traditions' (the recent mass rearing and release of pheasants in Scotland is another case in point), but it is actually a fairly new activity on Malta, produced out of the twin phenomena of more leisure time and affordable repeating shotguns. Neither of those was available to the modern shooter's grandparents.

We were absorbing all this as quickly, we hoped, as our students were taking in the pearls of wisdom shared by Alan and myself. We arrived at the clifftops at Dingli, a very impressive series of terraces and cliffs falling hundreds of feet into the deep blue Mediterranean. What we were being shown, however, were little stone huts where, in full season, men would crouch, holding a string connected to a clap-net, waiting for birds lured in by live decoy finches, bird calls and scattered seed. Some birds could still be legally trapped: we were also learning about Maltese wildlife laws, some of which were soon to become international *causes celèbres*.

After being shown the various tricks of the trade used by the trappers, we returned to our minibus and headed along the coast to a high point in order to take a couple of team photographs. As we were getting ready to move on, I noticed Ray and Inspector Miruzzi having an intense conversation and occasionally pointing across the deep valley below us, which ran in from the sea. Ray walked up to me and said, hesitantly, 'We were wondering if it would be alright to catch a bird trapper during your course?' Of course, that would be ideal. 'Where are they?' I replied. I looked across the valley with my binoculars, to where Ray was pointing out a high stand of eucalyptus and where I could faintly make out some netting. To put this in context, we were looking over a distance of perhaps a mile into a landscape of white limestone rock, sectioned off into rough rectangles by stone walls and fences consisting of thorny bushes and prickly pear cactus. Ray's sharp eyes and experience had spotted something I would never have seen, just as I would always spot an eagle or peregrine perched on a rock high above a

Justin Vassallo and author at raptor shooting hide on ridge

Scottish glen long before any visitor would.

The mood changed immediately from one of pleasant near-lethargy in the June heat to the tense excitement I have so often experienced amongst a team about to carry out a search. We worked out a route which would take us through the maze of stony tracks and walls to a point close to the trees, and set off in a cloud of dust.

Alan Stewart with police and illegal clap net

At the locus, several of the police jumped out, ran down a path and disappeared behind the line of eucalyptus. When we arrived a minute or so later, I saw a man in shorts and T-shirt, running around, shouting in Maltese, being watched by two policemen, one of them holding a rifle or shotgun in its case. Next to the trees was the largest mist net set-up I have ever seen: fine netting, stretching perhaps 30 metres across and 10 metres in height, held up by very long poles set into concrete- filled tubs. Not what you'd call a casual trap site! In the net were fluttering several small birds. We all set about removing these and releasing them.

Illegally-set mist net and Maltese Police Officer near Dingli, Malta

The action then moved to an adjoining plot where we found a large clap-net bird trap, set and ready to be used, next to a small dark shed. We looked into the shed and saw a mix of species of small birds – wagtails, larks and finches – in tiny cages. These were removed by the police. This second raid on the clap net and hut all happened very quickly, a little too quickly for my liking. During the ten minutes or so we had all

Time and again on searches in Scotland I had seen vital evidence found at the last minute, and on one or two annoying occasions only mentioned some time later by inexperienced police or Agriculture Department officials. After one unsuccessful poison search on a Highland estate, one of the Department officials casually mentioned having seen a Larsen trap with a live pigeon in it in the gamekeeper's yard. On another poison search, I found a plastic fork covered in alphachloralose on a sill when I put up my hand to steady myself when leaving a shed: five minutes later I watched the suspect gamekeeper deliberately tread on the same fork when the constable's back was turned. I lost count of the number of times that I was the person on a search who spotted poison, traps or some arcane piece of illegal equipment, before the police started deliberately keeping me and my colleagues away from buildings during searches as a sop to the shooting lobby. What's a simple way to make yourself more inefficient? Keep your expert witness well out of the way.

been trying to gain entry to the shed, I had not seen any of the policemen look round the back, so I had a look myself. Attached to the back wall was a wooden box with a flap of cloth nailed over it. I lifted this up and came face to face with an adult scops owl (*Otus scops*) blinking at the sudden light. I called the police back. I'm afraid I used that incident mercilessly during my lectures. Always have a good look round and don't be distracted by the obvious, as you will never get a second chance at a search.

So we all left in a jubilant mood: a major trapping site had been closed down, with several birds rescued and the probability of a much-needed, high profile court case for the ALE team (including possession of an unlicensed firearm). Inspector Miruzzi treated

everyone to an ice cream on the way home – a very welcome hot weather variant on the celebratory sticky buns and pies I've enjoyed in many Scottish police offices.

At some point, I plucked up the courage to ask Ray what the accused was saying as he ran about in front of his confiscated mist net. I was hoping for some new swear word or phrase to add to my international vocabulary, perhaps something along the lines of 'Son of a camel!' Ray translated it for me. 'Why me? What have I done? Have I murdered somebody? Who are all these people?' Yes, unlucky. Just another day's idle bird trapping and he's suddenly descended on by a dozen police, several military officers, a couple of customs officials, two conservationists and a Scottish policeman.

The rest of the week's training was pretty dull after that, I'm sure, no matter how much

Local birders and raptor camp volunteers sea-watching, Valletta

Alan and I tried to liven things up. I feel we did a good and useful job there, though, and helped the reputation of the RSPB, the UK WLO network and British conservation at one fell swoop.

I returned that same September (using all my leave for a change: it was 2001, the year of foot and mouth disease and so there was no fieldwork to be done) to help out as a volunteer at the annual Raptor Camp at Buskett. This international camp is run by BirdLife Malta and volunteers from all over the world get to watch and count hundreds of fabulous migrating birds, in particular raptors such as honey buzzards, marsh harriers, hobbies and kestrels, then get to watch them being blasted out of the skies by Maltese hunters who kill them and have them stuffed. It's a bizarre mix of intense pleasure at watching beautiful birds on a beautiful island carrying out a visible migration, which will have lasted thousands of years, and seeing all that destroyed in seconds by a bunch of ignorant macho clowns. These people talk about this being their traditional right, while deliberately destroying something which is far, far more ancient than their own presence on Malta, predating the British, French, Turkish, Roman and even Phoenician occupations. The BirdLife Malta people are immensely brave (cars have been bombed and burned) and I would go and help them every year if I could afford it – several friends do just that.

It's 2005 and I've had enough. Each field season is beginning to feel like *Groundhog Day*, in which the main character wakes up each morning to find that nothing has changed and that his day is going on exactly like every day before. I was seeing the same list of poison victims, the same estates involved, the same hassle getting the police and courts to do anything as I was seeing in the 1980s. The big difference was that then I was naive enough to think that involving the police would actually help conservation.

I have one more sabbatical to take, though. I've seen enough bird killing and it's time for something different. I start to ask around. One autumn afternoon, I'm driving around the Scottish countryside when I get a mobile phone call from someone I've never heard of at the Lodge. By 2005 that was the norm. In one sentence that sums up the enormous change in conservation from my earliest days in 1981 to my final months at the RSPB.

Chris Bowden had heard that I was looking for a sabbatical project and that I had experience of India. He started to tell me about the Indian vulture crisis. The drastic decline in vulture numbers is, of course, not the only serious conservation crisis taking place in the world, or even in India, where tigers are also now seriously endangered, but it is unusually clear-cut in being the result of one seemingly small change to the environment by man.

In December 1981, I spent a peaceful afternoon at my wife's uncle's farm a few miles outside Bombay (now Mumbai). While he pottered about indulging his hobby – he was a wealthy successful lawyer – I was birdwatching. At one point I lay on my back on a grassy slope and turned my binoculars up to the clear sky. Very high up, a speck to the naked eye, I saw a soaring Indian white-backed vulture (*Gyps bengalensis*), then another, then another. I realised that at regular intervals, almost as if in a grid pattern, the entire sky was covered, at a great height, by vultures. On our journey back into the city I counted over 100 white-backs on a single large electricity pylon. Their population in India was then estimated to be in the tens of millions.

Early in the 1990s, members of the Bombay Natural History Society (BNHS – India's highly respected and most active local conservation NGO) began to notice a lack of vultures.

This led to a roadside count, organised by volunteers and professional biologists, which soon confirmed that this most common of species was in severe decline. That started a remarkable conservation detective story, as remarkable in its scope and resolution as the DDT story mentioned in an earlier chapter. At first it was thought to be a pathogen, a disease, which targeted this species alone. A great deal of effort went in to finding fresh corpses and carrying out laboratory analysis. The work became international, with a great deal of help from the RSPB. Many people were aware of how key an element of the environment was disappearing. Finally, the scientists began to home in on the idea that this was a chemical problem which was causing terminal kidney damage. The chemical was isolated – diclofenac, a blood-thinning agent used in both human and veterinary medicine, but only recently in the latter in India.

All this took years to implement and resolve. In the meantime, the white-backed vultures declined by an estimated 99.9% since 1992. Drastic measures were needed to save the species from extinction. In a joint initiative by BNHS, the Ministry of Environment and Forests Government of India, the RSPB, the Zoological Society of London and several other smaller local and international organisations, a plan was put together involving the capture from the wild of the three closely-related species of *Gyps* vultures now known to be affected. These birds would then be housed in huge total seclusion enclosures and encouraged to breed in a diclofenac- free environment. When the outside environment was judged to be free of the chemical and enough birds had been bred, they would be re-introduced to the wild. This involved many logistical problems, not least of which was the fact that no one had succeeded in breeding this species in captivity.

By the winter of 2005 – 2006, two enormous seclusion aviaries had been built using expert advice from the UK falconer and raptor breeder, Jemima Parry-Jones. The first groups of white–backed, long-billed (*Gyps indicus*) and slender-billed (*Gyps tenuirostris*) vultures had arrived and hopes were high for successful breeding.

Sunday, 15 January 2006

A waiting room in New Delhi railway station. I had recently acquired a mini-disc recorder and a good-quality stereo microphone. Later, back at home, as I listen to the recording I have made that day, I can clearly see the crowd of Indian families spread out with their piles of bedding and belongings all over the few seats and the polished stone floor. I can hear the voices of Indian matriarchs scolding children, barely pausing for breath in long, seemingly endless sentences in what might be Hindi, Gujerati, Punjabi, Urdu, Maharashtrian or any one of the hundreds of local languages of this ever-moving population. No one pays a blind bit of attention to the pale Scotsman, clutching his rucksack and bag, drinking in the sights and sounds around him and reminiscing over earlier journeys.

Eventually, I made it through the organised chaos and onto my numbered seat on the Shatabdi Express to Kalka, an easy ride with a great meal provided. By ten o'clock at night, I walked out of Kalka station and met Saravanan, a PhD student, BNHS vulture biologist and my guide and minder. We drove through the night-time main road into Pinjaur (or Pinjore: variable spelling seems to be the norm in India) and the Forest Lodge, a compound of run-down houses with dusty gardens close to the centre of the town. Saravanan makes me the first of many superb potato and lentil curries and, for the first of many times, apologises for the poor standard of food. Later in my trip, when I heard the same apology for the umpteenth

CCTV photo of sitting white-backed vulture

CCTV vultures feeding on goat carcass inside breeding enclosure

time, I tried telling my Indian hosts how much such a quality vegetarian curry would cost back in Scotland. I don't think they believed me.

Pinjaur is in Haryana state, to the north of Delhi and close to the startling change of landscape that comes with the Himalayan foothills, one minute densely populated plain, the next a wall of deeply-fissured brown hills, soaring up into the distance. This is a frontier town, where the road and rail links to the old hill station of Shimla and the interior of the Himalayas meet the lowlands. A constant roar of trucks passing through mingles with the chanting of prayers at the Hindu temple and the call to prayer at the mosque. Early morning alarm calls were unnecessary.

After a slightly chilly night – Delhi experienced its coldest January night on record – I was driven past steppe eagles (*Aquila nipalensis*) on roadside trees, across wide riverbeds, through villages and fields, a forest road bordered by langur monkeys – regularly fed, as descendants of the Hindu monkey god Hanuman, much to the annoyance of the authorities – then down a bumpy track through dry jungle to a large fenced-off clearing with three huge concrete structures and a series of smaller buildings, some still in construction. This was the vulture breeding centre. I was shown round by Saravenan and a tough-looking local man who I knew only as Jaki. It was a very impressive set-up. I was delighted to find a CCTV monitor, linked up to cameras in the main breeding buildings, and even more delighted to see that several nests had been built, using provided branches, and that a couple of birds appeared to be sitting. This was a world first and I would be part of it! I was determined to be useful to the project rather than an idle spectator and I began to think in terms of recording the birds' behaviour, as I had learned to do all those years before when studying for my M.IBiol.

When Chris Bowden lured me into taking my sabbatical in India, it was with promises of fieldwork, finding and monitoring nesting vultures. It was, after all, the thing I liked to do best. However, India, as always, was anything but predictable. The head of the station, Dr Vibhu Prakash, arrived that evening and it was decided that I would accompany Saravanan on his research into known vulture concentrations in Rajasthan. That sounded fine to me.

THURSDAY, 19 JANUARY 2006

West Rajasthan. I woke up and looked out of the sleeper train window to see a desert landscape with crops planted in sand. The Thar desert. All we saw was the occasional thorn tree and miles passing by without any signs of habitation, which is very unusual in India. We arrived in Bikaner three hours late, piled into a tuk-tuk and dumped our bags at a small hotel full of wedding guests, dressed in bright saris and flashy suits and making an unbelievable amount of noise.

There was no rest for the wicked. (The Indian work ethic, by the way, is a shock to a visitor like me. When I asked the BNHS guys what they did at weekends, they looked puzzled. 'We work every day.') We were soon on another tuk-tuk heading for the edge of town and were dropped off to the side of a camel breeding station, an impressive government building surrounded by trees and flower beds. Behind that, however, was open semi-desert studded with thorn trees. We walked along a dusty track next to the railway line, which disappeared into the hummocky distance. It was a hot day and, of course, completely dry. As we crossed the railway line, apparently in the middle of nowhere, I noticed two steppe eagles and an immature Egyptian vulture (*Neophron percnopterus*) sitting together on a thorn tree, a taste of what was to come.

We trudged on through the sand until we reached the edge of a level plain. In front of me, I saw one of the most bizarre sights I had ever seen: a huge pile of cow carcasses, many stripped to the bone but some with flayed skin showing bright pink in the sunshine. A pack of several hundred, curly-tailed and mainly fawn-coloured dogs milled around the fresh carcases and among the bones waddled and flapped groups of vultures – Egyptian, Eurasian griffon (*Gyps fulvus*), Himalayan griffon (*Gyps himalayensis*) and the superb, huge, cinereous or black vultures (*Aegypius monachus*). On every thorn tree top were groups of steppe eagles, tawny eagles (*Aquila rapax*) and a variety of vultures. Most of these birds were winter migrants from the Himalaya and Pakistan mountains. A closer inspection showed a scattering of smaller birds, some quite unexpected in such a place – house crows and ravens but also black ibis (*Pesudibis paillosa*), black drongo (*Dicrurus macrocercus*) and southern grey shrike (*Lanius meridionalis*).

In amongst this hellish scene, four Indian men worked with small curved knives, skinning the freshly-dumped carcasses of cows which lay in grotesque poses.

Saravanan pointed out small, sandy hummocks of blue-and-white plastic covering several acres of desert. These were the stomach contents of previously-dumped cows, reduced to their non-degradable and possibly fatal last meals. Cows in Hindu India are regarded as sacred and are allowed to wander the streets of large towns. No-one can afford to give them pasture or fodder but some people feed them small amounts. Many cows eat the ubiquitous plastic shopping bags, which block their stomachs. Every night dead cows are removed and dumped at places like the Bikaner dump. Some animals are treated with diclofenac for visible health problems such as arthritis, which can have short-lived beneficial effects but don't cure the cows, which die.

Saravenan was at the dump to count vultures – we saw no white-backed vultures – but also, importantly, to count the feral dogs. The worry is that with lessening competition from vultures, the numbers of feral dogs are increasing. In India they are well-known carriers of rabies. The dogs at Bikaner dig burrows in the sand to have their pups. They were the best fed dogs I saw anywhere in India and we counted over 350. As I helped with the count, I again switched on my recorder to catch what was a remarkably peaceful scene. The dogs made very little noise and I seldom saw any aggression: all I could hear was the cawing of crows and the sound of the breeze in the microphone.

A walk beyond the dump was remarkable for only two things: we met a man, wearing a Rajasthani turban, out for a ride on a very large camel, and, far out in the desert, I saw a herd of wild chinkara gazelle.

We spent two full days at Bikaner, visiting the dump for counts several times, before leaving on a train on the Saturday evening. We made a long, slow night- time journey east.

Sunday, 22 January 2006

After a fairly sleepless night of travel, with passengers getting on at Jaipur and, at a chilly 5.30 a.m., a change at Bharatpur to the third class travel of a crowded local train, we arrived at the small town of Bayana. We loaded our luggage onto two cycle rickshaws and were slowly carried the half mile, to our accommodation, the upper floor of a large house in a back street with fantastic views of the hill ridge, scattered with ancient forts, that dominates the area.

We were in real small-town India, with pigs and buffalo in the streets, monkeys in the trees – and occasionally trying to plunder houses – and peacocks strutting about on a ruined temple roof. This was the wedding season, a mixed pleasure resulting in a hideous but somehow happy din of music every night. Out it blared from huge speakers loaded onto a cart and wired up to battery-powered amplifiers, the sound echoing off the narrow stone walls as the groom's procession moved through the town.

We were there to work, and headed off to the nearby cliffs with the local BNHS worker, Timon Singh, a quiet man with a thoughtful expression and little English. I found a stark contrast with the level desert landscape I had just left. This extreme western edge of Rajasthan has flat river valleys, full of fertile irrigated fields and tall roadside trees. The attractive red sandstone of the area was being actively quarried and the town was full of stonemasons' yards, piled up with enormous stone blocks. As always in India, there were sights which would make the most blasé traveller stop and stare: a man, dressed all in black, wearing a loose black Rajasthani turban and carrying an antique flintlock, short-barrelled gun, covered in mother-of-pearl inlay. He walked, very proud and upright, carrying the rifle, apparently casually parallel to the ground, weaving between the usual trucks, cars and camel carts and the shops advertising everything from gold bangles to Internet access. When I pointed him out to Saravanan, he just said, 'Oh yes, those people are allowed to carry their weapons around,' as though it was utterly normal.

Saravanan in front of vulture breeding enclosure, Pinjaur

As we left the town and were cycled along the main tree-lined road – a luxury, we walked to the cliffs every other day – I saw a sight which I will never forget. Walking towards us on the long roadside path was a tall, turbaned Indian man, wearing flowing robes and carrying a bag across his back, from which protruded the head of a many-stringed musical instrument. He walked with a steady rhythm and a fierce expression. Behind him were two small Indian women in identical yellow saris and carrying cloth bundles. It was a wedding musician and his family, walking the highway between gigs – a sight that would pre-date the trucks, cars and even bicycles, which he completely ignored – carrying on a family or caste tradition going back hundreds of years. As a musician, I found that very moving.

From the very edge of the town, a hugely impressive line of cliffs ran parallel to the road, although they were fringed here by a barren, rocky and dusty strip of uncultivated ground. As we left the rickshaws and headed straight towards the cliff, my experienced raptor worker's eye immediately picked out, high up, the tell-tale 'whitewash' streaks of nesting or roosting birds. When I started using my binoculars, I began to pick out a few sitting vultures, looking for all the world like shags or cormorants on a Scottish seacliff, a bundle of untidy-looking sticks with a large tail sticking up at one end. That illusion was soon shattered, however, when the first soaring bird appeared above us: even at a distance, it's obvious that a griffon or long-billed vulture is a very big bird indeed.

Even without having my eye in, I could easily have found these nests, as previous vulture workers had painted reference numbers on the rocks below. I couldn't quite envisage that back home: quite apart from encouraging pests such as egg thieves, I doubt whether it would meet our sense of aesthetic enjoyment of the countryside. Here, though, it was just another example of what, to an outsider, is the bizarre experience that is India.

As we walked along the base of the cliff, noting down the state of each of the nests high above us, Timon and Saravanan told me about these birds and the general area. Although we saw several nests, many more had become disused in recent years as the population of vultures declined. These were Indian long-billed vultures' nests while the other vultures we saw were wintering Eurasian griffons. At one point, Saravanan pointed out a huge paw print in the sandy soil and told me that it was from a hyena. 'Don't worry, they only come out at night.' I then noticed that some of the nearby smallholdings had thick barriers of thorn bush around them and was told that this was to keep out leopards, which came close to houses to kill dogs and other livestock. I resolved to be a bit more careful when walking around in the early mornings. Although I've always found that wild animals are more afraid of us than we are of them, I wouldn't want to accidentally disturb a leopard – I had felt the same thing when walking alone in the bush in Zimbabwe.

I got to know these cliffs quite well over the next couple of days and we also travelled a few miles along the ridge to look, unsuccessfully, for more nests. Those trips were very special, though, and included walking round the walls of a thousand-year-old fort, high above the plain, and meeting Timon's family in a beautiful village of blue-walled thatched houses, with buffalo and cattle wandering around. The air of peace about those places was wonderful. At one point, we took a short cut along the ridge at the edge of an irrigated field, and a man jumped up as we walked around the back of his tiny hut. He had a transistor radio and announced, to smiles all round, that India had just scored another six against Pakistan.

I remember our early morning ginger tea, drunk from earthen cups at a roadside stall in the mist; talking to our elderly landlord about his youthful duck-poaching days, a flint-lock rifle leaning against a corner of the best room, while eating sweets made from sugared pumpkin; the constant chirrup of sparrows and the scream of peacocks; narrow alleyways, turned into 'wedding tunnels' with coverings of cloth and flowers; young girls and women, their faces covered by their saris, all staring as I walked by; black buffalo chained up against a bright blue wall in a backyard in the centre of the town, and eating guava, sprinkled with a mix of chilli and salt, bought from a street vendor while waiting at a railway crossing in a hired jeep.

But all too soon it was time for the all-day rail journey back to Kalka and Pinjaur. We arrived late at night.

For the next week, I got into a rhythm of travel to the vulture centre, monitoring the sitting birds, helping weigh the meat to feed the vultures (a flock of diclofenac-free goats were kept specifically to feed the birds at the centre, the birds' rations meticulously divided up and recorded by Jaki) and generally keeping an eye on things. During my stay, there were several visits by media and print journalists which had to be carefully handled.

One big worry was bees. I saw several swarms attached to branches just outside the compound. These were no ordinary bees; for a start, they were about twice the size of our honey bee. The previous season, a honey buzzard had attacked a swarm close to one of the breeding buildings. The enraged bees had poured inside the building and managed to kill two of the vultures before a very brave Jaki (who was badly stung) managed to rescue the other birds. Now any bees found swarming inside the compound were removed immediately, as happened during my second week.

Although this was a pleasant life, made even more pleasant by the daily lunch of daal and thin chapattis at the Centre – I longed to see the Himalayan mountains, just out of reach. I decided to take a short break and headed off for two days to Shimla. I travelled on the famous 'toy railway', a hundred-year-old single track narrow gauge line which looped up and up, through steep grass slopes, crowded villages on the edge of ravines and pine woods. Eventually I reached Shimla, after a couple of stops at perfect whitewashed stations, with immaculately-painted fire buckets and monkeys sitting on rooftops. I arrived in the dark and walked a mile or so through a very un-Indian town, always upwards, until I came to my hotel. I booked in and walked upstairs to my room, following an open corridor with pinpoints of light showing through the pitch black night. When I woke in the morning, it was to the most stunning scenery I had ever seen. My hotel was perched several hundred feet above a grass-lined ravine and in the distance was a wall of snow-covered mountains. It was difficult to comprehend any mountains being that large and, at first, I was sure I was looking at a line of clouds.

A few things stick in my mind from that short stay: monkeys trying to mug tourists at a temple hilltop viewpoint; yak rides for a few pennies; incongruous English- style buildings; the bazaar area clinging on to the hillside; shy, just-married Indian couples holding hands. I had been warned that it would be very cold up there – Shimla is over 7,000 feet (2,200 metres) above sea level – but there had been no snow that winter. That was a worry as it is relied on both as a water supply and as a draw to Indian tourists.

Steppe eagles were common, drifting past at eye level in this town perched on a ridge, and I was pleased to see vultures at the town dump. All too soon, though, I was heading back down on the superb railway.

The rest of my last sabbatical held few surprises. I spent a delightful afternoon with Nikita, Vibhu Prakash's wife, a Gujerati and former vulture researcher. She asked me to edit a pamphlet she had written to publicise the vulture programme and we had fun comparing the way in which Indian people (and British and American) use the English idiom. I hope my suggestions were helpful. I was disappointed to see that no vulture chicks had hatched by the time I left. (All that year's nesting attempts failed, in fact, but 2007 saw the first successful breeding and this now seems to be a regular event. The fight against diclofenac use goes on in India). As the first RSPB sabbatical volunteer to the BNHS, I would like to think I helped in a small way with what is one of the great cooperative conservation projects of our time. It was a reminder of what I could have been doing for the previous quarter century if it hadn't been for the disgraceful levels of wildlife crime back home.

I arrived home in Edinburgh at 11 p.m. on the night of Thursday, 9 February 2006. Within a few days I had given a talk at a police conference in Fife, attended the annual staff conference in Pitlochry and picked up a suspected poisoned buzzard near Elgin. It was back to business as usual and India very quickly seemed very far away.

9

WORKING WITH THE MEDIA

As I fumbled around in my first months in the job as RSPB Investigations Officer, I took a very cautious line on publicity. I made sure that my photograph did not appear in public, reasoning that I did not want to be identified by crime suspects as I wandered the countryside or staked out some egg thief's house. They were very real worries at the time, but I have to say that after nearly three decades of newspaper, radio and TV exposure, including several specials on my work, I am rarely recognised, in the street or anywhere else. I must have an eminently forgettable face. The only exception was in police offices, where I had several 'You're that bloke off the telly!' conversations.

My change of heart over publicity was a gradual one. As I began to realise the extent and blatant nature of much of the crime I was dealing with and the repeated denials by criminals and their apologists of its very existence, I knew we had to do more to show the public a little

of what was really going on. For the first 15 years or so, I had no press or publicity officer to guide me and had to play it by ear. I did have a couple of big advantages, though: I was a performer, unafraid of microphones and was a Scot with a Scottish voice. The latter was a bit of a rarity in conservation in those days, although I'm glad to say that things have now changed.

The press and media have an insatiable appetite for stories involving wildlife, no doubt due in part to the excellent picture and film opportunities they present and in part

Inspector Gordon Nicoll and the author with Meritorious Conduct Awards from Tayside Police, 1999

Sgt Willie Hannah WLO and Australian TV crew. Heads of Ayr, 2000

PC Ronnie Sewell and Australian TV crew

to the public's fascination with the subject. Add to that the frisson of criminal activity and you've got a winning formula, as a journalist might say. As I became more adept at working with these people – a simple matter of satisfying each other's professional needs – I was able to get quick access to the public when I needed it. And I needed it a lot. Poisoned eagles, trapped buzzards, huge egg collections, international falcon smugglers – I constantly needed to get the reality of what was happening into the public eye in order to put pressure on police and the justice system, and on politicians when new legislation was being debated.

One of my early lessons in the speed of communication and the early ability of the RSPB to harness the media came in 1987.

SATURDAY, 30 MAY 1987

The large Highland Police sergeant sat back in his chair, as the hot summer sun streamed in through the window of Tongue police office. In his left hand he held a small box, which he was idly tapping on the table top beside him. I was discussing the day's events with his fellow officer, PC Jim Neil, and wondering what charges they would be able to lay against an egg thief, now released (there was no power of detention back then). Suddenly, we all heard an unfamiliar squeaking sound. 'What's that?' 'Jesus! They're hatching out! The eggs are hatching!'

That morning, Tom Talbot had been sleeping in his car in a small quarry above a loch near Tongue in Sutherland. Tom became an experienced fieldworker, specialising in divers, but this was one of his first conservation jobs. Like most of us back then, he lived frugally and sleeping in the car was quite normal practice. He woke up and looked out in time to see a man walking round the edge of the loch. This was unusual behaviour and Tom began to think he was looking for divers' nests. Suddenly, the man became distracted from his lochside ramble and started walking off into the moor. Tom saw him pick something up from the ground then walk rapidly back to where his car was parked in a lay-by. He then watched the man lift up the bonnet of the car and fiddle about, before making throwing actions, as if chucking something into the heather. Tom witnessed all of this from his car, using binoculars. His evidence was to prove essential. The car drove off towards Bettyhill but not before Tom had got the number. Tom drove straight to Tongue police office and roused out Jim Neil, both of them then heading back in pursuit of the red Cortina. They soon found it, a few miles east of Tongue.

By great good fortune, I had spent the previous night in an RSPB-rented farmhouse a few miles away. I was driving along, watching for birds and trouble, when I had the great pleasure of seeing Doug Young standing at the side of the road as his car was being searched by Jim Neil. I stopped beside them and got out. Jim looked up from his work. 'Oh, hello Dave, this is Mr Young. He is suspected of taking eggs.' 'Yes, I know Mr Young, he's from Norfolk, I helped your colleagues in Thurso search him last year, he's got a conviction for possession of a kite's egg.' If looks could kill! As so often, I was glad of the presence of a large policeman. The search of the car turned up a counter-sink drill (which would have been left, had I not been there); a diary mentioning 'kites in Germany' and a small, unlabelled, brown-ribbed bottle (which a policeman would also probably have left). I asked Jim to seize all these items. We drove in convoy to Tongue where the sergeant joined us.

I told Jim that the drill and bottle were part of an egg thief's kit. The drill bit is used to hole the egg (by slowly twisting it against the middle of the egg) to allow for the contents to be blown or shaken out. The egg would then be stashed for later retrieval. We seized several drill bits like that from eggers – a simple, easily overlooked but essential tool. The brown bottle was even more interesting – and sinister. I had seen such bottles before. Originally, up to the middle of the 20th century, they were made to hold medicine, the ribbing being useful identification, occasionally as a warning, even for a blind person. I also knew that identical bottles were being supplied by a firm of 'Natural History Suppliers' called Watkins and Doncaster. If I was correct, this bottle contained something called embryo solvent, a highly-alkaline solution designed to dissolve a developing chick inside an egg without damaging the shell. That description alone has always reminded me of the horrifically callous nature of egg collecting. You've arrived too late for a freshly laid egg? Never mind, just dissolve the developing embryo with our patented solution! It's as sure a way of killing birds as shooting them.

Back at the police office, Doug Young tells Jim that the bottle contains his eye drops. He wasn't aware of my conversation with the policeman. 'Alright, Sir, you won't mind putting a few drops in your eye to demonstrate, then?' Doug decides to come clean.

While Jim and the sergeant are processing Mr Young, it's decided that Tom and I should go back to the original lay-by where he saw Young throw something away. Within a couple of minutes we've found three cracked and cold eggs, not divers eggs as expected but something equally rare: a full clutch of greenshank (*Tringa nebularia*) eggs. We photograph everything in situ. The eggs end up back at the police office as evidence.

We move on a few hours to that outbreak of panic in the sunny office. We all stare down at the tiny, moving shape of a chick, wriggling inside the most badly cracked egg. What are we going to do now! Our nice clean capture has suddenly got very complicated indeed. These are rare birds, a Schedule 1 species and we must try to keep them alive, but how? I've a basic knowledge of feeding seized or orphaned raptor chicks but a greenshank? These things eat tiny invertebrates! Right, phone Roy Dennis, it's his patch anyway so he'll want to know about the egger. I'm in luck: when I phone, he's in. 'Roy, you're the expert. What are the chances of hand-rearing greenshank chicks?' 'Very low indeed, I would have thought. Why?' I explain the situation. Eventually he says, 'I think you've got one chance. The off-duty adult bird comes back to the nest area in the evening, after feeding all day. If you can put the hatching eggs back before then, they may accept them.' Great, all we have to do now is find the greenshank nest. Greenshank are a favourite with egg thieves because they are so hard to find and therefore present a challenge. Doug Young would have been elated to have found these eggs and then disgusted when he saw they were almost hatching. Even embryo solvent wouldn't fix that.

We have to give it a try. Tom and I – joined by a young Mark Hancock, also destined for a long life of RSPB contract work – race back to the loch. Tom showed us where he saw the man find the nest, in a featureless heather-, sphagnum- and lichen-covered bog. It takes us about an hour but I eventually spot a hollow with a single tiny greenshank feather in it. Two of the eggs are now 'chipping' and the chicks' faint squeaks can be heard. Reluctantly, and with great pessimism, we place the eggs in the nest and walk away. Poor things: if they don't freeze something will eat them, I thought as I drifted off to sleep that night. It had been another very long day – it was after 11 p.m. by the time my statement was fully written up.

SUNDAY, 31 MAY 1987

It's 8.30 a.m. and Tom and I are back at the loch. We slowly walk towards the nest. An adult greenshank jumps up and starts calling, 'tchew, tchew, tchew… tchew, tchew, tchew!' In the nest lie two healthy chicks. We run back to the road. Fan-bloody-tastic! We had the best possible result. I was already so used to finding smashed eggs, empty nests with distressed parents calling or pathetic corpses on top of poisoned baits, that the reality of helping save the lives of those chicks had me walking on air. We rushed off and told Jim Neil, and I phoned Roy, my family and anyone else I could think of.

That was on a Sunday, I spent the rest of the day patrolling the north coast as far as Thurso, after a fascinating chat with Jim Neil about what were obviously (to me) gangs of egg thieves and whom Jim and his colleagues had thought were 'some weird kind of poachers'. Of course, these aren't poachers – they aren't stealing private property. But they are worse, stealing something that belongs to all of us – wild birds' eggs. After 1987, Northern Constabulary became fully aware of these 'weird poachers' and of the kudos and public appreciation involved when they were very publicly caught.

The next afternoon I phoned my office to be told that the HQ press office were desperate to get hold of me. I immediately phoned my colleague Chris Harbard (using a Button A and Button B roadside callbox, I remember. It was the last one I ever used and at the time emphasised to me the remoteness of the area). 'Hi Chris, I heard you were looking for me.' 'Dave, where the hell have you been?' adding, just before I could tell him exactly where I had been, 'Listen! Listen! It's just come on! I'll put the phone against the TV…' and I heard the voice of John Craven talking live on *Newsround* about my greenshank case. Fantastic! I was really impressed by that – such an immediate dissemination of information to millions of viewers. That opened my eyes and meant no more hiding from the media.

On 13 January 1988 at Dornoch Sheriff Court, Young pled guilty to possession of items capable of being used to take eggs – the egger's kit I had described – and fined £150. His plea of not guilty to taking the eggs was accepted. Unlike poaching offences in Scotland, single eye-witness evidence was not enough to convict an egg thief in 1987.

My mantra became 'a case is only as good as the publicity it attracts'. My job was, after all, about protecting birds. One offender being punished may well affect how he goes about his work as a gamekeeper or fish farmer or how he practices his hobby of pigeon fancier, aviculturist, shooter or egg thief, but if no one else gets to hear about it, then where is the real deterrent effect?

Publicity surrounding alleged criminal activity and court proceedings, of course, has to be handled very carefully. I soon realised that unless you kept on top of a case, then it was very easy to lose any chance of useful publicity. Journalists, by their own rules of engagement, will only cover a live story – it's no use going to them several months after an incident, or even two days after a court result, and expecting them to get excited about your story. These were lessons either wilfully ignored or simply misunderstood by some police officers. I learned these lessons from the journalists I worked with, some of whom I became quite friendly with over the years, although it was always understood that each other's professional priorities might occasionally clash.

So once a poisoned eagle, red kite or peregrine has been retrieved, rapidly but expertly analysed and a follow-up search has taken place, it is essential that the media are informed as quickly as possible. Any information such as exact location or the type of poison used, which will be needed for an efficient and tight investigation, must of course be protected. I stress the need for speedy communication with the media because this may be the only opportunity to publicly mark the crime. The press won't want to hear about it later when searches have turned up nothing or when a Fiscal has put his pen through the case due to lack of evidence. A crime did take place – and if you don't believe that, then you're in the wrong job.

What was getting lost by the time I left the field in 2006 was any real sense of urgency after an estate-based crime was reported. There were two reasons for urgency, as far as I was concerned – firstly, to protect wildlife which continued to be at risk, particularly from poison (that continuing risk was all too often forgotten by police officers busy following protocols and systems developed for less urgent crime); and secondly, to make the most of the media opportunities.

If I had a pound for every time some poisoning, shooting or trapping, ending in a failed search or an unreported court case, led to a police officer saying, 'Well, they won't do that again in a hurry! That's given them a fright!' I would have free guitar strings for life. That attitude was simply wrong. Without publicity you are wasting your time. The publicity has to be carefully targeted, too, and not take the form of some half-hearted slap on the wrist suggesting that what are often well-planned, routine and callous acts of cruelty are somehow 'a technical oversight' or 'over-zealous vermin control'.

The world of press and media in Scotland back then, like that of conservation, was a small one. We all knew each other and became well used to each other's foibles. After the first fifty or so radio and TV interviews, I lost any real fear of the microphone or camera, which is particularly easy when you've been chatting to the interviewer like an old friend immediately beforehand. By the time we got the mid-1990s, Louise Batchelor, Mike Scott or Euan McIlwraith would be contacting me as often as I contacted them. Louise, a charming woman with a gorgeous smile, became adept at suckering me in with soft questions before bowling a googly straight at me at the end of an interview. In would come the rapier-thrust question, Louise still smiling sweetly, and I, for my part, would try to distract her or make her laugh. It was all part of the game and she wasn't the only BBC reporter who could do it.

WEDNESDAY, 27 JULY 1994, MID-ARGYLL.

One of the most hilarious interview moments I ever had was in one of the most spectacular locations. Ever the professional, Euan McIlwraith had decided that if he was going to make a programme including golden eagles, he would go to the eagles to make it. This particular item was going out live on Radio 5 Live. Even as early as 1994, the era of three-person BBC crews was long gone and Euan had to rig up his own live link, a satellite dish on top of his car. We could see this car, several hundred feet below us in the main glen, as we stood on the lip of a hanging valley, having puffed our way up a steep grass and bracken slope. Grateful to be now above the midgie line, we were able to take a leisurely look up this side valley where, in the near distance, a golden eagle chick had recently fledged, leaving a blizzard of 'chick fluff' feathers at its nest.

Being interviewed by Ewan McIlwraith, mid-Argyll

Euan got into position with his microphone and right on cue for the handover began our live interview. Things went well – I never tired of talking about golden eagles, far and away my favourite Scottish bird – until around the third or fourth question when I started to hear a familiar rumbling sound. Without any more warning, one of the RAF's finest shot past, below us, in the main valley. The noise was incredible: it must have come as a big surprise to the radio listeners as it certainly surprised us! Euan, however, with a smile on his face, carried on as soon as was possible with, 'Well Dave, what about that then, that can't be good for nesting eagles?' I could have throttled him but smiled back. That's it, Euan, I thought, drop me in it with the RAF and the many country folk who object to low flying. 'Well, it's no doubt a shock but it's over very quickly and it can only happen quite rarely.' Forgetting of course, that the b****rs always go round in pairs! No sooner were the words out my mouth than, with a tremendous roar, the second jet flew past, if anything even closer. We were helpless with laughter. I don't remember how the interview finished but I was glad when it did.

As I have already strongly hinted, there are many people unnecessarily nervous of the use of publicity when it comes to naming and shaming wildlife criminals. The police – a necessarily conservative organisation and always under scrutiny – are an obvious example, but I was also disappointed by the lack of commitment in this area from conservationists. My own organisation vacillated wildly between naming and not naming estates where wildlife crimes had taken place, depending on who was in charge of the RSPB at the time. To say that I found this frustrating would be a serious understatement. I had seen the success of open public attacks on poisoning in both Islay and Arran in the 1980s. Those two islands, even now, 20 years later, have an almost unblemished record since the exposés of the BBC's *Watchdog* on Islay and the printed anger of locals against the estates in response to a front-page story on Arran. Before the raptor issue became as polarised as it is today, I knew that bad publicity was what many estates feared most.

I was therefore delighted in 1993 when I was approached by a *Scotsman* journalist, responding to yet another spring crop of poisoned eagles, buzzards and kites. Auslan Cramb became a regular transmitter of wildlife crime stories but this time was concentrating on golden eagles. A second UK golden eagle survey in 1993, in which I was very much involved as a coordinator, had just very clearly shown those areas where eagles were not doing well – the grouse moors of central and eastern Scotland. It might have come as a surprise to a naive ecologist, as these were the areas with best food supply for chicks in the form of grouse and hares, but was not news to an already experienced wildlife crime investigator. I discussed the situation at length with Auslan and we homed in on the killing fields of the Monadhliadh Mountains, lying in the centre of the north of Scotland between Fort Augustus and Aviemore. I gave him chapter and verse on the many recorded persecution incidents in the area.

THURSDAY, 11 MARCH 1993

Late in the evening of 10 March 1993, I got an unusual call at home – it was Auslan. 'We've got a map drawn up with all the estate names and incidents on it. My editor wondered if you could look it over, just before it goes to press'. Twenty minutes later I am being ushered in through a side door of the old *Scotsman* building in the centre of Edinburgh and am looking, with a mixture of surprise, pleasure and trepidation, at a map of the Monadhliadhs, with a numbered key describing the names and locations of 20 incidents of eagle killing and the finding of poisoned baits within the previous 15 years. No changes were needed.

The next day, a full two-page spread appeared in *The Scotsman*, complete with map, incidents analysis and quotes from me. For a week I metaphorically held my breath. If the doom-mongers in the RSPB and beyond were right, if our enemies were to be believed, then a storm of legal threats would fall upon me. Nothing. No, that's not strictly true. I got one aggrieved phone call from a landowner in the south of the area. 'What's this about poisoned eagles on my ground?' (It had been five years earlier). 'Didn't your keeper tell you about it? He was interviewed by the police at the time?' 'No!' Oh dear, I expect there was a bit of an atmosphere at the next shoot.

I had, of course, openly mentioned estate names before with reference to proven poisonings, shootings and trappings but never on this scale. Call me naive (although what you've read so far should suggest I'm not) but you can't libel someone by telling the truth. Those in conservation and in authority are doing no one any favours by concealing from the public the full facts of wildlife crime in the Scottish countryside. When it comes to concealing the location of deadly poisoned baits, I would suggest they think very, very carefully about what they are doing.

By the late 1990s, it was seldom necessary to have to start with the real basics when discussing wildlife crime with a journalist. There were some understandable old wives' tales doing the rounds – Arabs paying tens of thousands of pounds for every peregrine egg or chick stolen; estate-based bird of prey killing being 'a few rotten apples in the barrel'; or that the RSPB went around charging and prosecuting criminals – but a decade or so of intensive publicity on many of the issues had brought some rewards. Decision makers such as MPs had listened and some laws had been tightened up. The downside, however, was that publicity had also attracted bureaucracy and the type of time-wasting instant experts that proliferate around any success story. The press and media were also beginning to be used by those who were vehemently opposed to wildlife laws being enforced in Scotland. For me the bottom line was always 'Are our endangered wildlife populations growing in numbers and stability?' By the end of the decade, there were still very few breeding golden eagles across much of Scotland's south, central and eastern uplands. Had we made any real difference out there?

10

INTO THE NEW MILLENNIUM

B y the year 2000, I felt that a watershed had been passed. Although we had our successes after that date, things were not changing for the better when it came to progressing bird conservation through the use of the Scottish justice system. The elephant in the room was always the raptor debate.

I have time now for reflection and a rational appraisal of those two decades, which I certainly didn't have as the millennium began. Increasingly, my time was being used up by political in-fighting with police forces, with every court case turning into a struggle against Fiscals on one side and defence QCs on the other, and by taking time out to help lobby for better legislation which, ironically, was being less efficiently used. The press and media had become nervous of the clout of the pro-gamekeeping and pro-landowning lobbies. In 1997 the rather weak Scottish Landowners' Federation (SLF) gave way on the lobbying front to the Scottish Gamekeepers' Association (SGA), founded by a millionaire undertaker/landowner in response to the growing pressure on shooting as the true facts of illegal activities were revealed. It was an astute move, ensuring that no dangerous split appeared between employer and front line workers, presenting the killing of birds of prey as simply a desperate attempt by downtrodden working men to save their livelihoods. It is, of course, a combination of an attempt to maximise estate profits and the continuation of the feudal management and vermin control practices, of the Victorian era. Despite wild claims to the contrary, very, very few keepers were ever sacked, even after successful prosecutions. That should in itself show any newcomer to this issue where the problem lies.

By the new millennium, there was little or no investigative journalism going on, due partly to the new economics of the internet era but also to political pressure from the shooting lobby. For my part, I was suffering health problems, undergoing two knee operations and one for angina, alongside the inevitable onset of energy-sapping middle age. All around me a growing army of virtual conservationists argued about hypothetical policy changes, while I continued to pick up poisoned eagles on rainy mountain tops and get criticised for it by politically-bent police officers. It would have been easy to get a little depressed.

I believe that the present lack of action which I still observe closely, thanks to the internet and a few old contacts, is in stark contrast to the successes we all had in the 1980s and 1990s. And it's because those successes are being wilfully ignored, forgotten or buried.

Keith Brockie cartoon showing the real cost of grouse shooting

That is to be expected: life moves on and people fit the facts to suit their own agendas. What I am not prepared to countenance, though, is to hear some idiot in the near future say 'Well, we've tried the criminal justice route and it didn't work – we need to negotiate with these wildlife criminals'. I was involved in over 350 cases which either went to court or were at least reported to a Fiscal – that may sound a lot and it certainly felt like a lot to me, but in the context of all reported crime in Scotland between 1984 and 2006, it was a drop in the ocean – and I can say that using the criminal justice system to stop wildlife crime in Scotland has not been tried. We've simply dabbled in it.

If I would like to be remembered for anything, it would be that 'I showed you the way'. I showed you the way to work a wildlife crime scene, how to use cameras and videos, how to identify victims, the identification and treatment of baits, the layout of bait and victim, the methods of trapping, the predation of victims, aspects of bird and animal behaviour in relation to a crime; how to find a cause of death using expert scientific analysts and how to get them to give evidence in court; how to discuss a case with a prosecutor so that the conservation/public interest is accepted and promoted in court; how to record and disseminate information on criminal techniques; how to profile wildlife criminals; how to make sure that previous convictions are put before a court; and how to handle pre- and post-court publicity.

I am not for one minute saying that I invented all of the above, although some of it, I did, but I was certainly the first person to put it all together, again and again and again. I then spent many, largely wasted, years teaching police/Procurators Fiscal/SNH those hard-won techniques and procedures. They were wasted years because, with the growing exclusion of civilian experts like the RSPB and, latterly, the SSPCA, thanks to interference from the very interests responsible for the crimes in the first place, cases have become fewer and fewer and less and less successful in court, while horrific poisoning incidents, in particular, continue apace.

There is also a shameful lack of even the pretence of a level playing field in our courts, with the lowliest under-keeper being represented by Counsel, highly-paid QCs with attendant solicitors. They bring all the pomp of their usual habitat, the High Court, where they deal with the most serious criminal cases, but play it out in provincial Sheriff Courts, under Summary case law, against overworked depute Procurators Fiscal. At the same time, we are repeatedly told by these people that the poisoning and illegal trapping of wildlife are not serious crimes and that this is all a waste of precious court time. I wonder how many people reading this would agree with that? I wonder how many would have such expensive legal representation paid for them by employers, who would then continue to employ them, no matter what the outcome? Where is the Crown Office response to this? Where are the Crown Advocates who could be brought in to even things up on an issue which is of such huge public interest?

And so I watch with growing weariness as politicians and my successors in conservation cry 'How can we solve wildlife crime?' by which they mean bird of prey persecution, as everything else is swamped by it. Go back and look at the early 1990s, I say: there was a time when we were winning this battle. There is a sequel to be written to this book, but it will be a hard-edged and ultimately depressing story of political interference with the justice system by those with an agenda at odds with the law, the political rise of people who purport to be defenders of the countryside but who in reality are trying to take us all back to a time when game birds were king and everything else was disposable. They do not share the sentiments of your average Scotsman, dare I say it: the man in the street who, in my experience, does really care about Scotland's wildlife, contrary to those people who would have us all turn a blind eye to the killing on our hills.

There was, of course, another side to the work of anyone involved with the investigation of wildlife crime, a side which received a disproportionate amount of interest and publicity when its actual effect on bird and animal populations are considered. The plundering of our wildlife by egg thieves, falcon thieves, unscrupulous taxidermists and dealers of all kinds took up a large amount of my time. In some of these areas, where cooperation between agencies was never a serious problem, large successes were achieved. Rare bird egg theft and the theft of wild peregrines and eagles have become rarely-recorded events in Scotland, although it would take a foolish person to think that it couldn't start up again very easily. I am clear in my mind that this change in the last 30 years or so was due to the strict application of the law, including the full use of penalties such as imprisonment, now available to the courts. This is a lesson still to be learned in the fight against what has always been the most important area of wildlife crime in this country, the persecution of birds of prey. While I am all for a fair hearing for anyone accused of wildlife crime, or any crime, I don't remember any egg thieves being defended by QCs.

In this book, I have written about my part in attempting to prevent the whole range of crimes against wild birds. This was not about revenge for deeds done, or even merely about punishment: it was always about how to allow wild birds to flourish through preventing their direct destruction. In that, I shared the goals of my colleagues in areas such as education, advocacy and the running of reserves. I always saw my work as having its closest connection with our education departments – I helped educate criminals by helping to catch them and making sure they saw the law used against them. At the same time, the widest use of publicity meant that others knew what would happen if they broke wildlife laws and, most importantly, that there was a good chance they would get caught, anywhere in the country. There was never any positive effect from waving the big stick: giving warnings and telling each other 'That'll make him think twice!' was a proven waste of time. Change came about when the big stick, in the form of the justice system, was actually used.

MONDAY, 15 APRIL 2002

It's a bright sunny Monday afternoon in mid-April, at a deserted crossroads on the island of Mull. I'm sitting in my car, idly watching a golden eagle soaring along a ridge about two miles away. Its 20 years since I first 'hunted' these birds, back across the water in mid-Argyll, and I have half a lifetime of chasing wildlife criminals behind me. So I have no problem in identifying the adult goldie in the distance or the two young men in the battered estate car passing me at speed. Or so I thought.

I had just experienced what I've heard older police officers refer to as 'the click', an indefinable sense of recognition when they see someone up to no good. I was on high alert at the end of that long month when both golden eagle and the very rare sea eagle's eggs are at risk from the strange and perverse predators called egg thieves, so when two intense-looking young off-islanders drove past in an unknown old car with English number plates, my first instinct was to write the number down and phone Finlay.

PC Finlay Christine, a Strathclyde policeman, formerly of the heavy squad in the Glasgow Gorbals, who ended up as the eagles' best defender on a Hebridean island. He had been a good friend and colleague since that memorable day in March 1995 when he caught three notorious egg thieves as they were about to leave the island with a car load of evidence.

'Fin, I've just seen a red estate, H-reg, drive past me, heading down the north side of Scridain' 'Aye, saw them, they came off the one o'clock ferry. I'm checking them out now. Nothing gets past me!' 'OK, I'll keep an eye out. See you later.'

5.20 p.m. and I'm leaving Mull on the wonderful Fishnish to Lochaline crossing, after saying goodbye to Finlay and Janet, my hosts for yet another session of eagle watching. Another ferry and a couple of hours later and I'm passing the village of Onich, on the mainland, when I get a call on my mobile from Finlay. 'See those guys we both clocked this afternoon? You'll never guess what they're into!' 'No, I won't, what's that, then?' 'We answered a call from a concerned resident about some funny lights and found these guys camping, with a set moth trap beside them.' 'Moths?' 'Aye, they're pretty knowledgeable, come from down in Englandshire, seem OK, definitely not into eggs, knew nothing about the eagles.' 'Dear God, moths, what will we get next?' 'Aye, ah know! Well, sorry to bother you, safe home.'

Tuesday, 16 April

In to work at 9.30 a.m., having got home towards midnight after another 15-hour day. It's business as usual and I'm being filmed for BBC *Newsnight*, yet another exposé on the slaughter of birds of prey in Scotland; every new TV producer seems to think this is a new story. When will they learn that it's endemic throughout Scotland? I faced another load of daft, naive questions – 'Who do you think is killing these birds?' I often tell these people to go into the first pub they can find in shooting country and ask the same question. They'd get the same answer as mine, but in much stronger terms. Long before this, though, I'd become aware that if we are ever going to get the killing stopped, we need the media to get the truth out to the public. So it's grit the teeth and on with the show. Back at my desk about 11 a.m., the phone rings.

'Dave, its Mike McGregor from Ardnamurchan, I've got a wee problem.' Mike McGregor is a wildlife photographer and naturalist and part of the splendid Liz Macdonald's group of Morvern and Ardnamurchan eagle watchers.

'What's happening?'

'You know the xxxx eagle site?'

'Sure, it got robbed a couple of years back. They left a line hanging from the tree...'

'Aye, that's the one. Well, there's a couple of lads walking across the hill, they're about 300 yards from it. I've called the police in Fort William and they're coming out, but they won't be here for hours yet. What I need to know is, will they be violent if I approach them? If I give you the car number, you might recognise who they are and know what sort of people I'm dealing with? I'm not asking you for names or anything, I know you can't do that...'

'Sure Mike, but my strong advice is not to go near them, leave that to the police – apart from anything else, they'll make up stories about what you said and did and before you know it, you'll be the one getting hassle in court. What's the number?'

'It's a red estate ...' and he read out a familiar H-reg number.

'God, Mike, that's the same car Finlay checked on Mull yesterday. They're just moth nuts.'

'Oh, you're sure they're not eggers?'

'Finlay says not, and I've never heard of them, which is a good sign. So you can relax.'

Luckily, we had not spoken for a very long time and spent a couple of minutes catching up on mutual acquaintances and bird news, until Mike suddenly interrupted me.

'Moths?'

'Yeah, moths. Why?'

'Well, they're now within yards of the only surviving site in the UK for the New Forest burnet moth. I help to look after them.'

'Amateur moth nuts all the way up from the south of England within yards of the only site of an incredibly rare moth... I don't think that's a coincidence, do you? Are they a protected species?'

'Yes, they're on the Wildlife and Countryside Act.'

'OK, Mike, I'll deal with this. Got to hurry. Keep an eye on them.'

I was on a very steep learning curve. A vertical one, in fact. I knew my colleague Duncan McNiven in Bedfordshire had successfully helped with a butterfly collecting and sale case in England but I had little knowledge of the subject. I checked the 1981 Act. Yes, there it was: Schedule 5, Moth, New Forest Burnet, *Zygaenaviciae*. I checked the text: 'If any person intentionally kills, injures or takes any wild animal included in Schedule 5… he shall be guilty of an offence… if any person has in his possession or control any live or dead wild animal included in Schedule 5… he shall be guilty of an offence.' So far, so good.

I needed to know more about these things, fast. The clock was ticking, police were on their way. So, who would know?

Would SNH? Scottish Natural Heritage, the government's nature conservation advisers, were not usually my first port of call on casework, as they were notably shy of getting involved in anything resembling enforcement. But I picked up the phone to their local Edinburgh office. I asked to speak to an entomologist and was put through.

'Hello, this is Dave Dick from RSPB Investigations, I need to know everything about the New Forest Burnet Moth. Can you help?'

'Well, I wrote the Biodiversity Action Plan – but how do you know about them?'

'Fantastic! Well, there's someone at the site in Ardnamurchan and we think they might be about to interfere with them so… would anyone want to collect them?' And the questions kept on tumbling out. 'What stage are they at right now? What do they look like? How would you carry them? What do they eat?'

He was extremely helpful, although sounding rather alarmed by the end of the call, particularly after I quizzed him about the world of moth collectors.

Right, that was the easy bit done – now came the fun part, telling the police.

I got through to the duty inspector at Fort William police office.

'Hello, Dave, it's Colin Soutar! Don't worry, we've got the eagle eggs under control, they're on their way.'

This was a minor miracle. I had known Colin since he was a constable working out of Strontian in the mid-1980s, when we hunted egg thieves together in Morvern. But even knowing the officer, I wasn't looking forward to the next bit.

'Aye, I know, but Colin, I've got a bit of a surprise for you. You're not looking for a couple of eggs the size of a goose egg. You're now looking for a boxful of caterpillars, bright green with yellow spots and about 2 – 3 mm long!' A pause followed. 'We think these guys are moth collectors. They're at the site of a very rare moth species, and apparently there's a network of collectors same as with bird's eggs. This one's called New Forest Burnet and it's on Schedule 5 of the 1981 Act, illegal to take or possess'.

To his great credit, Inspector Soutar didn't quibble and managed to get a call through to his men just as they arrived on site. The two collectors were found to be in possession of a large quantity of caterpillars, not taken from that site but from a nature reserve on Mull. As a result of this case, the police are now aware of the potential problem of rare moth theft and, importantly, are also aware of the sites at risk. It was a very good example of the importance of a rapid response to wildlife crime and the real need for good communication between police and knowledgeable civilians, and vice versa!

The species taken on Mull, slender Scotch burnet *Zygaena loti* ssp. *scottica*, despite its great rarity in the UK – SNH lists just five or six sites, all on Mull and Ulva – had no legal protection from thieves in 2002 but was at last recommended for full protection by the December 2008 SNH Quinquennial Review of Schedule 5 (1981 Act) species. Compare and contrast this situation with that of rare birds and their eggs. I was always aware that conservation colleagues working on little-known, non-bird species had an even bigger uphill struggle than I did. Now I could hold my head up in their company!

Anyone who wants to see successful wildlife crime investigations in Scotland – and it's not a rhetorical question to ask who might not – should realise that those in authority need to work closely with the people who really know about wildlife and its problems, such as staff members of RSPB and the Scottish SPCA, Raptor Study Group members and other experts who will actually stand up and be counted. Don't waste time and resources on protocols, partnerships and jargon-led initiatives, just get out there and do it. Don't listen to those who would tell you that wildlife cases are too complex or too difficult – in my experience, those are the words of those with an interest in such cases failing.

If we are to call ourselves a civilised country, then let's make proper use of the legislation that was so hard won in the first place, rather than go back to the destructive, ignorant and primitive practices of yesterday.

Poison case sheriff issues warning to landowners

Scotsman (front page) 24/5/89

By FRANK URQUHART

ESTATE owners tempted to turn a blind eye to the setting of poisoned bait or illegal traps to kill wildlife were given a stern warning yesterday by a sheriff.

Sheriff Alastair Stewart declared that owners of shooting estates who condoned illegal actions on their land should be pursued with the utmost rigour of the law.

He gave the warning at Aberdeen Sheriff Court when he fined George Rodenhurst, a gamekeeper, a total of £2,600 for the illegal actions he took on the Haddo estate, Aberdeenshire. Rodenhurst, who was head gamekeeper at the 8,000-acre estate, had pled guilty to five charges on indictment, including the use of poisoned baits and illegal gin traps to kill wild birds, two of which were protected species.

The prosecution, the first poisoning case brought under the Wildife and Countryside Act, was hailed as a victory for conservation by the Royal Society for the Protection of Birds.

Rodenhurst, 39, was said to have been fined the equivalent of half-a-year's salary. He issued a statement through his lawyer as he left the court, alleging that the acquisition of one of the poisons, which he had admitted using, was widespread throughout estates in Scotland.

Rodenhurst claimed he was aware of about 400 estates which had purchased alpha-Chloralose, a narcotic rodenticide. Four dealers were said to be making a full-time living dealing in it.

Sheriff Stewart said, "I find it rather ironic that Parliament permits the imprisonment of those who poach game but does not permit the imprisonment of those who set illegal traps or use illegal poisons to preserve it."

He continued, "I find the use of poisons particularly distasteful. Poisons are worse than traps because it is possible for poisons to get into the animal food chain and possibly affect, not just wild life, but ultimately, conceivably, humans."

The sheriff, commenting on claims that Haddo estate was not without blame, stated, "I don't think I can really comment on that. But I would say, if it be the case that those running the estate were either condoning what was going on, or turning a blind eye to it, I find that utterly reprehensible."

Captain Colin Farquharson, factor on the Haddo estate and Lord Lieutenant of Aberdeenshire, said he would have to see a full transcript of what was said before making any comment.

Rodenhurst article

QUOTATIONS

'I only use alpha for the hoodies.'

Perthshire shepherd/stalker referring to alphachloralose poison while talking to the author, who had recently found a golden eagle nearby, poisoned with alphachloralose, Spring 1982.

'You'll never stop the gamekeepers.'

Pete Ellis, former RSPB Investigations Officer (Scotland),
during the author's induction, January 1984.

*'This is just a poor man's hobby. You should be after those b***s with the pheasants!'*

South Lanarkshire finch trapper during a house search, 1984.

'It's Spring and the bottle's out.'

Perthshire gamekeeper referring to poisoning, in conversation with RSPB fieldworker, 1985.

'Three this year, Dave!'

Message chalked onto a rock above robbed peregrine nest in Moffatdale, 1988.

'Have you ever seen a crow peck the eyes out of a live lamb?'
'Have you ever talked to a little girl whose dog took 16
hours to die from strychnine poisoning?'

Exchange between the Convenor of the Scottish Landowners' Federation (SLF) and the author during a radio debate following the poisoning of a golden eagle, c. 1989.

'What you don't realise, Mr Dick, is that shooting three buzzards
is no different to me than shooting three crows!'

A major northeast Scotland landowner, in phone conversation with the author, c. 1990.

'I know you don't like me but I'm not like those other
b*stards. I've never taken a re-lay.'

Convicted Liverpudlian falcon thief while giving information about raptor poisoning by phone
to the author. A re-lay is a second clutch of eggs, sometimes laid if a first
egg theft occurs early enough in the season, c. 1995.

'Bob has been a gamekeeper for 35 years and has worked on estates all over the
country. He said 'I would say that 99% know exactly what their keepers are doing
on their behalf, but now they are not prepared to back them... so, if the owner
doesn't get any grouse and he sees the skies full of peregrines, the keeper will lose his
job. If the keeper does something about it and gets caught, he loses his job.'

Quote from an article in *The Scotsman*, 22 October 1996.

'Derek, a head keeper with 27 years experience, said: 'Of course birds of prey are
killed. Some keepers don't have to do it but the vast majority must have been
forced to do it at one time or another. But it is not the slaughter the RSPB
say it is. We only do it on a one-off basis when we have identified
a particular bird, or pair, causing us a problem.'

Quote from an article in *The Scotsman*, 22 October 1996.

'We've all done daft things when we were lads.'

Michael Skelly, gamekeeper, after the author pointed out eight years'
worth of wildlife crimes recorded in his diaries, 1997.

'They shoot every eagle that tries to overwinter on those moors,
they hunt them down till they get them, they call them 'turkeys'.'

Newly-retired gamekeeper, talking to raptor group worker and WCO, south Scotland, 2002.

'How many are at it? Who isn't?! I would say more than 97%.'

Retired gamekeeper in conversation with police WCO, 2006.

'Get a life!' Offences against animals are 'not even on the second page' after serious crimes such as robbery and assault.

Sheriff Kevin Drummond, chairman of the government's Partnership for Action against Wildlife Crime (PAWCS) legislation sub-group, when asked by Mark Rafferty of the Scottish SPCA whether offenders should get tougher sentences for wildlife crime, WLO Conference, Tulliallan, 17 February 2010. *The Herald*, 7 March 2010.

REFERENCES AND FURTHER READING

Abram, D. *et al. The Rough Guide to India.*

Scottish Raptor Study Groups (1998) *The Birdwatchers' Yearbook.* Buckingham Press.

Brown, P. and Waterson, G. (1962) *The Return of the Osprey.* Collins.

Gordon Booth, C. (reprinted 1981) *Birds in Islay.* Argyll Reproductions Ltd.

Brown, L. (1976) *British Birds of Prey.* Collins, New Naturalist Series.

Carson, R. (1962) *Silent Spring.* Reproduced in *Animals* magazine.

Cummings, J. (1990) *Thailand – a travel survival kit.* Lonely Planet Publications.

Cummings, J. *et al.* (1990) *Indonesia – a travel survival kit.* Lonely Planet Publications.

Dick, D. (April 1990) 'As I See It,' in *The Scots* magazine.

Dennis, R.H., Ellis, P.M., Broad R.A., and Langslow, D.R. (1984) *The Status of the Golden Eagle in Britain.* British Birds, 77: 592-607.

Durrell, G. (1959) *My Family and other Animals.* Penguin.

Blackman, D.E., Humphreys P.N. and Todd, P. (eds.) (1989) *Animal Welfare and the Law.* Cambridge University Press.

Gordon, S. (1980 reprint) *The Golden Eagle.* Melven Press.

Green, R.E., (1996) 'The Status of the Golden Eagle in Britain in 1992.' *Bird Study* 43, 20-27.

Grimmett, R., Inskipp, C. and Inskipp, T. (2001) *Pocket Guide to the Birds of the Indian Subcontinent.*

http://www.islayinfo.com/portnahaven.html

Love, J.A. (1983) *The Return of the Sea Eagle.* Cambridge University Press.

Lovegrove, R. (1990) *The Kite's Tale.* RSPB.

Lovegrove, R. (2007) *Silent Fields – the long decline of a nation's wildlife.* Oxford University Press.

Macintyre, D. (1936) *Wildlife of the Highlands.* Phillip Allan and Co. Ltd.

Mackinnon, J. (1990) *Field Guide to the birds of Java and Bali.* Gadjah Mada University Press, Indonesia.

Owen, M. (1980) *Wild Geese of the World.* B. T. Batsford Ltd.

Ogilvie, M.A. (1978) *Wild Geese.* T. and A. D. Poyser.

Poole, A.F. (1989) *Ospreys – A Natural and Unnatural History.* Cambridge University Press.

Ratcliffe, D. (1980 and 1993) *The Peregrine Falcon*. T. and A. D. Poyser.

Ratcliffe, D. (1997) *The Raven*. T. and A. D. Poyser.

Ratcliffe, D. (2000) *In Search Of Nature*. Peregrine Books.

Robinson. P. (1982) *Bird Detective*. Elm Tree Books/RSPB.

'Legal Eagle' and 'Annual Bird Crime Reports' online at http://www.rspb.org.uk/ourwork/policy/wildbirdslaw/legalpublications.aspx?c=&t=&r=Law&start=40&end=59%20-%2038k (RSPB).

Round, P. and Lekagul, B. (1991) *A Guide to the Birds of Thailand*. Saha Karn Bhaet Co. Ltd., Bangkok.

Scottish Raptor Study Groups website: http://www.scottishraptorgroups.org

Wildlife Investigation Incident Scheme. Annual reports online at http://www.sasa.gov.uk/pesticide_wildlife/wiis/reports.cfm. Scottish Agricultural Science Agency.

Samstag, A. (1988). *For Love of Birds: the Story of the RSPB*. RSPB.

Shiels, R. *Reports to the Procurator Fiscal: a Guide for Non-Police Reporting Agencies*. 1st edition.

Wilson, N. (2000) *Malta*. Lonely Planet Publications.